WHAT MATTERS IN JANE AUSTEN?

JOHN MULLAN is Professor of English at University College London. He writes the regular 'Guardian Book Club' column on fiction in the *Guardian* and frequently appears on the BBC's *Review Show*. He was a judge of the 'Best of the Booker Prize' in 2008 and a judge of the Man Booker Prize itself in 2009. He has taught Austen to university students for over a quarter of a century, and has lectured widely to lovers of her fiction in both the UK and the US.

WHAT MATTERS IN JANE AUSTEN?

Twenty Crucial Puzzles Solved

JOHN MULLAN

BLOOMSBURY

LONDON • NEW DELHI • NEW YORK • SYDNEY

First published in Great Britain 2012
This paperback edition published 2013

Bloomsbury Publishing Plc
50 Bedford Square
London WC1B 3DP

www.bloomsbury.com

Bloomsbury Publishing, London, New Delhi, New York and Sydney

A CIP catalogue record for this book is available from the British Library

ISBN 9781408831694

10 9 8 7 6

Typeset by Hewer Text UK Ltd, Edinburgh
Printed and Bound by CPI Group (UK) Ltd, Croydon CR0 4YY

In memory of Tony Tanner

CONTENTS

A Note on References

Quotations from Jane Austen's fiction are taken from the Oxford University Press edition of *The Novels of Jane Austen*, edited by R. W. Chapman, 3rd edition (1965–6). References are given within the text, by volume and chapter number. References to *Lady Susan* and *Sanditon* are given by chapter number. The aim has been to enable readers easily to locate passages, irrespective of the editions they might be using.

Quotations from Jane Austen's letters are taken from the Oxford University Press edition, edited by Deirdre Le Faye. As pagination differs between the third (1995) and fourth (2011) editions, references are given within the text by letter number.

Introduction

Did Jane Austen know how good she was? It is a question often asked by her aficionados, struck on each new reading by the intricate brilliance of her fiction and perhaps aware that many of her first readers just did not see it. Contemporary reviewers might have been generally complimentary, but their very compliments show their failure to grasp what they were reading. 'Whoever is fond of an amusing, inoffensive and well principled novel, will be pleased with the perusal of *Emma*.'[1] 'If *Emma* be not allowed to rank in the very highest class of modern Novels, it certainly may claim a least a distinguished degree of eminence in that species of composition.'[2] Though she compared herself confidently with other novelists, especially other women novelists, of her times, there is no evidence that Austen herself dreamed of posterity. Her famously modest description of her own art in a letter to her nephew James Edward – 'the little bit (two Inches wide) of Ivory on which I work with so fine a Brush' (*Letters*, 146) – is so arch that some have taken it as a kind of boast: surely she did not think her work was such a small thing. Yet there is something incongruous about her latter-day status. Shakespeare and Dickens, the only other English authors who can rival her continuing, international appeal, were successful candidates for fame in their own day. They were also conscious innovators in the forms they used, whose audacity was widely – by rivals, grumpily – recognised. Here is the reason why that question about Austen's creative self-awareness is irresistible: she did things with fiction that had never been done before. She did things with characterisation, with dialogue, with English sentences, that had never been done before. Is it possible that she had no particular idea of how singular her novels were? Or did she have some hunch that her fiction was unlike that of any of her contemporaries, and would duly outlive all her rivals?

'Few so gifted were so truly unpretending,' wrote Henry Austen in his posthumous Biographical Notice of his sister.[3] Critics and biographers of recent times have tended to bridle at the version of the author that came down from her family: a woman who wished nothing of fame and whose writing was undertaken more to amuse her relations than to reach out to any public. Yet the widespread resistance to the image of a modest lady has been allowed to obscure an important truth: she was in some ways the most surprising genius of English Literature. She lived in an age distinguished by its literary intimacies and exchanges: we cannot think of the so-called Romantic period without thinking of the networks of friendship among its leading writers. Jane Austen knew not a single notable author, even distantly. Her most renowned female predecessor, Fanny Burney, had conversed with men and women of letters, and had been befriended by Samuel Johnson, no less. Her best-known female contemporary, Maria Edgeworth, may have lived in seclusion in Ireland, but when she did come to London she consorted with Jeremy Bentham and Walter Scott. The thoroughly eccentric William Blake, much of whose work was produced in very limited editions for a small number of patrons, was still known by a circle of London artists and literati, and his writings were discussed by fellow poets such as Wordsworth and Coleridge. Even the so-called peasant poet John Clare became acquainted with Coleridge, Hazlitt and Lamb, and had his high season in the salons of literary London. Not Austen. There are a couple of poignant passages in her letters where she looks forward to the possibility of meeting the poet George Crabbe – then acknowledges that she has missed her chance of doing so. In his memoir, Henry Austen recalls a planned meeting with the French novelist and intellectual Germaine de Staël, which duly never took place.[4] Though her books sold well in her lifetime, Jane Austen was utterly unknown to her great literary contemporaries. Her one encounter with a leading author came when *Emma* was reviewed at length in the *Quarterly Review* by Walter Scott. Yet the review, while admiring, was anonymous. In a letter to her publisher John Murray, Austen expressed regret that 'so clever a Man' as the reviewer should have left *Mansfield Park* out of his survey of her work (*Letters*, 139). It is unclear whether this means that Austen knew she was reading the considered response of the novelist who had burst on to the scene with *Waverley* less than two years earlier.

Jane Austen's obscurity among her contemporaries is all the more striking when one considers her technical audacity. There was nothing so surprising about the fact that she wrote novels. There was something miraculous about the fact that she wrote novels whose narrative sophistication and brilliance of dialogue were unprecedented in English fiction. She introduced free indirect style to English fiction, filtering her plots through the consciousnesses of her characters. She perfected fictional idiolect, fashioning habits of speaking for even minor characters that rendered them utterly singular. She managed all this with extraordinary self-confidence and apparently without the advice or expert engagement of any other accomplished writer. She had had access to books, of course, and the conversations of a bookish family, but no circle of fellow authors. It might be a wrench to think of Austen, the conservative literary genius in a revolutionary age, as an experimental writer, but such she was. This has nothing to do with her subject matter: indeed, provide some bare plot summaries of her novels, and they can be made to sound rather less daring than those of contemporaries such as Maria Edgeworth or Mary Brunton. Her brilliance is in the style, not the content. Even when it comes to her characters, her success is a matter of formal daring as much as psychological insight. We hear their ways of thinking because of Austen's tricks of dialogue; their peculiar views of the world are brought to life by her narrative skills.

Virginia Woolf, a reader completely alive to Austen's fictional intelligence, said that 'of all great writers she is the most difficult to catch in the act of greatness'.[5] Woolf meant that it was nearly impossible to take a single scene, or single paragraph, as an epitome of that greatness. The apparent modesty of Austen's dramas is, though, only apparent. Look closely, and the minute interconnectedness of her novels is a bravura achievement. This interconnectedness is the reason why, when you re-read her novels, you have the experience of suddenly noticing some crucial detail that you have never noticed before, and realising how demanding she is of your attention. One of the special delights of reading Jane Austen is becoming as clever and discerning as the author herself, at least for as long as one is reading. And when you do notice things it is as if Austen is setting puzzles, or inviting you to notice little tricks, which do justice to the small, important complications of life. Readers of Austen love quiz questions about her novels, but the apparently trivial pursuit of the answers invariably reveals the intricate machinery of her fiction. Are there any scenes in Austen where only men are present? Who is the only married woman in her novels to call her husband by his Christian name? How old is Mr Collins? Among the pleasures of knowing Jane Austen's novels is trying to answer such questions, but in this book I hope to show that doing so also reveals the true depths of her fictional world.

This book tries to catch her in the act of greatness, by scrutinising the patterns and puzzles that she builds into her novels. 'I hope somebody cares for these minutiae,' she wrote in a letter to her sister Cassandra, joking about the particulars of a recent journey – the distances and the times – with which she found herself filling her letter (*Letters*, 84). In life, such details may be inert; in Austen's novels, never. How far is it from Kellynch to Uppercross in *Persuasion*? The answer, three miles, is significant because Anne Elliot's short journey from one place to the other is 'a total change of conversation, opinion, and idea' (I. vi). What time do John Thorpe and James Morland set off from Tetbury to Bath in *Northanger Abbey*? Ten o'clock: we need to be clear because John Thorpe is an absurd braggart obsessed with the unlikely speed of his horse, and his bending of every fact to his purpose ('It was eleven, upon my soul! I counted every stroke') is the essence of his character. Little things matter, not because Austen's interests are trivial, but because the smallest of details – a word, a blush, a little conversational stumble – reveal people's schemes and desires. Austen developed techniques that rendered characters' hidden motives, including motives that were hidden from the characters themselves, and gave the novel reader new opportunities to discern these from slight clues of dialogue and narrative. The talk of Austen's 'miniature' art should not be a way of shrinking her achievement, but of drawing attention to its beautiful, exacting precision (which is why the metaphor of the ivory and the fine brush is indeed a boast). Almost a decade after her death, Walter Scott recorded in his journal that he had just read 'Miss Austen's very finely written novel of *Pride and Prejudice*' for at least the third time, and marvelled at her unmatched 'talent for describing the involvements and feelings and characters of ordinary life'. 'The Big Bow wow strain I can do myself like any now going but the exquisite touch, which renders ordinary common-place things and characters interesting from the truth of the description and the sentiment, is denied to me.'[6]

'Exquisite touch' is a generously precise appreciation of Jane Austen's precision. Accuracy is her genius. Noticing minutiae will lead you to the wonderful connectedness of her novels, where a small detail of wording or motivation in one place will flare with the recollection of something that went much earlier. This is one of the reasons they bear such re-reading. Every quirk you notice leads you to a design. The boon of Austen's confidence is that the reader can take confidence too, knowing that if he or she follows some previously neglected thread it will produce a satisfying pattern. Look at the presence of the weather in her novels and you will find her circumstantial exactitude, but also a carefully planned insertion of chance into her plots. Attend to her descriptions of her characters' blushes and you are shown how they become interpreters – often misinterpreters – of each other's unspoken thoughts. To follow one of these topics is to catch her narrative technique in action. Over and over again, it has seemed to me that as I have pursued some theme through Austen's fiction I have been finding a pattern that she has made to please and amuse us. So when I look at the characters in her novels whose speech is never quoted, or at scenes from which her heroines are absent, I am discovering what the novelist designed, not exercising my ingenuity but revealing the author's.

My book asks and answers some very specific questions about what goes on in her novels, in order to reveal their cleverness. The closer you look, the more you see. This sometimes means discerning what the author would have taken for granted, so this book tries to make explicit some of the matters of fact that, after two centuries, do need some explaining. Reading Austen it is important to know how much money was worth, or what conventions of mourning might have been, or how polite people addressed each other. I hope that I interestingly illuminate some of these matters of social history. A little knowledge will reveal the peculiar role that Austen gives to seaside resorts, or her expectation that we register the presence of servants, even when they are not mentioned. Yet it is also easy to lose yourself in scrutiny of the mores of Regency England. It is salutary for the Austen researcher in need of historical background to find, over and over again, that Austen's novels are themselves consistently invoked by social historians as 'evidence' of this or that custom. It is doubly salutary, as Austen invariably uses conventions, rather than merely following them. A book about the customs of the time will tell you that a young lady would not normally walk out alone, but we are surely not to side with Miss Bingley in her disapproval of Elizabeth Bennet's walk across the fields to visit her ailing sister at Netherfield. We can still sense that Elizabeth was doing something unconventional, and that Austen's contemporaries, like Mr Bingley, would have relished her doing so.

The themes that I have pursued are trails of the author's intent. How did she manage to produce such complex yet unified novels? The sparse manuscripts that have survived from Jane Austen's mature years as a published novelist – some cancelled chapters of *Persuasion*, the beginnings of a novel called *Sanditon* – give us few clues as to her methods of composition. Except that they suggest that she did have a design to follow when she wrote. We do not have the equivalent of Dickens's number plans or Nabokov's card indexes, but any attentive reader will feel that final intent is encoded in early beginnings. We will never know whether Austen made plans on paper, or whether she simply had a great writer's ability to hold in her head the details of what she had already written. The lack of evidence about her habits of composition has allowed a long tradition of condescension to her. Henry James seemed to think that Austen had not known what she was doing, technically speaking. While conceding that her stature was assured – she was 'one of those of the shelved and safe' – he thought that she 'leaves us hardly more curious of her process, or of the experience that fed it, than the brown thrush who tells his story from the garden bough'.[7] She had all the 'grace' of 'her unconsciousness', he thought, finding for her process of composition the metaphor of a woman with her work basket, making her tapestry flowers and occasionally dropping stitches as she 'fell a-musing'. There has hardly been a novelist more conscious of his methods than James, whose prefaces to his novels are evidence – and are meant to be evidence – of the rigour of his art. He knew just what he was doing, but then what he was doing was built on Jane Austen's fearless innovations. It was Austen who had taught later novelists to filter narration through the minds of their own characters. It was Austen who made dialogue the evidence of motives that were never stated. It was Austen, a Jamesian *avant la lettre*, who made the morality with which her characters act depend on the nice judgements of her readers. Why should she not know what she was doing?

In truth, literary critics who admire Austen rather relish the many examples of great literary minds who have been baffled by her hold over intelligent readers. 'What is all this about Jane Austen? What is there *in* her? What is it all about?' wrote Joseph Conrad to H.G. Wells in 1901.[8] This book might take its motto from Vladimir Nabokov, who said in his lecture on *Mansfield Park* that 'the beauty of a book is more enjoyable if one understands its machinery, if one can take it apart'.[9] Yet this great, thoroughly sophisticated novelist had initially failed to understand Austen's greatness, confessing his antipathy to her and, apparently, all women novelists in a letter to his friend, the critic Edmund Wilson. 'I dislike Jane, and am prejudiced, in fact, against all women writers. They are in another class. Could never see anything in *Pride and Prejudice*.'[10] Wilson explained to him that he was entirely 'mistaken' about her.[11] 'Jane Austen approaches her material in a very objective way.' Under his influence Nabokov was soon studying *Mansfield Park*. Wilson knew that Austen was an entirely conscious artist, believing that she shared with James Joyce 'the unique distinction in English novels of having a sense of form'.[12] When we see how good she is, we can hardly doubt that she knew it herself. This book was written in the firm belief that Austen rewards minute attention, that hardly anything in her novels is casual or accidental. Discussing *Pride and Prejudice* in a letter to Cassandra, Jane Austen adapted a couple of lines from Scott's narrative poem *Marmion*: 'I do not write for such dull Elves / As have not a great deal of ingenuity themselves' (*Letters*, 79). That ingenuity is the subject of this book, and worth examining because Austen hoped (or is it expected?) that her reader would share it. The self-indulgent purpose of the book has been to convey my own pleasure in reading Jane Austen. Its less selfish aim is simply to sharpen the pleasure of other readers of her novels.

ONE

How Much Does Age Matter?

. . . she was fully satisfied of being still quite as handsome as ever; but she felt her approach to the years of danger . . .
Persuasion, I. i

So reliable are the misjudgements of casting directors as to the appropriate ages of actors chosen to perform in film and TV adaptations of Jane Austen's novels that new conventions have been established. Even in the minds of many who have read *Pride and Prejudice*, an impression of the age of Mrs Bennet, say, or of Mr Collins has become settled. It would surprise many to be told that Elizabeth Bennet's mother is probably only a little way past her fortieth birthday (her eldest daughter is twenty-one, and it is likely that she married when not much more than eighteen). The matter is significant early in the novel, when Mr Bennet makes a joke about the risk of Mr Bingley being attracted to her instead of one of her daughters (I. i). The joke would be empty if his wife were in her fifties or sixties. Instead, Mrs Bennet's easy dismissal of his suggestion ('I do not pretend to be any thing extraordinary now') bespeaks her confidence that she does still possess allure. Equally, many admirers of *Pride and Prejudice* think of Mr Collins as middle-aged. In the 1940 Hollywood film the role was taken by British character actor Melville Cooper, then aged forty-four. The trend was set. In Andrew Davies's 1995 BBC adaptation Mr Collins was played by David Bamber, then in his mid-forties. In the 2005 film the role was taken by a slightly more youthful Tom Hollander, aged thirty-eight. Yet Mr Collins is introduced to us as a 'tall, heavy-looking young man of five-and-twenty' (I. xiii). Adaptors miss something by getting his age wrong. His solemnity and sententiousness are much better coming from someone so 'young'. Middle-aged is what he would like to sound, rather than what he is.

Age naturally matters to characters in Austen's novels because these novels are about getting married, and the age of a young woman (but perhaps also a man) will determine her (or his) marriage prospects. Age matters to the novelist because she uses it to shape the reader's expectations. The facts that Austen gives us about her characters' ages are like dramatic instructions. Take *Sense and Sensibility*. In Ang Lee's 1995 film, Emma Thompson, then aged thirty-six, played Elinor Dashwood; Gemma Jones, then aged fifty-two, played her mother. But Elinor is nineteen. Readers have long differed over whether her composure is admirable or unsettling, but it is all the more striking given her age. Austen's own phrasing acknowledges the prematurity of Elinor's 'strength of understanding, and coolness of judgement' (I. i). These qualify her, 'though only nineteen', to guide her mother. Equally, Mrs Dashwood is just forty, a fact that matters a good deal in the novel's dialogue. In the second chapter of the novel, Mr and Mrs John Dashwood discuss how much Mrs Dashwood might cost them if they settle an annuity – an annual payment for the course of her life – on her. 'She is very stout and healthy, and hardly forty', points out Mrs John Dashwood (I. ii).

Later, after we and the Dashwoods have first met Colonel Brandon, a 'silent and grave' man who is 'the wrong side of five and thirty', Marianne and her mother discuss Mrs Jennings's jokes about a possible romance between him and Marianne. Mrs Dashwood, 'who could not think a man five years younger than herself, so exceedingly ancient as he appeared to the youthful fancy of her daughter', tries to convince her daughter that Mrs Jennings is not actually ridiculing his age (I. viii). When Marianne talks of Colonel Brandon's 'age and infirmity', her mother laughs at the apparent 'miracle' of her own life having been 'extended to the advanced age of forty'. We know from Mrs Dashwood at the end of Chapter iii that Marianne is 'not seventeen'. She is youthfully absurd in her sense of the importance of age, going on to say that a twenty-seven-year-old woman could only marry a thirty-five-year-old man in order to perform 'the offices of a nurse', in return for financial security. Elinor, even while she disagrees with her sister, concedes that 'Perhaps ... thirty-five and seventeen had better not have any thing to do with matrimony together.' It is an unnecessary fragment of dialogue if Austen had not wanted the reader to feel some sense of compromise at the end of the novel. We are supposed to remember this judgement when Marianne and Colonel Brandon do eventually marry, so that we know just how far Marianne has been aged, metaphorically speaking, by her errors and her sufferings.

Austen's is an age-sensitive world, in which some people's age sensitivity is wrong-headed. Modern readers do not have to study any social history to understand how the novels use information about characters' ages. Any social historian, on the other hand, who tried to extract social conventions from the novels would have to be very wary. A good example is the most extraordinary reflection on the significance of a woman's age in all of Austen's novels, in the fourth chapter of *Persuasion*. We have just been told of Lady Russell's response, eight years earlier, to the engagement of Anne Elliot to Captain Wentworth. She was dismayed to see her favourite 'throw herself away at nineteen, involve herself at nineteen in an engagement with a young man, who had nothing but himself to recommend him' (I. iv). Anne's age is repeated, as Lady Russell must have repeated it to herself. Not, as we might now think, because she was too young to be getting married, but because she would have been turning her back on the prospect of a finer match. Anne was 'so young; known to so few'. That 'so young' is Lady Russell's thought, and the next phrase, 'known to so few', clarifies her logic: 'at nineteen' she has every chance of attracting a grander and richer husband – a husband, if Lady Russell is to be gratified, with aristocratic pedigree. But this was not to be. Persuaded to break off her engagement to Captain Wentworth, Anne lost 'bloom and spirits' and no noble suitor appeared. When she was 'about two-and-twenty' she received a proposal from Charles Musgrove, eldest son of a local landed gentleman. Lady Russell was in favour of her accepting, and the novel's explanation of this gives us an alarming glimpse of a young woman's wasting assets: 'however Lady Russell might have asked yet for something more, while Anne was nineteen, she would have rejoiced to see her at twenty-two so respectably removed from the partialities and injustice of her father's house, and settled so permanently near herself.' When she was nineteen, Charles Musgrove would not have been good enough; when she is twenty-two, he is entirely desirable. At twenty-two she must, according to Lady Russell's think-ing, already be prepared to compromise. Her allure is fast diminishing.

This must surely be Lady Russell's anxious judgement rather than the author's. Charlotte Heywood, the heroine-to-be of *Sanditon*, is 'a very pleasing young woman of two and twenty' when the novel begins (Ch. 2). There is no suggestion that she is anything other than 'young'. Jane Bennet is twenty-two at the beginning of *Pride and Prejudice*, and clearly still glowing. Yet there is a hint in one of Austen's letters that nineteen is indeed thought to be the prime age for a young woman, when she characterises a Hampshire acquaintance. 'Miss H. is an elegant, pleasing, pretty looking girl, about 19 I suppose, or 19 & ½, or 19 ¼, with flowers in her head, & Music at her fingers ends' (*Letters*, 73). The joke seems to be that her appeal rather depends on her not yet being twenty. Without this sense of the brevity of a young woman's maximum allure, there would be no point to Elizabeth Bennet's brilliant riposte to Lady Catherine de Bourgh's impertinent enquiry as to her age: 'With three younger sisters grown up . . . your Ladyship can hardly expect me to own it' (II. vi). Lady Catherine responds that, being no more than twenty, Elizabeth has no reason not to declare her age: she is still at her marketable peak.

In fact, the average age of women marrying for the first time in Jane Austen's lifetime was probably twenty-three or twenty-four.[1] We should not trust the judgement of Anne's highly fallible adviser and surrogate mother Lady Russell. It was she who 'persuaded' the heroine to relinquish the man she truly loved. But we are to think that her reasoning is narrow-minded rather than merely absurd. Her concession to the match with Charles Musgrove would make no sense if it were irrational. Three years might make a big difference to a woman's marriageability. And, indeed, twenty-two would already be older than any of Austen's other heroines when they receive their proposals. Elinor Dashwood is nineteen at the beginning of *Sense and Sensibility* and is engaged to Edward Ferrars nine months later. Elizabeth Bennet is twenty when Mr Darcy first proposes to her, and she accepts him after another six months have passed. When the Crawfords arrive at Mansfield, in July, Fanny Price has 'just reached her eighteenth year' (from later references, this evidently means that she is eighteen years old). Henry Crawford proposes to her six months later. At the end of *Mansfield Park* we do not know how long it is before Edmund asks her to marry him because the author has decided to 'abstain from dates upon this occasion' (III. xvii). We might infer a year or so, in which case Fanny would be nineteen or twenty when she is finally claimed by the man she loves. Emma Woodhouse is twenty at the beginning of *Emma* and is united to Mr Knightley a year later. Catherine Morland is the youngest bride of all: engaged to Henry Tilney at the age of seventeen, and married less than a year afterwards. (One of the peculiarities of these novels is that most last about a year, though not one of them mentions any heroine having a birthday.)

Age sensitivity is no mere social convention: it is built into the structure of Austen's novels. Never more so than in *Persuasion*, with the early vanishing of Anne's 'bloom' and Sir Walter's certainty that she would never now be courted by any aristocratic suitor. His folly in thinking his favourite daughter Elizabeth 'as blooming as ever' at the age of twenty-nine is the insensitivity to age of mere vanity (I. i). Age cannot be evaded. Elizabeth's 'approach to the years of danger' is both her thought and the author's confirmation of it. The pressure is cranked up by our knowledge that Elizabeth yearns for a proposal from a suitably elevated suitor 'within the next twelvemonth or two'. She thinks of herself in a race against time. She hates seeing that page in the Baronetage, 'with the date of her own birth' but without the record of a marriage. While Sir Walter believes his and his daughter's ageing to be suspended, he is highly attentive to the ages of others. To illustrate his antipathy to the navy he tells Mr Shepherd of the Admiral whom he imagines past sixty, when he is truly only forty (I. iii). When he hears of Admiral Croft's reputed gout, Sir Walter calls him 'Poor old gentleman', though he is considerably younger than Sir Walter himself (II. vi). He calls Mrs Smith 'old and sickly', thinking her forty – though she is in fact thirty (II. v). Even when Anne tells him her true age, he insists on describing her as 'between thirty and forty' – when she is but a year older than his precious, 'handsome' eldest daughter.

Judgements of what is inevitable at any given age are invariably ridiculous failures of imagination.

There is no dodging age, and Austen provides the facts of her characters' ages as primary information – rather like newspapers of today, which conventionally append the age of a person to the first mention of his or her name. She was unusual in doing this. In novels of the period it is conventional to be told the age of a heroine in the opening chapters, but rare to be told the age of any other character. Austen is singular in requiring us to notice the ages of almost all her major characters. The information is interesting because of the dramatic use she makes of it. Her characters think and talk about how old people are, and her novels are comically true to the self-centredness of their different ideas of age. What is old? Emma's protégée Harriet Smith, aged seventeen, has her own ideas about this, ideas strong enough for her almost to contradict the wisdom offered by her mentor. Harriet is appalled to hear Emma's recommendation that Robert Martin should wait six years before he think of marrying. 'Six years hence! dear Miss Woodhouse, he would be thirty years old!' (I. iv). The recommendation is deceitful:

Emma pretends to disinterested judgement when in fact she is trying to put Robert Martin's marriage beyond Harriet's hopes. Clearly thirty seems an advanced age to Harriet. She goes on, later in the same conversation, to describe the newly married Mr Weston as 'almost an old man', being 'between forty and fifty'. Given Mr Weston's sprightliness – he is always walking somewhere – Harriet's horror at the vale of age that he is entering is comic. Yet her sense that thirty is very late to be marrying is not so foolish. Emma talks as if marriage were merely a prudential undertaking, while Harriet unguardedly speaks from deeper needs. If the choice of a sexual partner is all or nothing, why not choose when you are in your prime?

Judgements of what is inevitable at any given age are invariably ridiculous failures of imagination. 'A woman of seven and twenty ... can never hope to feel or inspire affection again,' declares Marianne Dashwood (*Sense and Sensibility*, I. viii). *Persuasion*, in which the heroine who has lost her bloom is exactly this age, might be a retort. Except that age still matters. In *Pride and Prejudice* Charlotte Lucas is twenty-seven when she snares a husband, and her age spurs her to waste no time when he hoves into view. She becomes the only woman in all Jane Austen's fiction to marry a man younger than herself. The novelist expects us to notice the slight difference between her age and that of her husband (of about two years). It further emphasises Charlotte's achievement, with little money and no beauty to assist her. It is not clear that in Austen's world it was any more unusual for a wife to be older than her husband than it might be today. In 1792 her brother James married thirty-year-old Anne Mathew, his first wife, when he was twenty-seven. Her brother Henry married his cousin Eliza in 1797 when he was twenty-six and she was ten years older than him. James Austen, whose wife

Anne died in 1795, had already proposed to Eliza unsuccess-
fully in 1796.[2] The pattern was to continue after Austen's
death. A year after his first wife, Mary, died in July 1823, her
naval brother Frank married his second wife, Martha Lloyd
(elder sister of his brother James's second wife Mary). When
they married, Frank was fifty-four and Martha was sixty-
two or sixty-three. Jane Austen herself was almost twenty-
seven when she received a proposal from twenty-one-year-
old Harris Bigg-Wither in 1802, and might have received a
proposal aged twenty-nine from clergyman Edward Bridges,
three years younger than her, in 1805.[3]

The predatory protagonist of Austen's *Lady Susan* (an
early epistolary tale unpublished in the author's lifetime) is
said by her sister-in-law to be thirty-five but to look ten years
younger (Letter 6). She is well able to ensnare the twenty-
three-year-old Reginald De Courcy, and most of the other
characters worry that he will indeed marry her. 'Our difference of age must be an insuperable objection,' he reassures
his father (Letter 14). Yet the story relies on the possibility that he is wrong. Contradicting even more resoundingly
Marianne's judgements about a woman's marriageability after
her mid-twenties is the union that opens *Emma*. The new Mrs
Weston, who first joined the Woodhouses as a young governess for the infant Emma and her sister, was with the family
for sixteen years, so must be in her mid-thirties. Our reali-
sation of this matters. We are to acknowledge the luck for
Miss Taylor, apparently embarked on a lifetime as a superior
servant, in finding what Mr Knightley calls 'independence' so
late in the day. The novel opens into a discussion of this luck,
with Mr Knightley telling Mr Woodhouse that his daughter 'knows how very acceptable it must be at Miss Taylor's
time of life to be settled in a home of her own' (I. i). 'Miss
Taylor's time of life' is, implicitly, not the usual one at which

to be netting a husband. Later, we should be aware again of Mrs Weston's age so that we see the suspect glitter of Frank Churchill's gallantry when he tells Emma in their first conversation that, anticipating meeting his father's new wife, he had 'not expected more than a very tolerably well-looking woman of a certain age', but had found his stepmother to be 'a pretty young woman' (II. v). At the age of thirty-five, the author was herself the object of a similar flourish of flattery on the part of Wyndham Knatchbull, who, at a London evening gathering, apparently called her 'A pleasing looking young woman' (*Letters*, 72). She reported the comment to Cassandra, adding 'that must do—one cannot pretend to anything better now—thankful to have it continued a few years longer'. Coming from Knatchbull, a London merchant in his sixties, the compliment was more genuine than if it had come from a Frank Churchill, a keen-eyed young man in his early twenties.

For most of *Emma*, Mrs Weston is pregnant. It is not clear when exactly she tells anyone, but widespread knowledge is suggested in the course of one of Miss Bates's effusions at the ball at the Crown Inn. 'She was now met by Mrs. Weston.—"Very well, I thank you, ma'am. I hope you are quite well. Very happy to hear it. So afraid you might have a headach!—seeing you pass by so often, and knowing how much trouble you must have"' (III. ii). The 'trouble' here seems likely to be the endurance of a first pregnancy in middle age. By now Mrs Weston is in the seventh month of pregnancy, so her condition is likely to be evident to all. We can infer the pleased surprise at her news among her friends, including Emma, and share the apprehension as the expected birth of her baby approaches. Her age gives an extra force to the manner in which the arrival of her daughter is announced. 'Mrs. Weston's friends were all made happy by her safety.' 'Safety' would always be a consideration – two of Austen's sisters-in-law and any number of acquaintances had died following childbirth – but here it signals her friends' worries about her having a first child so late. Mr Weston's age is also noticed. When we are told in the novel's first chapter that he is a 'suitable age' to marry Emma's friend, it sounds much like Emma's own judgement. Well into his forties, he is the right age to be marrying a woman who is well out of youth. When he becomes a father again, more than two decades after his first wife gave birth to Frank, we find Emma considering how his daughter will be 'a great comfort to Mr. Weston as he grew older—and even Mr. Weston might be growing older ten years hence' (III. xvii). As she entertains herself with the warming thought of the more sedentary Mr Weston solaced by 'the freaks and the fancies' of his child, we are invited to contrast the image with her relationship with her own elderly father. The gap of years here is a kind of chasm. 'The evil of the actual disparity in their ages (and Mr. Woodhouse had not married early) was much increased by his constitution and habits' (I. i).

Elsewhere in Austen's fiction, marriages between middle-aged women and older men look less commendable. In *Sanditon* Mr Parker tells Charlotte the full marital history of Lady Denham, who married her first husband, 'an elderly Man' with 'considerable Property', when she was 'about thirty'. We are to infer that her husband, Mr Hollis, might have been in his sixties, and it seems that from the beginning her duty was to 'nurse him' (Ch. 3). 'After a widowhood of some years, she had been induced to marry again.' Her wealth attracts Sir Harry Denham; his title attracts her. Her age at marriage is left unspecified, but we could guess that she was in her forties. Resourceful women are certainly able to find husbands once they themselves are middle-aged. *Persuasion* relies on our knowing this, for Sir Walter Elliot, in his mid-fifties, is the prey of Mrs Clay, who is called 'a clever young woman' and is a widow in her thirties. Anne thinks of her as 'between thirty and forty' (II. v). When she does so she is comparing her with her friend Mrs Smith, who is just thirty, so we might suppose that Mrs Clay is not so much older. Yet no one in the novel cites age as a reason for thinking their marriage unlikely. Both Anne and Lady Russell fear that it might be entirely possible, and even Elizabeth scorns the idea not because of the age disparity but because Mrs Clay has freckles. Meanwhile it is clear to the reader that Mrs Clay and her father, Mr Shepherd, are calculating on her catching the vain Baronet.

Age matters very much to women, but to men too. Henry Crawford's reflection is characteristically self-regarding, when he tells his sister that he is staying in Mansfield not only for the hunting. 'I am grown too old to go out more than three times a week; but I have a plan for the intermediate days' (II. vi). (His plan is to make Fanny fall in love with him.) He is called 'young' by the narrator and must still be in his early twenties, but likes to talk as if his youth were fled. Mr Knightley feels his age in *Emma* with better reason. There is a light suggestion of how a man's age does and does not matter in the very manner of telling us about his age at the beginning of *Emma*, when we are introduced to him as 'a sensible man about seven or eight-and-thirty' (I. i). The narrator sounds as if the character has got beyond precision in these matters. Yet he himself is rather accurate about years and dates. He smiles when he points out that he is sixteen years older than Emma, as if this means that he will always be right in their differences of opinion (I. xii). The disparity in their ages has made some readers feel uncomfortable about their eventual marriage, though Mr Knightley himself likes to draw attention to it. After they have become engaged, he mocks himself for his past censure of Emma, the only good of which was to fix his affections on her: 'by dint of fancying so many errors,' he says, he has been 'in love with you ever since you were thirteen at least' (III. xvii). It is an unsettling declaration, but evidence that the novel is determined to exploit and not try to forget the age difference between these two eventual lovers. The sixteen years between them allowed them not to notice what they felt towards each other. They have behaved as if the gap between their ages precluded romance, but we know that they should have known better. Age does shape their relationship, but not at all as they expected.

TWO

Do Sisters Sleep Together?

At night she opened her heart to Jane.

Pride and Prejudice, III. xvii

Are sisters not more intimate, more truly confiding, than any of Austen's lovers? Jane Austen's own most intimate relationship was with her sister, Cassandra, and a few years ago this gave rise to one of the peculiar controversies that periodically bubble up around Austen. In August 1995 a review essay by Professor Terry Castle of Stanford University on Deirdre Le Faye's new Oxford edition of *Jane Austen's Letters* appeared in the *London Review of Books* (*LRB*). It was concerned mostly with the evidence in surviving letters of the closeness between the two Austen sisters, including their physical closeness. That issue of the *LRB* carried the question 'Was Jane Austen Gay?' on its cover. Largely because of this surely mischievous headline, the review became the focus of a public controversy about the nature of the sisters' relationship that spilled into magazines and newspapers and other broadcast media. For several months the correspondence column of the *LRB* was able to rely on freshly provoked contributions from academics and Austen enthusiasts. In a letter of her own to the journal, Professor Castle denied that she had ever suggested that the novelist was 'gay', but pointed out that the two sisters shared a bed for the whole of their adult lives.

What did such intimacy mean? Sisterly chat, of which there is so much in Austen's novels, would surely be peculiarly significant for a writer who would have talked to her own sister in bed. Except that those academics earnestly debating the implications of bed-sharing were, like Emma Woodhouse, 'imaginists'. The *LRB* debate was brought to a resounding close by Bonnie Herron from the University of Alberta who wrote to point out that Edward Copeland had given a paper at the annual conference of the Jane Austen Society of North America in 1993 showing, from the records of Ring Brothers of Basingstoke, a home furnishing store, that Austen's father had bought the sisters two single made-to-order beds when they were young adults. 'Jane and Cassandra each had her own bed'.[1] The disputants would have been better focusing on the novelist Fanny Burney, Austen's most important female predecessor, whose fiction is notably devoid of sisterly intimacy, but who certainly did share a bed with her own sister, Susan. Their bed-sharing was clearly of some significance to them. Three weeks before Susan's marriage in 1782 to the ominously dashing Captain Molesworth Phillips, Fanny Burney wrote a letter to her expressing some of her mixed feelings about the forthcoming happy event. 'There is something to me at the thought of being so near parting with you as the Inmate of the same House – Room – Bed – confidence – life, that is not very *merrifying*.'[2]

Jane and Cassandra Austen did share a compact bedroom, which they occupied until the ailing Jane left the family home in Chawton for Winchester in May 1817, aged forty-one. Surely it was a place for *sotto voce* confidences at the end of the day. Any visitor to Jane Austen's house in Hampshire will be struck by the small sleeping space occupied by two middle-aged women. Indeed, so restricted is this that only one single bed is now placed in the room; if there were the original two, visitors would scarcely be able to enter. Jane and Cassandra might not quite have shared their bodily warmth, as Terry Castle had liked to imagine, but they would have ended and begun each day in intimate isolation from all others. What about the sisters in Austen's novels? Did the novelist assume that they too would have this place of joint retreat where talk would be intimate? The immediate answer is, sometimes – and that where they do, this intimacy is at the heart of the novel.

Most of Austen's sisters have their own bedchambers. There is no need to share bedrooms at Mansfield Park or Kellynch Hall, for instance. This is a fact of wealth and domestic architecture in *Mansfield Park* and *Persuasion*, but it is more than this. Both these novels are stories of sisterly alienation. *Emma* lets us infer a comparable history of sibling separation. Emma's older sister Isabella is long gone from Hartfield, but we know that it is a house large enough always to have allowed the sisters separate rooms. Would the distance of outlook and temperament between Emma and Isabella be imaginable if they had spent their teenage years sharing a bedroom? The Morlands in *Northanger Abbey*, with their ten children, would have to have a remarkably capacious rectory at Fullerton not to make some room-sharing necessary, and we might presume that Catherine shares at least a bedchamber, if not a bed, with Sarah, who, a year younger than her, has become her 'intimate friend and confidante' (I. ii). Sisterly communication, however, might have been limited to family matters or the pleasures of the latest Gothic novel. Catherine's dizzying encounter with Henry Tilney is her first romance and her three months away from home, first in Bath and then at Northanger Abbey, have transformed her. She has had some fond illusions expelled and she has fallen in love. Sarah's inability to grasp what has happened to her erstwhile confidante is signalled in the penultimate chapter, when Henry Tilney has unexpectedly arrived at the Morlands' rectory and, after initial conversation has given way to awkward silence, has asked if Catherine might show him the way to the Allens' house, that he might pay his respects to them. Sarah blurts out that their house can be seen from the window, producing 'a silencing nod from her mother' (II. xv). Sarah has no idea why Henry and her sister might need an excuse to be alone together.

What about *Sense and Sensibility*? Barton Cottage has four bedrooms as well as the garrets for the servants, so the Dashwood ladies could have a room each (I. viii). Yet we know that one of the bedrooms is 'spare' and unused, so Elinor and Marianne might indeed be sleeping in the same room. When the two sisters stay in London they are certainly sharing a bedroom. The morning after the party at which they meet Willoughby after his long separation and silence, and at which we witness his coldness to Marianne and his apparent attachment to another woman, Elinor is 'roused from sleep' by Marianne's 'agitation and sobs' and sees her sister 'only half dressed . . . kneeling against one of the window-seats' and writing a letter by the dim early morning light (II. vii). She begins to ask a question, but Marianne stops her short. 'No, Elinor . . . ask nothing.' The refusal to tell her anything presses all the more on Elinor because of the intimacy of their situation. It is in this shared bedroom that the revealing conversation between the sisters takes place a few hours later, when Elinor comes up after breakfast and finds her sister 'stretched on the bed' clasping Willoughby's terrible letter, in which he dishonestly professes surprise that Marianne should have imagined 'more than I felt, or meant to express'. Now Marianne can tell her that 'there has been no engagement between them', and can show her the increasingly anguished letters that she has sent to him. It is hard to imagine the conversation taking place anywhere but a bedroom. The bedroom is commonly Marianne's retreat. She has taken to this sisterly sanctum when the Steele sisters later arrive on a visit, and Elinor is nettled by Miss Steele's suggestion that, if Marianne is 'laid down upon the bed, or in her dressing gown', she and Lucy might go up to see her (II. x). 'Elinor began to find this impertinence too much for her temper' and the elder Miss Steele gets a 'sharp reprimand' from Lucy. Only Marianne's sister can visit her in their bedroom.

We know that Elizabeth and Jane Bennet also share a bedroom. In *Pride and Prejudice* (I. xxi) Jane receives a letter from Miss Bingley announcing the Bingleys' indefinite absence from Netherfield and she looks for an opportunity to tell Elizabeth about it: 'a glance from Jane invited her to follow her up stairs. When they had gained their own room, Jane, taking out the letter, said, "This is from Caroline Bingley . . . You shall hear what she says".' In their shared room, unhampered talk is natural. Jane tells Elizabeth everything. 'I *will* read you the passage which particularly hurts me. I will have no reserves from *you*.' Shut away together from the rest of their family, the two sisters can talk to each other quite explicitly of the prospect of Jane becoming Mr Bingley's wife. When Mrs Bennet talks to her daughters of this prospect, it is painfully embarrassing for them and comic for the reader; when Jane and Elizabeth discuss it in their bedchamber, we hear the truth of their feelings and uncertainties. Later, as the end of the novel approaches, with Lydia already married and Jane betrothed, Elizabeth tells Jane of her engagement to Mr Darcy in their bedroom. 'At night she opened her heart to Jane' (III. xvii). Confidences flow across the gap – as we might imagine – between their beds. 'All was acknowledged, and half the night spent in conversation.'

The bedroom is a sanctum, and only special people may enter. In all Austen's fiction, we never encounter a husband and wife together in a bedroom. We know that General Tilney and his wife had separate bedrooms because Catherine is caught by Henry Tilney sneaking a look at Mrs Tilney's bedroom.[3] Admission to a bedroom is a rare privilege, for the reader as well as for a character. For the sake of some show of 'tenderness', the baleful Bingley sisters visit Jane Bennet in her bedroom during her illness – but it is a Netherfield bedroom, and not Jane's personal domain. Solicitous though he is about her state of health, Mr Bingley does not visit Jane Bennet in her bedroom during her illness. When she is able to come down to the drawing room for a while, Mr Bingley sits with her and talks to almost no one else. But only his sisters are permitted to entertain Jane with their conversation in the bedroom. Elizabeth, meanwhile, signals her closeness to her sister by spending much of her time in the bedroom. When she is first tending Jane, she passes 'the chief of the night' in her room (I. ix).

Sisterly closeness is not necessarily to be admired.

Think of Jane and Elizabeth Bennet and we might suppose that unreserved sisterly talk is admirable. But Austen knows that such confidential talk can allow malign confederacy too. Think of the conversations between sisters that we do not hear – the sisterly chat going on just off stage, perhaps in bedrooms that we never get to visit. In *Sense and Sensibility*, the Steele sisters talk together, and have always lived in close proximity, even though they are peculiarly divided associates. Miss

Steele – Anne – is 'nearly thirty' and 'very plain'; Lucy Steele is 'two or three and twenty' and 'pretty' (I. xxi). There is a special friction that has come from their life together and that is evident when they first converse with Elinor. With superb crassness Miss Steele asks Elinor if she had 'a great many smart beaux' in Sussex, while Lucy looks 'ashamed of her sister'. Anne always says something tactless or inapposite, so Lucy 'generally made an amendment to all her sister's asser- tions' (I. xxi). Privately, however, in exchanges that we must imagine, they tell each other things. This is crucial to the plot of *Sense and Sensibility*, for clever, dishonest Lucy makes the mistake of sharing with her sister the secret of her engage- ment to Edward Ferrars. Anne (or 'Nancy', as Mrs Jennings likes to call her) lets Mrs John Dashwood know, prompting the latter's 'violent hysterics' (III. i). Her mistake (for she has none of the subtlety of calculation that Lucy possesses) is characteristic of the Steele sisters' twisted intimacy. Even what the two do not share still gets shared. During a stroll in Kensington Gardens, Anne Steele cheerfully tells Elinor about the lovers' chat between Edward and Lucy. Elinor is surprised that this exchange should have taken place in her presence.

> 'La! Miss Dashwood, do you think people make love when any body else is by? Oh, for shame!—To be sure you must know better than that.' (Laughing affectedly.)—'No, no; they were shut up in the drawing-room together, and all I heard was only by listening at the door.' (II. ii)

When Elinor expresses her dismay at this behaviour, the elder Steele assures her that such eavesdropping is more or less what her sister would expect. 'I am sure Lucy would have done just the same by me; for a year or two back, when Martha Sharpe and I had so many secrets together, she never made any bones of hiding in a closet, or behind a chimney-board, on purpose to hear what we said.' Theirs is a relationship of mutual espionage. The Steele sisters have lived so close to each other that such prying has become their way. Only when she has been badly bitten by her sister's indiscretion does Lucy change her policy of confiding in her sister. She conceals her engagement to Robert Ferrars from Anne, and even takes some money from her under false pretences before disappearing with her new paramour.

Sisterly closeness is not necessarily to be admired. Perhaps the closest sisterly conversationalists in Austen's fiction are Kitty and Lydia Bennet. They are habitual companions, a cameo of their companionship given us when they wait in the upstairs room of an inn for Elizabeth's return from Kent. As they travel back from there to Longbourn, Lydia gossips and jokes, 'assisted by Kitty's hints and additions' (II. xvi). Kitty's talk is hooked to Lydia's. Later, when Elizabeth is trying to explain her sister's elopement, she comments on Lydia's preoccupation with 'love, flirtation, and officers': 'She has been doing every thing in her power, by thinking and talking on the subject, to give greater—what shall I call it? susceptibility to her feelings, which are naturally lively enough.' This 'talking' has largely been with Kitty. Kitty is unsurprised at the news of Lydia's elopement and Jane's letter tries to excuse her for having 'concealed their attachment' (III. iv). Kitty knew about their being 'in love' – but not (Jane thinks) before they went to Brighton (III. v) – she knows from letters, not talking. Talking about it would have made her Lydia's abettor. Once Lydia has been rescued from disgrace, the chat between the sisters must be brought to an end. 'From the further disadvantage of Lydia's society she was of course carefully kept' (III. xix).

More poisonous sisterly confederates are Caroline Bingley and Louisa Hurst. Caroline Bingley is the more powerful, but they come as a pair. In Chapter viii of *Pride and Prejudice*, when Elizabeth leaves the company after dinner to attend to her sick sister, they speak with peculiarly unified intent.

> 'She has nothing, in short, to recommend her, but being an excellent walker. I shall never forget her appearance this morning. She really looked almost wild.'
> 'She did indeed, Louisa. I could hardly keep my countenance. Very nonsensical to come at all!' (I. viii)

This is a performance for the benefit of their brother and Mr Darcy. Listen to this almost rehearsed unanimity and you know that these sisters have already been talking, agreeing about their efforts to denigrate Elizabeth. Discussing with Jane Mr Bingley's later neglect of her, Elizabeth certainly takes for granted that both sisters are behind it: '"You persist, then, in supposing his sisters influence him." "Yes, in conjunction with his friend."' (II. i). They are quite a pair. In Miss Bingley's original invitation to Jane to come to Netherfield, she refers to the amount of time that she and Mrs Hurst spend together, and pretends that they are often at loggerheads, 'for a whole day's tête-à-tête between two women can never end without a quarrel' (I. vii). But this is a blind. The sisters are always together and always of a mind.

When Jane visits Miss Bingley in London, she is made to realise that she cannot stay long 'as Caroline and Mrs Hurst were going out' (II. iii). The implication, unperceived by Jane, is that Caroline Bingley has pre-arranged with her sister to extract her from a tricky interview. Again, they have been talking together. When Elizabeth and her aunt, Mrs Gardiner, arrive at Pemberley to visit Georgiana Darcy, she is in the saloon, 'sitting there with Mrs Hurst and Miss Bingley' (III. iii). They have clearly arranged to try to fight Elizabeth off. Miss Bingley confesses the confederacy when she deplores to Mr Darcy the supposed alteration in Elizabeth's appearance since their last meeting. 'She is grown so brown and coarse! Louisa and I were agreeing that we should not have known her again' (III. iii). The fact that this malign pair are always scheming together should allow us to correct what is surely a printer's error in all the standard editions of *Pride and Prejudice*. In Volume III Chapter xiii, where Jane recognises how she and Bingley were kept from meeting each other while both were in London, she explains, 'It must have been his sister's doing' (III. xiii). But she immediately adds, 'They were certainly no friends to his acquaintance with me.' 'They' were up to something: she and Elizabeth are thinking of both sisters, who have always been scheming together, and Austen must surely have meant 'sisters'' (plural possessive) not 'sister's' (singular possessive).

Sisterly togetherness can be deceptive. Maria and Julia Bertram seem to come as a pair, until we see that they are really rivals. They have 'their own apartments' at Mansfield Park (I. xvi) – all the grandeur that space can provide – and true apartness becomes natural to them. They begin in concert, alternating in their reports of Fanny's ignorance (I. ii). They go out together as 'belles of the neighbourhood' (I. iv). But then come the Crawfords, and the casting of that play. The intimacy between the sisters is what allows Julia to know that she is being fobbed off with an undesirable part. When Henry Crawford asks her to play Amelia, she looks at Maria. 'Maria's countenance was to decide it; if she were vexed and alarmed—but Maria looked all serenity and satisfaction' (I. xiv). Theirs is an antagonistic union: they know each other, as we say, all too well.

The sister with whom she was used to be on easy terms was now become her greatest enemy . . . With no material fault of temper, or difference of opinion, to prevent their being very good friends while their interests were the same, the sisters, under such a trial as this, had not affection or principle enough to make them merciful or just, to give them honour or compassion. (I. xvii)

These are sisters reared together as a proud pair who have long since ceased to talk to each other.

Persuasion offers us the one hint of sisterly talk that excludes the heroine but is neither conspiratorial nor rivalrous. Henrietta and Louisa Musgrove may be fairly empty-headed girls, but Anne envies them 'that seemingly perfect good understanding and agreement together, that good-humoured mutual affection, of which she had known so little herself with either of her sisters' (I. v). Close in age (nineteen and twenty) and schooled together, they have an easy – we might imagine somewhat giggly – closeness. When Captain Wentworth becomes a regular visitor to the Musgrove home and the dancing begins, we glimpse the possibility of a Bertram scenario: 'as for Henrietta and Louisa, they both seemed so entirely occupied by him, that nothing but the continued appearance of the most perfect good-will between themselves could have made it credible that they were not decided rivals' (I. viii). But the potential rivalry evaporates exactly because of their habit of talking to each other. On the walk with Anne, Mary Musgrove, Charles Musgrove and Wentworth, they find themselves suddenly in sight of Winthrop, where Henrietta's discarded suitor Charles Hayter lives. Mary, disliking this liaison, wants to turn back.

Henrietta, conscious and ashamed, and seeing no cousin Charles walking along any path, or leaning against any gate, was ready to do as Mary wished; but 'No!' said Charles Musgrove, and 'No, no!' cried Louisa more eagerly, and taking her sister aside, seemed to be arguing the matter warmly. (I. x)

This moment of pressing sisterly talk – of witnessed intimacy – enables Henrietta's change of heart. We naturally assume from the exchange that Louisa knows her sister's true feelings: Henrietta has talked to her of them before now. Her awkwardness conquered, Henrietta goes with her brother to call on the Hayters and her future is happily decided.

All Austen's heroines have sisters. *Sense and Sensibility* is unique is giving us, at first, the thoughts of both of them when they talk privately together. Marianne smiles 'within herself' when Elinor says that Edward has a taste for drawing (I. iv). Then later in the same conversation Elinor 'was sorry for the warmth she had been betrayed into, in speaking of him' (I. iv). This is confidential talk indeed: the sisters discuss Elinor's feelings for Edward, and Marianne finds out that they are not engaged. Yet despite the movement between viewpoints the conversation is unbalanced. Elinor's measured sentences are set against Marianne's histrionic exclamations: 'Cold-hearted Elinor!' It will not be long before private speech between the sisters is reported entirely from Elinor's point of view. In a novel so concerned with secrecy, it is telling that, while Elinor and Marianne are often alone together, attempts at conversation are often stopped short. '"Marianne, may I ask?"—"No, Elinor," she replied, "ask nothing; you will soon know all."' (II. vii). When Marianne does finally tell Elinor the truth about her relationship with Willoughby, it is an outpouring that permits no actual exchange between the two. After her recovery from her near-fatal illness, Marianne has, notoriously, learned to talk to her sister in an entirely new way. Back in Devon, the two sisters go for a walk together, Marianne 'leaning on Elinor's arm' (III. x). The younger sister embarks on a flow of self-reproval couched in balanced Johnsonian sentences such as she would once have scorned.

There are, in fact, only five significant conversations between Elinor and Marianne in *Sense and Sensibility*. In *Pride and Prejudice* we are given twelve private conversations between Elizabeth and Jane. Their retreat into each other's company is a recurrent feature of the novel. Volume II Chapter xvii begins, 'Elizabeth's impatience to acquaint Jane with what had happened could no longer be overcome . . .' (the news is Darcy's proposal and Wickham's perfidy). This is typical. The sisters are constantly looking for opportunities to be alone together. Jane is Elizabeth's 'willing listener' (II. xvii), even if their conversations commonly stage the clash between Elizabeth's candour (in our sense of unsentimental truth telling) and Jane's 'candour' (in Austen's sense of thinking the best of people). In their crowded house, they have to spend time finding places to talk. One of their haunts is the shrubbery, where Elizabeth tells Jane about Darcy's supposed cruelty to Wickham (I. xvii). They take their moments in what spaces they can, sometimes simply having to 'walk out' from the house in order to be able to communicate with each other (III. vii).

Such communication is unusual in Austen's fiction, even where sisters like each other. In *Mansfield Park* Fanny Price returns to her family home in Portsmouth, to find, as well as much discord, a new 'intimacy' with her sister Susan (III. ix). 'Susan was her only companion and listener' (III. xiii). But Austen strangely muffles the relationship. Before this conversational kinship is established, we do hear Susan speak, complaining mostly about the running of the household. Once she and Fanny become companions, no word of dialogue between the sisters is given us. There is some sisterly talk similarly missing from *Emma*. When Emma's sister Isabella visits Hartfield for Christmas, she speaks a good deal, but from Chapters xi to xvii she says no word of directly quoted dialogue to Emma herself. The sisters speak at opposite ends of a crowded room, or through intermediaries. Emma, we have been told, has had seven years without Isabella's company since her sister got married. The sisters are not well matched, but the separation is also a narrative requirement: in this novel Austen needs to isolate her heroine from advice and confidences and private conversation.

In the end, in *Persuasion*, Austen has abandoned the idea that sisterliness might permit the warmest kind of intimacy. Though its plot is as sister-influenced as that of *Pride and Prejudice* – it too turns on an estate that will go to a more distant relative because a father has produced only daughters – its heroine has just one reported conversation with her elder sister, Elizabeth. This is when Anne warns her that Mrs Clay might have designs upon their father. Sisterhood makes the conversation possible, but also difficult. Anne is coldly rebuffed, though she hopes that her sister might be 'made observant' by this private exchange (I. v). With her other sister, Mary, in contrast, there is no shortage of one-to-one conversation, though this usually casts Anne as a tactful therapist, listening to Mary's complaints and talking her round into cheerfulness. It is Mary, naturally, who causes her sister peculiar pain when she happily reports Wentworth saying, 'You were so altered he should not have known you again' (I. vii). No wonder that sisterly chat holds no allure for Anne. It is often remarked that *Persuasion* marks a new departure – taking its heroine off to sea and leaving the landed gentry to their houses and their fates. It is also the end of sisterhood. When Anne becomes engaged once more to Wentworth, she cares 'nothing' about the 'disproportion in their fortune', but a different imbalance does pain her:

> to have no family to receive and estimate him properly, nothing of respectability, of harmony, of good will to offer in return for all the worth and all the prompt welcome which met her in his brothers and sisters, was a source of as lively pain as her mind could well be sensible of under circumstances of otherwise strong felicity. She had but two friends in the world to add to his list, Lady Russell and Mrs Smith. (II. xii)

Anne has escaped her family and can feel a melancholy relief. There is no more need for talking to her sisters.

THREE

What Do the Characters Call Each Other?

...in the whole of the sentence, in his manner of pronouncing it, and in his addressing her sister by her Christian name alone, she instantly saw an intimacy so decided, a meaning so direct, as marked a perfect agreement between them.

Sense and Sensibility, I. xii

Only one married woman in all Jane Austen's novels calls her husband by his Christian name. The wife in question is Mary Musgrove (née Elliot) in *Persuasion*. Not only does she refer to her husband as 'Charles' when talking to her sister Anne, she calls him 'Charles' when she speaks to him directly.[1] Are we to take this as a commendable modern intimacy? Or is it an unwonted breach of domestic decorum? It is likely that anything Mary says will be a little wrong, and we note that she first addresses him as 'Charles' to oppose his wish to leave her with her sick child in order to go to meet Captain Wentworth. 'Oh! no, indeed, Charles, I cannot bear to have you go away' (I. vii). Such informality seems to make dispute all the easier for Mary, as when her husband tells Anne that Captain Benwick is full of her virtues. 'Mary interrupted him.

"I declare, Charles, I never heard him mention Anne twice all the time I was there'" (I. ii). She is always ready to make an objection. 'Good heavens, Charles! how can you think of such a thing? . . . Oh! Charles, I declare it will be too abominable if you do . . . But you must go, Charles. It would be unpardonable to fail' (II. xxiv). Charles Musgrove in turn addresses his wife as 'Mary' when he wishes to contradict her. 'Now you are talking nonsense, Mary'(I. ix); 'Now Mary, you know very well how it really was. It was all your doing . . . Now Mary, I declare it was so, I heard it myself, and you were in the other room' (II. ii).

Any keen reader of Austen will register, though perhaps only half-consciously, the weight of this. For even the fondest of Austen's other wives find some alternative to using their husbands' Christian names. Mrs Croft may be 'Sophy' to her husband, but he is 'my dear admiral' to her. Mr Weston may address his wife as 'Anne, my dear', but she calls him 'Mr. Weston'. The Weston example is particularly striking as we are hearing this recently married couple talking without any witnesses and therefore without any need for formality. We never know Mr Weston's forename – nor Mr Allen's, Colonel Brandon's, Mr Bennet's, Dr Grant's, or Admiral Croft's. Even Mrs Elton has to find a nauseating endearment – 'Mr. E' – rather than brandish her husband's Christian name (*Emma*, II. xiv). Will none of Austen's heroines use their beloved husband's first names after marriage? Elinor Dashwood might do so when she has become Elinor Ferrars, as her husband has long been 'Edward' to her family. He has qualified by already being a relative by marriage. Elizabeth Bennet might be put off doing so by her husband's cumbersome Christian name, Fitzwilliam. But surely Anne Elliot will call Captain Wentworth 'Frederick'? At least in private? We cannot know, but nothing in the talk between married couples in the novels encourages us to think that she will.

The nature of the Musgrove marriage is revealed to us by this small touch: their use of each other's first names. It is no sign of amorous feeling (Charles has married Mary, after all, because Anne would not have him). Rather, it dramatises the companionable disrespect of their relationship. They complain about each other, but in a fatalistic vein, and they also complain in unison, about the failure of Charles's parents to give them more money. They cannot agree about many things, but are not afraid to disagree. They bicker, but they take their social pleasures together. Neither admirable nor wholly improper, their informality in naming each other epitomises this relationship. In Austen's novels, as here, we should notice conventions about how people name others in order to see how they are disobeyed – or to see that different characters follow different conventions. Charlotte Heywood in *Sanditon* notes Lady Denham's 'oldfashioned formality' towards her young companion, and distant relation, 'of always calling her *Miss Clara*' (Ch. 6). But clearly some conventions have a near-moral force. After Maria Bertram gets married, she is always 'Mrs. Rushworth' to both Fanny and the narrator. To call her anything else, even in one's thoughts, would be to undo her marital ties. And this is just what Henry Crawford desires. Encountering her coldness, 'he must get the better of it, and make Mrs. Rushworth Maria Bertram again in her treatment of himself' (III. xvii).

Informality between spouses is not symmetrical. In the second chapter of *Sense and Sensibility*, John Dashwood calls his wife 'My dear Fanny', though she addresses him as 'My dear Mr. Dashwood' (I. ii). 'Shall we walk, Augusta?' says Mr Elton to his wife in front of the group at Box Hill. This is almost ostentatious. 'Happy creature! He called her "Augusta."

How delightful!' says Harriet Smith, after first meeting the vicar's new wife (II. xiv). Her exclamation indicates that the Eltons are behaving in an unusual, perhaps modish, manner. Mr Elton's flourishing of 'Augusta' is made the more repellent by Mrs Elton's mock-coy revelation that he wrote an acrostic on her name while courting her in Bath. Yet it is not simply 'wrong' to use your wife's Christian name. Admiral Croft addresses his wife Sophia as 'Sophy' as he sits in his gig with her and Anne (I. x). She addresses him as 'my dear' and, with an anxious exclamation as he steers erratically, 'My dear admiral, that post!' When Admiral Croft talks to Anne he commonly quotes or cites the support of his wife, and invariably calls her 'Sophy'. We are to notice this as a marked informality: he is the only husband in Austen's novels to call his wife by an affectionate shortening of her Christian name. Yet this is surely at one with his breezy good-heartedness, and a sign of the couple's closeness. His uxoriousness is such that, at one point, as he struggles to remember Louisa Musgrove's name, he frankly wishes that all women were called Sophy.

Equally enamoured of a special name is Fanny Price in *Mansfield Park*: 'there is nobleness in the name of Edmund. It is a name of heroism and renown . . .' (II. iv). A person's Christian name is a kind of magic word. The heroine-centred novels of the eighteenth century invariably gave their protagonists singular names. The trend was set by Samuel Richardson with *Pamela* (1740) – a name previously to be found only in literary romance. Other heroines of successful eighteenth-century novels were called Clarissa, Evelina, Emmeline, Cecilia and Camilla.[2] Austen chooses traditional English names for her heroines, but for other female characters she chooses names that sometimes seem to announce unreliability. The range of female names in Austen's fiction is far wider than the range of male names (twenty-six male versus fifty-five female, even though there are scarcely more named female characters than named male characters).³ The wider lexicon allows for romantic names that bode ill: Maria, Julia, Lydia, Augusta and Selina. Marianne, a recent importation from France, should give us pause.⁴ The Musgrove sisters, bubbly provincial aspirants to fashion, come as a named pair: Henrietta and Louisa. These are new names. The Musgroves, in their state of change, 'perhaps of improvement', enshrine their family ambitions in their daughters' names. One of the running jokes in *Persuasion* is Admiral Croft's inability to remember Louisa's Christian name, which is really a sign of her failure of character. 'And very nice young ladies they both are; I hardly know one from the other' (I. x). Before he tells Anne the news of Louisa's engagement to Captain Benwick, he says, 'you must tell me the name of the young lady I am going to talk about' (II. vi). A few minutes after Anne has done so, and he has confidently referred to her as 'Louisa Musgrove', he is saying that Captain Wentworth's letter to his sister did not indicate 'that he had ever thought of this Miss (what's her name?) for himself'.

In Austen's novels as in her family, names are often handed down to signify continuity. 'Henry is the eldest, he was named after me,' says Mr Woodhouse of his grandson. 'Isabella would have him called Henry, which I thought very pretty of her' (*Emma*, I. ix). In *Mansfield Park*, Tom Bertram, the eldest son, has been named after the *pater familias*, Sir Thomas. In *Persuasion*, Charles Musgrove's eldest son is called Charles, while Mr Elliot carries the name Walter, which he despises (II. ix). Eldest daughters often get their mother's names, as Cassandra Austen did: Maria Bertram and Fanny Price in *Mansfield Park*; Elizabeth Elliot in *Persuasion*. Some names peculiarly meant something to Austen. *Northanger Abbey* opens with a private joke about the name Richard – 'a very respectable man, though his name was Richard' – that the centuries of annotation have not clarified. Perhaps there are other examples of names that had some family meaning to the Austens. It is difficult not to think that the characters in Jane Austen's fiction who shared her author's name – Jane Bennet and Jane Fairfax – thereby acquired a special interest for knowing readers.

As well as those married men whose forenames we never know, think of the women: Mrs Dashwood, Mrs Bennet, Mrs Allen, Mrs Norris, Mrs Grant, Mrs Dixon, Mrs Smith. The last of these is particularly significant, as she is Anne Elliot's old and intimate friend, and the two women are usually found talking alone together. The formality perhaps tells us something of the original age gap between the friends and suggests a distance that remains. Mrs Grant's name remains unknown because in each of several private conversations, Mary Crawford calls her 'Mrs. Grant' or 'sister', while being called 'Mary' – sometimes 'dear Mary' or 'dearest Mary' – in return. The women are some ten years apart in age, so Mrs Grant is a semi-maternal figure, and she is married, so Mary Crawford is speaking in a proper way. Yet the younger woman is a good deal more worldly and more penetrating than her half-sister. The asymmetry of their forms of address helps create the sense that Mrs Grant is an indulgent, fond attend-ant on Mary, who need not exactly requite her attentions.

Such asymmetry is often telling. The famous example is in *Emma*, where Mr Knightley uses the heroine's forename, but she never uses his. This serves the plot: his use of Emma's forename signifies that he is an honorary family member and a kind of father figure, and therefore out of the romantic running. It helps to sustain Emma's own failure to think of him in romantic terms. (Mr Weston – licensed by his wife's intimacy with Emma perhaps – also uses her forename, without any suggestion of offence.) Emma, in turn, always addresses Harriet Smith as 'Harriet', but Harriet, with all that proper respect that Emma so enjoys, never uses her Christian name, always addressing her as 'Miss Woodhouse'. Emma simply assumes that Harriet's name is hers to use. It is inconceivable that Harriet would have invited Emma to use her Christian name. Here the asymmetry enacts a power difference. It also enables Emma to avoid the damning ordinariness of Harriet's surname. ('Mrs. Smith, such a name!' exclaims Sir Walter Elliot in *Persuasion* (II. v).) But how does it feel to Mr Elton, who always calls her 'Miss Smith'? Every time he does so he thinks of the lowness of her origins. When he proposes to Emma, who tells him that he should be addressing himself to her protégée instead, his disbelief is measured by the number of times he repeats the name 'Miss Smith!' How could he couple himself to someone with such a name – which, as she is illegitimate, is almost certainly not the name of her unknown father.

Comparably, in *Persuasion*, Elizabeth Elliot calls Mrs Clay 'Penelope', but the pseudo-respectful Mrs Clay addresses her as 'My dear Miss Elliot' (II. x). Elizabeth's use of Mrs Clay's first name is evidently improper when she never calls her own sister 'Anne'. It is doubly so when Elizabeth has extended her intimacy to a woman whose interest in her is entirely predatory. In *Sense and Sensibility* the Miss Steeles so wheedle their way into the John Dashwood establishment that Elinor hears 'accounts of the favour they were in' from Sir John Middleton. 'Mrs. Dashwood had never been so much pleased with any young women in her life as she was with them; had given each of them a needle book, made by some emigrant; called Lucy by her Christian name; and did not know whether she should ever be able to part with them' (II. xiv). Lucy will not be calling Mrs John Dashwood by her Christian name, but the power imbalance is not as obvious as it seems. Lucy Steele is working on her new patroness. More evidently subordinate is Fanny Price, who calls Maria Bertram 'Miss Bertram', while Maria Bertram calls her 'Fanny'. More unsettling is the asymmetry by which Edmund always calls Fanny by her forename, but Fanny never calls him Edmund. *In extremis*, she will exclaim, 'Oh! Cousin . . .' (e.g. II. ix). The imbalance is calculated by the novelist. What Fanny has most to suffer is the torment of Edmund's easy intimacy with her: 'My dear Fanny . . .' She preserves the possibility, unlikely though she believes it, of moving to some greater intimacy. If she ever calls him Edmund, it will only be at the moment when he ceases to be her cousin.

Familiarity can be contemptuous. When Miss Bingley tells Elizabeth Bennet at a ball that she is foolish to be charmed by Mr Wickham, she refers to him as 'George Wickham' three times in one short paragraph, and the very use of his forename is scornful. Names are used by Austen, as well as by her characters, as though they are precious material, so we sometimes hear only once, glancingly, what someone's name is. Thus the label on the trunk seen by Harriet Smith, directed to Mr Elton at his hotel in Bath, which names him as Philip (II. v). Or the signature on Mr Collins's letter to Mr Bennet that shows him, for the only time in *Pride and Prejudice*, to be called William. There is the signature 'John Willoughby' at the foot of the letter that cruelly disclaims any attachment between himself and Marianne Dashwood (II. vii). Or the one passing endearment from Mr to Mrs Weston that reveals her to be called Anne. We only find out Captain Benwick's Christian name for the first time late in *Persuasion*, when Admiral Croft refers to him as 'James Benwick' (II. vi). Is this the privilege of seniority? Or a further example of the Admiral's bracing informality? What about Mr Elliot? Eventually we read the letter where, for the only time, we see he is called William – and hear him say that he hates the Elliot name (II.ix). (William Walter Elliot is the only character in Austen's completed fiction to be given two forenames, burdening him with the reminder of his lineage.)

As narrator, Austen shares the sensitivities of
her characters in the matter of names.

The mere use of a person's Christian name is a rare privilege and can carry great weight. The famous example is in *Sense and Sensibility*, where Elinor overhears Willoughby discussing the gift of a horse with her sister and saying, 'Marianne, the horse is still yours' (I. xii). Elinor knows what to think: 'in the whole of the sentence, in his manner of pronouncing it, and in his addressing her sister by her Christian name alone, she instantly saw an intimacy so decided, a meaning so direct, as marked a perfect agreement between them. From that moment she doubted not of their being engaged to each other.' A woman who lets a man speak her name has given him a special power. We hear Willoughby's loss of this privilege when he turns up at Cleveland to explain himself to Elinor. He declares that his purpose is 'to obtain something like forgiveness from Ma—from your sister' (III. viii). He used to call her 'Marianne', an acknowledgement of intimacy, and now – married to another woman – he has forfeited the right to do so.

Between two young women, the habit is easier. The 'quick' progress of the friendship between Catherine and Isabella in *Northanger Abbey* means that, on their second meeting, 'They called each other by their Christian name' (I. v). But the quickness is suspect. Isabella is interested in Catherine as a way to her brother, and all her warmth is feigned. In contrast, it is a long time before Catherine calls Eleanor Tilney by her Christian name. Although we may not realise it until we search the text, 'it is not until the very night of the General's barbarously turning Catherine out of doors that we hear Eleanor and Catherine use each other's Christian names'.[5] The sense of decorum with which Henry Tilney's sister is addressed is emphasised by the the narrator's habit of calling her 'Miss Tilney'. It is a long time before even the novelist can dare to use Miss Tilney's forename, well into the second volume of the novel, when Catherine hears Captain Tilney 'whisper to Eleanor' (II. v). Catherine waits even longer before using Eleanor's name. After their acquaintance in Bath and four weeks' stay at Northanger Abbey, the first occasion recorded by the novel is one of high feeling. Eleanor has come to Catherine to tell her that her father has decreed that she must leave. Eleanor begins her mortifying announcement, 'My dear Catherine . . .' (II. xiii). Catherine responds with the same, new informality. '"My dear Eleanor," cried Catherine . . .' (II. xiii). Now the intimacy has been hazarded, and Catherine can have confidence in it. 'Do not be distressed, Eleanor . . .' A crisis has pushed them to this closeness. 'You must write to me, Catherine' . . . 'Oh, Eleanor, I will write to you indeed.' Few readers will be conscious that the two women are now naming each other in a new way. The novels employ nuances such as this that shape any sensitive reader's understanding, but that only text-searching can reveal.

In *Mansfield Park* Mary Crawford calls Fanny by her Christian name for the first time in a note, written with the (false) assurance that Fanny is about to become engaged to her brother (II. xiii). Though Mary Crawford may be expert at infiltrating people's affections, she is clever enough to know when she is risking familiarity, and explicitly draws attention to her new assumption of intimacy. 'My Dear Fanny, for so I may now always call you, to the infinite relief of a tongue that has been stumbling at *Miss Price* for the last six weeks'. 'Stumbling' because it is a formality, she implies, that hinders confidence and affection. From here on, her use of Fanny's name is a constant assault on her defences, often in phrases such as 'dear Fanny' or 'Good, gentle Fanny' (III. v). Mary Crawford is herself called 'Mary' by the narrator in scenes with only her brother or Mrs Grant, who both use her Christian name, but is called 'Miss Crawford' by the narrator in scenes with Fanny. Fanny is resolute against her blandishments and the novelist is with her. This just begins to change in the third volume, in a scene where Miss Crawford is reminding Fanny that her brother has helped William Price gain promotion. '"I cannot imagine Henry ever to have been happier," continued Mary presently, "than when he had succeeded in getting your brother's commission." She had made a sure push at Fanny's feelings here' (III. v).

If familiarity is noticeable, nicknames and shortenings are potentially jarring. Some can be disdainful. Sir Thomas Bertram's son becomes 'Tom' to everyone because he is himself no respecter of tradition or obligation. When the Musgrove sisters start lamenting 'poor Richard' the author informs us that they are in fact referring to 'a thick-headed, unfeeling, unprofitable Dick Musgrove' (*Persuasion*, I. vi). In fact he 'had never done any thing to entitle himself to more than the abbreviation of his name'. 'Richard' is respectful; 'Dick' dismissive. Fanny Price's father calls her 'Fan', a rough informality that is all the more striking as she addresses him as 'Sir' in reply (*Mansfield Park*, III. xv). She seems to be trying to tug him back to a gentility that he has forgotten.

Men in Austen use each other's surnames for informality. In *Sense and Sensibility*, Sir John Middleton calls his brother-in-law 'Palmer', at least in company (I. xix). In *Mansfield Park*, Henry Crawford calls Edmund 'Bertram' and Edmund calls Henry Crawford 'Crawford'. In *Emma*, Mr Knightley refers to Mr Weston as 'Weston' when he talks to Mrs Weston. It is a form of familiarity in which Austen joins. In *Sense and Sensibility*, the narrator from the first refers to 'Willoughby', not 'Mr Willoughby'. Soon Elinor, Marianne and Mrs Dashwood are also calling him this. After he has jilted Marianne and his history as a seducer has been revealed, he arrives for a confrontation with Elinor who, for the first time, resolutely addresses him as 'Mr. Willoughby': his privilege has been withdrawn. In *Pride and Prejudice* Mr Darcy is 'Darcy' to his friend Mr Bingley, but soon to the narrator as well. He is later called 'Darcy' by his cousin Colonel Fitzwilliam and his aunt Lady Catherine de Bourgh. Wickham refers to him as 'Darcy' in a dialogue with Elizabeth late in the novel, when he comes to Longbourn as Lydia's husband. We can take the familiarity as further evidence of Wickham's untrustworthiness. Elizabeth calls her future husband 'Darcy' just once in the whole novel, in confidential conversation with Jane, as she reveals his proposal (and Wickham's nefariousness). 'There is but such a quantity of merit between them; just enough to make one good sort of man . . . For my part, I am inclined to believe it all Darcy's' (II. xvii). Her informal use of his name is a stronger sign of her good will towards him than the judgement she is passing. Wickham, in contrast, is first called by his surname by the narrator, the sign of an impending familiarity (I. xvi). The first character who refers to him in this way is Mr Bennet, who jestingly and improperly tells Elizabeth, 'Let Wickham be *your* man. He is a pleasant fellow, and would jilt you creditably' (II. i). The next to do so is, tellingly, Lydia, who refers to 'dear

Wickham' when she is reporting to Elizabeth that he is not, after all, to marry the heiress Mary King. 'There is no danger of Wickham's marrying Mary King ... Wickham is safe.' It is a clue to Lydia's later attachment to him. And once the truth about him has been revealed, he becomes 'Wickham' to Elizabeth and Jane too (II. xvii).

In the fullest treatment of names in Austen, Maggie Lane suggests that this familiar use of men's surnames was a fashion left over from the 1790s, when early versions of *Sense and Sensibility* and *Pride and Prejudice* were first composed. 'We would never speak of Churchill or Elliot,' she observes.[6] The former is indeed always 'Frank Churchill', but surely for special reasons: not just because his adoptive father, Mr Churchill, is still alive, but also because the two elements of his social being – the name his father has given him and the name he has taken from his adoptive parents – have to be equally stated. He will never be 'Churchill' because it is not his true name. Meanwhile we know that Mr Elliot called Mrs Smith's husband 'Smith', so presumably did get called 'Elliot' in return. The issue is really whether women might use men's surnames, and is brought alive by Mrs Elton's evident impertinence in *Emma*. Who arrived when she was meeting the Westons for the first time? she asks Emma. '"Knightley!" continued Mrs. Elton; "Knightley himself!—Was not it lucky?"' (II. xiv) We do not need a social historian to explain why Emma is silently indignant. 'Absolutely insufferable! Knightley!—I could not have believed it. Knightley!—never seen him in her life before, and call him Knightley!' Mrs Elton does not only continue to talk of 'Knightley', she addresses him as such. '"Is not this most vexatious, Knightley?" ... "Pray be sincere, Knightley" ... "Yes, believe me, Knightley"' (III. vi). The convention of this familiarity has not changed; what is novel is Mrs Elton's singular presumptuousness in adopting it.

Unlike those much younger men from the earlier novels, Mr Knightley is always called 'Mr' by the narrator. He famously tires of the formality.

> '"Mr. Knightley."—You always called me, "Mr. Knightley;" and, from habit, it has not so very formal a sound.—And yet it is formal. I want you to call me something else, but I do not know what.'
>
> 'I remember once calling you "George," in one of my amiable fits, about ten years ago. I did it because I thought it would offend you; but, as you made no objection, I never did it again.'
>
> 'And cannot you call me "George" now?'
>
> 'Impossible!—I never can call you any thing but "Mr. Knightley." I will not promise even to equal the elegant terseness of Mrs. Elton, by calling you Mr. K.' (III. xvii)

Even being in love does not let you use a man's Christian name. Thus an added reason for Catherine Morland's distress as she is about to leave Northanger Abbey. Parting from Eleanor Tilney, she wants to mention 'one whose name had not yet been spoken by either' (II. xiv). She asks to be remembered to 'her absent friend', but at 'this approach to his name' she is overcome by emotion. The impossibility of Henry's name is all the greater as she has never used it, even to Eleanor.

To use a Christian name with amorous intent is hazardous indeed. The climax of the after-dinner evening at Mansfield Park, where Mr Crawford shows off his reading skills to Fanny and tries to pressure her into conversational exchange, is his first ever use of her Christian name. Expressing his 'warmest hopes' of some eventual return of his professed affection, he exclaims 'Yes, dearest, sweetest Fanny—Nay—(seeing her draw back displeased) forgive me.' He knows that she has been offended not by the endearments but by the use of her name. 'Perhaps I have as yet no right—but by what other name can I call you?' Austen does not need to describe Fanny's feelings; we are to sense vividly her embarrassment and displeasure when he goes on to tell her, 'it is "Fanny" that I think of all day, and dream of all night' (III. iii). What we perhaps hardly notice is the amorous hyperbole of his finding in her 'some touches of the angel' earlier in his speech. But we should, for we have heard Mrs Norris thinking Julia 'an angel' much earlier on in the novel. Mr Crawford is not so completely wrong as her, but is falling back on the same cliché. He talks as if modesty and principle were more than human. He never addresses her as 'Fanny' again.

A more subtle impertinence is his sister's addressing Fanny as 'my dear child'; it is a form of would-be endearment that is precisely calculated by the author. It catches Mary Crawford's fundamentally condescending attachment to Fanny, but it also shows us how unaware she is of Fanny's feelings. Fanny has grown into a womanly rival for Edmund's affections, no child any longer. The impertinent endearment is only used elsewhere in Austen by one other character, Mrs Elton, who addresses the powerless and humiliated Jane Fairfax as 'my dear child'. She takes possession of Jane Fairfax by calling her 'Jane', to Frank Churchill's evident surprise and distaste (II. ii). When he writes his long letter explaining his actions to Mrs Weston – and thus to Emma too – he expresses his anger at Mrs Elton's 'system of . . . treatment' of Jane Fairfax, and his protest focuses on her use of his fiancée's Christian name. '"Jane," indeed!—You will observe that I have not yet indulged myself in calling her by that name, even to you' (III. xiv). 'Think, then, what I must have endured in hearing it bandied between the Eltons with all the vulgarity of needless repetition, and all the insolence of imaginary superiority.' And this is the point: Jane Fairfax is certainly not going to call Mrs Elton 'Augusta'.

As narrator, Austen shares the sensitivities of her characters in the matter of names. So she has the peculiar habit of referring to a character formally and informally in the same stretch of narrative. When Charlotte Lucas sets about luring Mr Collins into a marriage proposal, we are told 'Charlotte's kindness extended further . . . Such was Miss Lucas's scheme' (I. xxii). The first statement seems to take us sympathetically into the character's thoughts; the second to view her with a colder detachment. 'Charlotte had been tolerably encouraging . . . Miss Lucas perceived him from an upper window . . .': these are in almost adjacent sentences. 'Miss Lucas, who accepted him solely from the pure and disinterested desire of an establishment . . . Charlotte herself was tolerably composed . . .' The reader is hardly conscious of the narrator's movement back and forth between formal and familiar names, but it conditions our odd mix of sympathy and horror at what the character is doing.

Formality can be painful, never more than in *Persuasion*, when Captain Wentworth addresses Anne as 'madam' in his first words to her that are actually quoted in the novel (I. viii). Then, in the crisis after Louisa Musgrove's fall, she overhears him exclaim, 'but, if Anne will stay, no one so proper, so capable as Anne!' (I. xii) It takes her a moment 'to recover from the emotion of hearing herself so spoken of' – and the emphatic use of her Christian name, twice, is partly what causes this emotion. The modern reader knows that Captain Wentworth is acknowledging her competence and care, but the name-sensitive reader knows that, by calling her 'Anne', he is releasing the energy of pent feelings. In the cancelled manuscript Chapter x, he exclaims 'Anne, my own dear Anne!', but in the finished novel he is never heard actually to address her by her Christian name. The avoidance of a name can be powerful too. After their first meeting, in a passage where

Anne is thinking about Captain Wentworth, he is called by his name and title. At a certain point, however, Anne starts avoiding his name in her thoughts, so the narrator starts avoiding it too. When Anne is introduced to Mr Elliot, we hear that 'his manners were so exactly what they ought to be, so polished, so easy, so particularly agreeable, that she could compare them in excellence to only one person's manners' (II. iii). That 'one person' is Captain Wentworth, but his name is suppressed. Or again, when Mr Elliot recalls looking at her at Lyme 'with some earnestness', 'She knew it well; and she remembered another person's look also.' The avoidance of 'Captain Wentworth' is a concession of feeling on the part of the heroine. Perhaps she once called him 'Frederick' and now declines the formality of his title and surname when she thinks of him. It is the comparison with Mr Elliot – the resexualisation of the heroine – that forces the suppression. When Lady Russell invites her to consider herself as the future Lady Elliot, she knows that she cannot accept Mr Elliot – partly because 'her feelings were still adverse to any man save one' (II. v). So much is in a name that the narrator, in imitation of the heroine, has to omit it. It is just too potent a word.

FOUR

How Do Jane Austen's Characters Look?

'She is a sort of elegant creature that one cannot keep one's
eyes from. I am always watching her to admire . . .'

Emma, II. iii

Jane Austen aficionados like to share their mild outrage at
the casting in some of the many film versions of her novels,
especially the casting of the actresses who play the heroines.
Sometimes this is prompted by the film-makers' provocative
neglect of Austen's characterisation – the choice, for instance,
of Billie Piper, energetic action girl, as Fanny Price in an ITV
Mansfield Park – but often the offence is a matter of looks.
Could Gwyneth Paltrow be Emma, as she was in the 1996
Hollywood film? Her accent was less a worry than her looks.
Not only the wrong-coloured eyes (blue instead of Emma's
'true hazle') but also a willowy frame that seemed not to match
Austen's insistence on her heroine's physical robustness. And
how could the thin and delicate Keira Knightley be chosen for
Elizabeth Bennet, famous for her three-mile walk down lanes
and across loamy fields? Such casting is often an affront to
our presuppositions about how Austen's heroines look. The

affront is telling, for these presuppositions are founded on so much that is only implicit in the novels themselves. We do not know, for instance, even the colour of these heroines' hair. How people look is often suggested rather than specified in Austen's novels. Why should she not tell us?

Perhaps because she would have us, like Laurence Sterne in *Tristram Shandy*, imagine an attractive woman to meet our own requirements: 'Sit down, Sir, paint her to your own mind—as like your mistress as you can—as unlike your wife as your conscience will let you.'[1] But Austen wants us to think not so much about how characters look, but how they look to each other. Her sparing use of specification when it comes to looks is striking when looks can be so important. Think of the Bennet girls, who must rely on their personal attractions to win them some kind of financial security and social standing. When Jane Bennet becomes engaged to Mr Bingley her mother exclaims, with embarrassing glee and yet also honesty, 'I was sure you could not be so beautiful for nothing!' (*Pride and Prejudice*, III. xiii). There is the sense confessed quietly throughout Austen's narrative that looks are hugely important (thus those words used so frequently about characters when we first meet them: handsome, pretty, gentlemanlike, elegant). Austen herself is too honest not to mention a character's looks when he or she is introduced to us. And yet there is often the sense for the reader that looks are difficult to catch, elusive, unspecifiable. This is partly because Austen wants to avoid the strained formulae of other novels. For most novelists of Austen's age and earlier, a heroine's looks belong with her predictable parcel of virtues. In the first chapter of a novel that Jane Austen certainly read, Mary Brunton's *Self-Control* (1810), we find that the heroine, Laura Montreville, is possessed of 'consummate loveliness', 'cheerful good sense' and 'matchless simplicity'. There is a ready vocabulary of superlatives for any novel heroine, for her virtues and for her attractiveness. Austen needed to escape such a vocabulary, and thus came her interest in the indefinability of some of her most important characters' looks. (One of her tricks is to save her precise descriptions for minor characters.)

The elusive qualities of Elizabeth Bennet's looks are explicitly discussed in *Pride and Prejudice*, taken up by Mr Darcy when he responds to Miss Bingley's sarcasm about adding her to the portraits in Pemberley: "'. . . what painter could do justice to those beautiful eyes?'" "It would not be easy, indeed, to catch their expression, but their colour and shape, and the eye-lashes, so remarkably fine, might be copied'" (I. x). The difficulty of catching the 'expression' of Elizabeth's eyes is evidence of their beauty, and the detection of this difficulty is proof of Mr Darcy's attraction to her. Later he talks to Elizabeth about her trying to 'sketch' his 'character', and she talks of trying to 'take your likeness', as if the most appreciative judges of other people – especially other people to whom they may be attracted – are those who know how hard it is to render a likeness.

Elizabeth's eyes in *Pride and Prejudice* captivate Mr Darcy. We remember finding out in Chapter vi that she does not please Mr Darcy's taste. 'But no sooner had he made it clear to himself and his friends that she had hardly a good feature in her face, than he began to find it was rendered uncommonly intelligent by the beautiful expression of her dark eyes.' That 'made it clear to himself' is wonderfully satirical: he convinces himself against the pressure of an unstated allure. The eyes have him. Mr Darcy's judgement also alerts us to the feature of a woman that we are most likely to find out about throughout Austen's fiction. We are told of Anne Elliott's 'mild dark eyes', and of Fanny Price's 'soft light eyes' (to be preferred by any properly discerning male judge to Mary Crawford's 'sparkling dark ones'). Catherine Morland's eyes are not specifically described like this, though in the opening pages of *Northanger Abbey* we are told of her transformation from tomboy to 'interesting' young woman, how, as she grows through her teens, 'her eyes gained more animation'. Marianne Dashwood's eyes naturally reveal her personality, but also have an unusual colour that makes her allure singular: 'in her eyes, which were very dark, there was a life, a spirit, an eagerness which could hardly be seen without delight' (I. x).

When we come to the looks of the Austen heroine whom we know best of all, Emma Woodhouse, eye colour is the one particular of which we can be sure. Emma is 'handsome', we know this from the first sentence, but we know rather little about her appearance, beyond her former governess's enraptured description. 'Such an eye! the true hazle eye—and so brilliant! regular features, open countenance, with a complexion! oh! what a bloom of full health, and such a pretty height and size; such a firm and upright figure. There is health, not merely in her bloom, but in her air, her head, her glance' (I. v). Mrs Weston's appreciation may be a little too exclamatory for comfort, but it is not in itself unusual, for how people appear in Austen's novels is inseparable from how they are looked at. And looking at others appreciatively – judging the attractiveness of their features – is a proper aesthetic activity. There is a kind of connoisseurship of looks in Austen.

Take Harriet Smith in *Emma*. 'She was a very pretty girl, and her beauty happened to be of a sort which Emma particularly admired. She was short, plump and fair, with a fine bloom, blue eyes, light hair, regular features, and a look of great sweetness' (I. iii). This is a description, but through Emma's eyes. Harriet's appearance is caught through Emma's appreciation of it. We soon know that she is so caught up

in her own appreciativeness that she can readily mistake as
intended for Harriet Mr Elton's later compliment about the
'soft eye' of a 'lovely woman' in the ingratiating rhyme that he
composes. Emma flatters herself on the score of her powers
of discrimination, and this includes her connoisseurship of
looks. Her appreciation therefore runs to Jane Fairfax, whom
of course she does not like, but whose looks she has to admire
in an aesthetic way.

> Jane Fairfax was very elegant, remarkably elegant; and she had
> herself the highest value for elegance. Her height was pretty, just
> such as almost every body would think tall, and nobody could think
> very tall; her figure particularly graceful; her size a most becom-
> ing medium, between fat and thin, though a slight appearance of
> ill-health seemed to point out the likeliest evil of the two. Emma
> could not but feel all this; and then, her face—her features—there
> was more beauty in them altogether than she had remembered; it
> was not regular, but it was very pleasing beauty. Her eyes, a deep
> grey, with dark eye-lashes and eyebrows, had never been denied
> their praise; but the skin, which she had been used to cavil at, as
> wanting colour, had a clearness and delicacy which really needed
> no fuller bloom. It was a style of beauty, of which elegance was
> the reigning character, and as such, she must, in honour, by all her
> principles, admire it:—elegance, which, whether of person or of
> mind, she saw so little in Highbury. (II. ii)

All this, like much of the novel, is in free indirect style,
where the narrative takes on the habits of thought and the
vocabulary of the character. That opening repetition – 'very
elegant, remarkably elegant' – lets us hear Emma thinking
to herself, complimenting Jane Fairfax but also her known
judgement. For a moment she can admire Jane Fairfax, whom
she does not like, as a compliment to her own discernment.

She likes to see 'elegance' because of its rarity, and because, by implication, so few in Highbury are qualified, like her, to recognise it.

The habit of one character looking at another with disinterested aesthetic regard is the more peculiar as looking can be charged with such significant feeling in Austen's fiction. Rarely is this sense stronger than in the scene at the concert in Bath in *Persuasion*, staged as Anne has begun to believe that Captain Wentworth still loves her. The singers sing, or Mr Elliot talks on, while in every interval of the two Anne looks for Wentworth, and tries to catch a look from him. For nothing more is possible. When speech is difficult, characters become so sensitive to looks that they feel them without looking themselves. Or they think they do so. In *Emma*, Frank Churchill takes his leave of Highbury after having stopped short of giving Emma a proper explanation of the state of his feelings. 'I think you can hardly be without suspicion,' he says, and she naturally misunderstands (II. xii). He is on the point of confessing his attachment to Jane Fairfax; Emma believes he is about to declare his love for her. 'She believed he was looking at her; probably reflecting on what she had said, and trying to understand the manner. She heard him sigh.' Most important of all are the occasions when characters will not look back when looked at. Thus the peculiar passage in *Emma*, shortly after Frank Churchill has blunderingly revealed his knowledge of Mr Perry's coach, where the narrative unfolds from Mr Knightley's perspective. 'Mr. Knightley's eyes had preceded Miss Bates's in a glance at Jane. From Frank Churchill's face, where he thought he saw confusion suppressed or laughed away, he had involuntarily turned to her's; but she was indeed behind, and too busy with her shawl' (III. v). Jane Fairfax is adept at turning her looks from others.

In *Persuasion*, it is the heroine who avoids meeting another's eyes. When Anne Elliot encounters Wentworth again after almost eight years the narrative mimics her own looking aside.

> Her eye half met Captain Wentworth's, a bow, a curtsey passed; she heard his voice; he talked to Mary, said all that was right; said something to the Miss Musgroves, enough to mark an easy footing; the room seemed full, full of persons and voices, but a few minutes ended it. Charles shewed himself at the window, all was ready, their visitor had bowed and was gone. (I. vii)

She looks down and away, only confusedly sensing what is happening. She sees only enough to mortify her the more, to notice that the years have given him 'a more glowing, manly, open look'. When she plays the piano as he dances with the Musgrove and Hayter girls she can look at the music or the keys, though not without an acute sensitivity to his glances. '*Once* she felt that he was looking at herself – observing her altered features, perhaps, trying to trace in them the ruins of the face which had once charmed him.' Only in the crisis of Louisa Musgrove's fall at Lyme is such painful restraint abandoned. In desperation, Wentworth does look at – and look for – Anne. 'Captain Wentworth's eyes were also turned towards her' (I. xii). The manoeuvres of looking and not looking are set aside. And then when, in Bath, she senses that his feelings for her are fully re-awakened, she and we discover a different kind of not-looking, seeing Wentworth in the street and looking and then 'not daring to look again' (I. vii).

This emotionally charged evasion of looks contrasts with the strange licensed looking that we have seen with Mr Darcy's inspection of Elizabeth Bennet or Emma's of Jane Fairfax. When Emma Woodhouse visits Jane Fairfax after the latter's two-year absence from Highbury, we are told first of her 'dislike' of the woman, and second of her admiration of her person. She looks at her with a 'sense of pleasure'. The next day she tells Mr Knightley, 'She is a sort of elegant creature that one cannot keep one's eyes from. I am always watching her to admire' (II. iii). This is not a confession, but a declaration that is supposed to exhibit her good taste. When Frank Churchill attempts to pre-empt suspicions of his relationship with Jane by commenting on her 'most deplorable want of complexion', Emma enters into the debate with 'a warm defence of Miss Fairfax's complexion' – as if the matter were not charged with significance. Emma says, 'there is no disputing about taste'. Even more cunningly, Frank Churchill confidentially mocks Jane's hairstyle:

she saw Frank Churchill looking intently across the room at Miss Fairfax, who was sitting exactly opposite.

'What is the matter?' said she.

He started. 'Thank you for rousing me,' he replied. 'I believe I have been very rude; but really Miss Fairfax has done her hair in so odd a way—so very odd a way—that I cannot keep my eyes from her. I never saw any thing so outré! Those curls! This must be a fancy of her own. I see nobody else looking like her! I must go and ask her whether it is an Irish fashion. Shall I? Yes, I will—I declare I will— and you shall see how she takes it;— whether she colours.'

He was gone immediately; and Emma soon saw him standing before Miss Fairfax, and talking to her; but as to its effect on the young lady, as he had improvidently placed himself exactly between them, exactly in front of Miss Fairfax, she could absolutely distinguish nothing. (II. viii)

Frank Churchill's *sotto voce* comments to Emma are an impro-
vised excuse for being caught in a lover's gaze. When he goes
to speak to Jane he naturally ('improvidently', Emma mistak-
enly thinks) blocks Emma's view of Jane's face.

> *It still surprises some readers to find that looks*
> *in Austen's novels can so openly express what*
> *we might call sexual attraction.*

Mr Darcy's aesthetic appreciation of Elizabeth Bennet's eyes
is amusing self-delusion, but this way of looking at women
can be more uncertain in its effects on us. For the modern
reader, there is, I think, something disconcerting about Mr
Knightley's appreciative discussion of Emma's 'person' in
the fifth chapter of *Emma*. 'How well she looked last night!'
exclaims Mrs Weston.

> 'Oh! you would rather talk of her person than her mind, would
> you? Very well; I shall not attempt to deny Emma's being pretty.'
> 'Pretty! say beautiful rather. Can you imagine any thing nearer
> perfect beauty than Emma altogether—face and figure?'
> 'I do not know what I could imagine, but I confess that I have
> seldom seen a face or figure more pleasing to me than her's. But I
> am a partial old friend.' (I. v)

We may detect here something more than the language of
an 'old friend'. He is sizing up her body as well as appreciating her features. It is important, however, that Mrs
Weston does not immediately detect anything in his relish
of Emma's 'face and figure'. Such relish is allowed, even of
a young woman's figure, which means nothing less than the
shape of her body as revealed and concealed by her dress.

The aesthetic appreciation of a woman's shape, or shape-liness, seems, in *Sense and Sensibility*, to have been shared by the author herself. Elinor Dashwood, we are told, has 'a delicate complexion, regular features, and a remarkably pretty figure'. Her sister is 'still handsomer'. 'Her form, though not so correct as her sister's, in having the advan-tage of height, was more striking' (I. x). The use of 'correct' here, which is surely the author's judgement, is strange to us, implying that there is some culturally agreed standard for body-shape, by which observers would reasonably judge actual women.

Egged on by Mrs Weston ('She is loveliness itself. Mr. Knightley, is not she?') Mr Knightley actually agrees with her superlatives. '"I have not a fault to find with her person," he replied. "I think her all you describe. I love to look at her."' These two characters could not have this conversation if either were conscious that Mr Knightley was a possible part-ner for Emma. He is indeed Emma's 'old friend' – and we might remember this when 'friend' becomes the word that prods him into proposing to her some nine months later: 'as a friend, indeed, you may command me,' she says to him. '"As a friend!" repeated Mr. Knightley. "Emma, that I fear is a word —No, I have no wish—Stay, yes, why should I hesitate?"' (III. xiii)

There is a kind of appreciative looking at a young woman – and not at her face only – that is a quite proper exercise in taste. It can be done foolishly or wrongly. We should note that Sir Walter Elliot greatly fancies himself a connoisseur of female beauty. And there is something wrong with Mr Darcy's first expression of what he sees in Elizabeth: 'Catching her eye, he withdrew his own and coldly said, "She is tolerable; but not handsome enough to tempt *me*."' (I. iii) He is fancy-ing himself an imperturbable judge. 'Though he had detected with a critical eye more than one failure of perfect symmetry in her form, he was forced to acknowledge her figure to be light and pleasing.' Elizabeth does not please his taste, having 'hardly a good feature in her face', but then 'her dark eyes' correct his judgement. Everyone knows about the tingling dialogue between the two of them, but the complexity of feeling between them is truly expressed in a drama of looking. It is through looks that the impression of something between them has been given.

Famously, it is really set in motion by Elizabeth's walk across the fields, and Mr Darcy's 'admiration of the brilliancy which exercise had given to her complexion'.

> Elizabeth could not help observing, as she turned over some music books that lay on the instrument, how frequently Mr. Darcy's eyes were fixed on her. She hardly knew how to suppose that she could be an object of admiration to so great a man; and yet that he should look at her because he disliked her was still more strange. (I. x)

She supposes it is all about taste or distaste, as when Miss Bingley invites her to walk up and down the room with her – perhaps, Mr Darcy suggests, 'because you are conscious that your figures appear to the greatest advantage in walking'. Yet it is about more than taste.

Even Mr Darcy senses that something is happening: on Elizabeth's last day at Netherfield, he 'would not even look at her'; when they meet in Meryton we find him 'beginning to determine not to fix his eyes on Elizabeth' (I. xv). Looks are risky. His looks escape his intentions. His looking indeed becomes so attentive that it make others observant. A great watcher of others' looks, Charlotte Lucas (now Collins) wonders explicitly if he is in love with her friend.

> She watched him whenever they were at Rosings, and whenever
> he came to Hunsford; but without much success. He certainly
> looked at her friend a great deal, but the expression of that look
> was disputable. It was an earnest, steadfast gaze, but she often
> doubted whether there were much admiration in it, and some-
> times it seemed nothing but absence of mind. (II. ix)

It still surprises some readers to find that looks in Austen's
novels can so openly express what we might call sexual attraction. Just such is the look that Anne gets from the unknown
gentleman on the steps to the beach in Lyme: 'he looked at her
with a degree of earnest admiration, which she could not be
insensible of' (I. xii). She has had 'the bloom and freshness
of youth restored', 'the animation of eye', and she knows just
how she is being looked at by this stranger in a public place.
It is a look that is open enough to be seen and interpreted by
Captain Wentworth too.

> It was evident that the gentleman (completely a gentleman in
> manner) admired her exceedingly. Captain Wentworth looked
> round at her instantly in a way which shewed his noticing of it.
> He gave her a momentary glance, a glance of brightness, which
> seemed to say, 'That man is struck with you, and even I, at this
> moment, see something like Anne Elliot again.' (I. xii)

It is a look of admiration that Mr Elliot later admits to,
though when he does so Anne remembers 'another person's
look also'. These looks keep coming back, as when Mr Elliot
enters the confectioner's shop in Bath.

> Captain Wentworth recollected him perfectly. There was no
> difference between him and the man who had stood on the steps
> at Lyme, admiring Anne as she passed, except in the air and look

and manner of the privileged relation and friend. He came in
with eagerness, appeared to see and think only of her. (II. vii)

Mr Elliot fusses away, unaware that his own role in the novel
is to spark Captain Wentworth's jealousy.

This idea of a man appreciating a woman, expressed in the
wordless encounter between Anne and Mr Elliot in Lyme, is
put to unsettling use in *Mansfield Park*, when Edmund reports
to Fanny his father's appreciation of her looks.

> 'Your complexion is so improved!—and you have gained so
> much countenance!—and your figure—nay, Fanny, do not turn
> away about it—it is but an uncle. If you cannot bear an uncle's
> admiration, what is to become of you? You must really begin to
> harden yourself to the idea of being worth looking at. You must
> try not to mind growing up into a pretty woman.'
>
> 'Oh! don't talk so, don't talk so,' cried Fanny, distressed by
> more feelings than he was aware of. (II. iii)

Edmund blunders, not knowing of Fanny's love for him,
and doubly so in talking of her being 'worth looking at'. He
alerts her both to the possibility of her being attractive, and
to the fact that he does not look at her with a lover's eyes.
This perceptive yet unseeing registering of another person's
physical attractions can even distinguish a woman looking at
a man, though this is much rarer. *Emma* is unique in allowing
its heroine to appreciate the masculine 'figure' in a comparably candid manner, when she looks at Mr Knightley at the
dance at the Crown. 'His tall, firm, upright figure, among the
bulky forms and stooping shoulders of the elderly men, was
such as Emma felt must draw every body's eyes; and, excepting her own partner, there was not one among the whole row
of young men who could be compared with him' (II. ii). It is

as close as Emma can go to recognising something beyond friendship.

In the scene where Mr Knightley and Emma finally acknowledge their true feelings for each other, looks take over. Looking in Austen is perhaps never more charged with meaning than when Mr Knightley declares himself to Emma and expects her response to what is implicitly a proposal. 'He stopped in his earnestness to look the question, and the expression of his eyes overpowered her' (III. xiii). It is an extraordinary grammatical usage: to 'look the question'. As if only looking can express meaning. Something similar happens when Captain Wentworth places his letter before Anne Elliot in the room at the White Hart, and she sees and cannot misinterpret his 'eyes of glowing entreaty' (*Persuasion*, II. xi). A substitute for speech, the letter concludes with an acknowledgement that speech will hardly be necessary to communicate her response. 'A word, a look will be enough,' it says. Soon they meet again, in the company of others. 'He joined them; but, as if irresolute whether to join or to pass on, said nothing, only looked. Anne could command herself enough to receive that look, and not repulsively. The cheeks which had been pale now glowed, and the movements which had hesitated were decided. He walked by her side.' Wentworth is right. After all the elusiveness of people's looks in Jane Austen's fiction – after all the uncertain, anxious, puzzled, mistaken looking that has gone on – here finally, satisfyingly . . . a look *is* enough.

FIVE

Who Dies in the Course of Her Novels?

A sudden seizure of a different nature from any thing fore-
boded by her general state, had carried her off after a short
struggle. The great Mrs. Churchill was no more.

Emma, III. ix

If we except the little pre-history of the Dashwood family
in the first chapter of *Sense and Sensibility*, and the odd case
of Lord Ravenshaw's grandmother (of which more later),
there are only two deaths that occur within Jane Austen's
novels, and one of these is of a character whom we never
meet. The two people who die are Dr Grant in *Mansfield
Park* and Mrs Churchill in *Emma*. Neither is lamented; both
deaths are indeed calculated to make us consider how we
might fail to grieve at others' mortality. In the case of Mrs
Churchill, the consideration is comic. She is the most powerful absentee character in all Austen's fiction. We never see
or hear her; she exerts influence over her adopted son, Frank
Churchill, mostly by feigning various illnesses, but always
off stage. Then suddenly she dies from an unspecified
'seizure', though we are told that it is something different

from anything of which she has long been complaining (III. ix). Even the *malade imaginaire* is susceptible to the reaper. She is dead, but she is vindicated. The inhabitants of Highbury, none of whom have ever met her, respond with peculiarly disingenuous feeling: 'Every body had a degree of gravity and sorrow.'

Dr Grant's death in *Mansfield Park* is more frankly unregretted. In the rounding-up that happens in the novel's closing phases, Dr and Mrs Grant, who first brought the amoral, chaos-causing Crawfords to Mansfield, have returned to London, where Dr Grant has found ecclesiastical advancement in Westminster. His self-satisfaction is not to last. Soon he 'brought on apoplexy and death, by three great institutionary dinners in one week' (III. xvii). It is thoroughly poetic justice: the gastronome clergyman kills himself with gluttony at the height of his contentment. We expect deaths like this in a different kind of novel – in Fielding, say, where the irascible Captain Blifil, who has married the wealthy Squire Allworthy's sister, also dies of 'an apoplexy ... just at the very instant when his heart was exulting in meditations on the happiness which would accrue to him by Mr. Allworthy's death'.[1] Dr Grant's demise is comically smuggled in from a different, moralistic and satirical, kind of narrative. And it is not just poetic justice. His death also serves the other characters' wishes and the author's narrative purposes. For it means that the two half-sisters, Mrs Grant and Mary Crawford, can live together in pretty perfect harmony. The novel says nothing of any sadness or sense of loss that we might hope Mrs Grant to have felt. At the beginning of the paragraph in which Dr Grant dies, we are told that Mrs Grant has 'a temper to love and be loved', so we may take the omission to confirm what we surely already suspect: that she never loved her husband.

Dr Grant was not yet fifty, but the flesh is frail. By dying he is rather surprisingly fulfilling the casual prediction made by the formerly feckless heir to the estate, Tom Bertram. When Dr Grant first arrives to take the living that was previously promised to Edmund Bertram, Tom convinces himself that the man who has purchased the position will, 'in all probability, die very soon' (I. iii). The prediction exhibits Tom's callous wishful thinking: the living has been snatched from Edmund's hands to cover his own gambling debts. Yet it is evidently a plausible guess. When Dr Grant appears 'a hearty man of forty-five' Tom is not to be dissuaded, and proves an accurate prognosticator. The apparently healthy divine does indeed make way for Edmund Bertram to take up the station – and to receive the income – for which he has been groomed. Dr Grant's demise from gorging suits everyone. The novel's penultimate paragraph tells us that, to complete Edmund and Fanny's happiness, 'the acquisition of Mansfield living by the death of Dr Grant' has occurred just at the moment when the young couple wanted a larger income and a home nearer 'the paternal abode' (III. xvii). His end could hardly have been better timed.

It is telling that the two characters who die are more conveniently dead than alive. Austen wants you to notice how deaths can suit the living. Mary Crawford and Mrs Grant must both be wearing full mourning as they begin a new life together, but we take it that, even in their black clothes, they are delighted to be rid of an irksome impediment to their sisterly friendship. At the end of *Emma* Frank Churchill consorts with his now acknowledged fiancée, Jane Fairfax, clad in sombre mourning garb. Mrs Churchill's death has made their marriage possible, but requires an interim. 'There must be three months, at least, of deep mourning' (III. xvi). Frank Churchill meets Emma again after the announcement of his engagement, smiling and laughing on this 'most happy day', but suited, we should realise, all in black. We are not told this, but Austen's first readers would have 'seen' this garb, and registered the clash of official sorrow and private happiness. The deaths of close kin usually required a period of full (often called 'deep') mourning – in which clothes were predominantly black – followed by an equal period of 'second' or 'slight' mourning.[2] Often the household servants would also be required to wear mourning.[3] For a woman, full mourning might involve not only a black dress but also the rejection of shimmering silk for duller bombazine. 'Short mourning for distant relations was comparable with second mourning and was expressed rather by lack of any colour than by wearing black.'[4] Second mourning could involve the wearing of grey clothing. Other signs distinguished second mourning: for women, black edging on dresses or black ribbons; for men, black bands on hats and cuffs, or black buckles. Conventions were not certain, however: there are many examples from the late eighteenth and early nineteenth centuries of men and women anxiously asking each other about the regulations currently governing mourning.

Periods of mourning were also disputable, though by the mid-nineteenth century it was de rigueur for a widow to wear full mourning for a year.[5] In Fanny Burney's 1778 novel *Evelina*, the young heroine is disapproving of the fact that her grandmother is out of mourning only three months after the death of her husband: she has been living in France and thinks that no one in England will know how short a time she has been a widow.[6] In *Lady Susan*, the amoral protagonist has been 'only four months a widow', so as she flirts and fascinates, she is presumably doing so, shockingly, in mourning garb (Letter 2). Austen's own life was full of deaths and wearing black must have become a habit. She remarks in one letter in July 1813 that she will not need to put on mourning for the recently deceased Thomas Leigh, her mother's cousin, as she is still wearing it for her sister-in-law Eliza, who had died just over two months earlier (*Letters*, 86). She can just carry on in black. The donning of mourning was a regular demand. It was not only worn for family members. In 1810, for instance, twelve weeks of national mourning was decreed to mark the death of George III's daughter Princess Amelia.[7] In June 1811 Austen described how her niece Anna and family friend Harriet Benn walked with her to Alton to buy mourning to be worn in the event of the King's death, and that she bought a black 'Bombasin' for her mother (*Letters*, 75). The mourning clothes adopted by Austen's characters would have been visible in the mind's eye of an early reader who took these habits for granted. In *Persuasion*, Captain Benwick is 'in mourning' for Fanny Harville's loss, which means not just that he is sad, but that he is actually wearing mourning, as the Harvilles are likely to be (I. xi). Anne learns the story of their shared tragedy, but then their clothes would have made her curious. If we do not see these clothes we lose something, for Captain Benwick must have either eschewed his mourning dress while paying his attentions to Louisa Musgrove, or courted her while wearing it. Either possibility gives peculiar force to Captain Harville's later exclamation to Anne, 'Poor Fanny! she would not have forgotten him so soon' (II. xi). Mourning dress is, after all, donned in order to stop you escaping from the memory of the dead person.

No one dies during the course of *Persuasion*, but the novel is full of the deaths that have mattered to its characters. As Linda Bree rightly says, 'most of the characters would have been wearing black, in some form, throughout the novel'.[8] The requirement to wear mourning alerts us to the possibility that people who thus advertise their loss are not always so very sad. On hearing the news of Mrs Churchill's death in *Emma*, Mr Weston shakes his head solemnly while thinking – Austen cannot resist telling us – 'that his mourning should be as handsome as possible' (III. ix). His wife, meanwhile, sits 'sighing and moralizing over her broad hems'. Thinking about the clothes is natural – sometimes more natural than actual mournfulness. In October 1808 Jane Austen told her sister, 'My Mother is preparing mourning for Mrs E. K.—she has picked her old silk pelisse to peices [*sic*], & means to have it dyed black for a gown—a very interesting scheme' (*Letters*, 57). Mrs E. K. might have been Elizabeth Knight, sister of Thomas Knight, who had adopted Edward Austen, henceforth Edward Knight, as his heir. The duties of mourning reached a long way – in *Persuasion* the Elliots wear black ribbons after the death of Mr Elliot's wife, a woman they have never met – and made necessary such adaptations of clothing.

Reading through Austen's letters you might think that she cared too much about the sartorial implications of the deaths of friends and relations. When the mother of the Austens' close friend Martha Lloyd died, her dressmaker was apparently slow to make up the mourning dress that she ordered, prompting Austen to send Martha 'Lines *supposed* to have been sent to an uncivil Dress maker'.

> Miss Lloyd must expect to receive
> This license to mourn & to grieve,
> Complete, er'e the end of the week –
> It is better to write than to speak –[9]

Mrs Austen even penned a facetious rhyming response from the imagined dressmaker, to divert their friend. But the business of attending to mourning dress was exactly a diversion from grief. Even when the death of Edward's wife Elizabeth

provoked Austen to shock and raw sorrow, she was soon turning to the costume implications.

> I am to be in bombazeen and crape, according to what we are
> told is universal here, and which agrees with Martha's previous
> observation. My mourning, however, will not impoverish me, for
> by having my velvet pelisse fresh lined and made up, I am sure I
> shall have no occasion this winter for anything new of that sort.
> I take my cloak for the lining, and shall send yours on the chance
> of its doing something of the same for you, though I believe your
> pelisse is in better repair than mine. One Miss Baker makes my
> gown and the other my bonnet, which is to be silk covered with
> crape. (*Letters*, 59)

Such detail can sound griefless to modern ears, but the peculiar requirements of mourning inevitably prompted such
practical considerations.

The adopting of mourning dress might, however, free the
mourner from any obligation to grieve. When encountered
at the inn in Lyme in *Persuasion*, Mr Elliot is in mourning,
as is his manservant (I. xii). But Mr Elliot is already looking
about him. There is that moment on the steps from the beach
when he pauses to gaze at Anne with 'earnest admiration'.
He does not seem to be a man dwelling on memories of his
recently dead wife. When Anne meets him again in Bath, she
asks herself why he is paying court to her family and wonders
if he has an interest in Elizabeth. But then she reflects that
'Mr. Elliot . . . had not been a widower seven months' (II.
iv). Every time she sees 'the crape round his hat' she considers that he cannot be pursuing any amorous scheme so soon
after the death of his wife. She should instead infer that he is
behaving like someone who has indeed forgotten about his
wife. He is not the only character to whom mourning is mere

convention. Lady Russell, noticing Mr Elliot's attentions to Anne, begins 'to calculate the number of weeks which would free him from all the remaining restraints of widowhood, and leave him at liberty to exert his most open powers of pleasing' (II. v). When Mrs Smith suggests that Mr Elliot might have an interest in her, Anne responds as if this were improper. 'Mr. Elliot's wife has not been dead much above half a year. He ought not to be supposed to be paying his addresses to any one' (II. ix). Her friend has no time for this argument – 'if these are your only objections . . . Mr. Elliot is safe' – and is sure that he will not let his mourning impede his courtship.

> *Mourning, as Austen's novels require us to*
> *realise, is not the same as grieving.*

How long should one grieve? It is a question at the heart of *Persuasion*. By Captain Harville's account, Captain Benwick is so distressed by news of Fanny Harville's death that Captain Wentworth has to stay with him for a week (I. xii). When Anne meets him it has been just over four months since he first received the news. Yet we should know that such consuming grief is suspect when we find him, in fact, already prepared to fall in love with someone else. Anne's judgement on him when she hears the news of his engagement to Louisa Musgrove is pragmatic and magnanimous. 'He had an affectionate heart. He must love somebody' (II. vi). It is less than six months from his hearing the news of his fiancée's death to his proposing to Louisa – no wonder Captain Harville feels that his sister would have slower to forget their love (II. xi). It is the subsequent discussion between him and Anne of how long grief should possess a person – of whether men or women have more 'retentive feelings' – that sparks Captain Wentworth's epistolary declaration of his own undiminished passion.

The business of dressing in mourning was so conventional that Austen could joke in her letters about those who took it to excess. Writing to Cassandra from Bath in 1799, she described bumping into a vicar from Hampshire whom they knew: 'at the bottom of Kingsdown Hill we met a Gentleman in a Buggy, who on a minute examination turned out to be Dr Hall—& Dr Hall in such very deep mourning that either his Mother, his Wife, or himself must be dead' (*Letters*, 19). Mourning, as Austen's novels require us to realise, is not the same as grieving. Characters who know all about the conventions of mourning do not necessarily know anything about grief. In the bleakly brilliant opening of *Persuasion*, Sir Walter Elliot's imperviousness to melancholy reflection is shown us. How could he so often view the page in his 'favourite volume', the Baronetage, which lists the deaths of both his wife and his son? Though there might be a good motive for adding the date of one's wife's death, Austen's wording makes sure we know differently. She tells us how he has supplemented the bare year recorded by the book by 'inserting most accurately the day of the month on which he had lost his wife'. The wording ('most accurately') lets us see his fussy respect for the facts of aristocratic family history. It is anything but sadness.

In this, the most elegiac of Austen's novels, some of the conventions for condolence are laid out in all their emptiness. The Elliots failed to send a letter of commiseration to their (literally) distant cousins the Dalrymples upon the Viscount's death, and thereby committed a grave offence. This is despite the fact that the two families had never met. In return and revenge, the Dalrymples scorn to send condolences on the death of Lady Elliot. These minor aristocrats are caught up in a petty tit-for-tat. Meanwhile the expression of real grief is difficult to find. Anne Elliot's sadness at the death of her mother, when she was fourteen, is left inexplicit, but it is intimated. When she is playing the piano for the unappreciative and philistine Musgroves, we hear that apart from her time with Captain Wentworth, she had not known real appreciation of her musicality 'since the loss of her dear mother' (I. vi). That 'dear' is like a flicker of her own feeling, hidden from others. The autumnal mournfulness of the book's first part is always associated with Anne's loss of love, but it also reaches back to this loss of her mother. The novel, following its heroine's own habits of fortitude and avoidance, will not say much about this. Something explicit emerges belatedly, when we find that Anne's friendship with Mrs Smith was formed many years earlier when she 'had gone unhappy to school, grieving for the loss of a mother whom she had dearly loved' (II. v).

The Musgroves are themselves grieving for their dead son Richard – or rather, they have just been reminded to do so again by the mention of Captain Wentworth (I. vi). Their son died two years earlier, and was 'scarcely at all regretted' when news of his death first arrived. This is an extraordinary sentence for a modern reader: if their son had been sent away to sea because he was 'unmanageable', should his parents not have felt some extra stab of guilt and regret? Returning to the only two proper letters that, under Captain Wentworth's influence, he had bothered to write to them while at sea, Mrs Musgrove is thrown into 'greater grief for him than she had known on first hearing of his death'. There is some sense that Austen is rigging our judgements here. When, some time later, Captain Wentworth responds to Mrs Musgrove's expressions of grief by showing 'the kindest consideration for all that was real and unabsurd in the parent's feelings', it seems that the author is also trying to show some consideration after her earlier asperity (I. viii). The consideration is passing, for soon we are hearing of 'her large fat sighings over the destiny of a son, whom alive nobody had cared for'. The novel is satirising her for acting up to grief now, not for failing to grieve before.

That failure would once have been more understandable because a death like Richard Musgrove's would not have been exceptional. Death was always possible. The question of life expectation indeed often occupies Austen's characters. No sooner has Charlotte Lucas become engaged to Mr Collins than her mother starts thinking about her best friend's father's death. 'Lady Lucas began directly to calculate with more interest than the matter had ever excited before, how many years longer Mr Bennet was likely to live' (*Pride and Prejudice*, I. xxii). Such was life. In the second chapter of *Sense and Sensibility*, Mrs John Dashwood is happy for her husband to calculate on the 'three thousand pounds each' that the Dashwood girls will receive 'on their mother's death'. He calls this 'a very comfortable fortune for any young woman' (I. ii). But of course this is killing the mother off rather easily. If she lives another twenty years the girls are 'young women' no longer. A few sentences later, in response to her husband's suggestion of an annuity for his stepmother, Mrs John Dashwood is observing that 'people always live for ever when there is any annuity to be paid them; and she is very stout and healthy, and hardly forty'. In these examples, the prospect of death matters because of its financial consequences and it is in these terms that characters most often mention death. In the midst of proposing marriage to Elizabeth, Mr Collins cannot help referring to the fact that he is 'to inherit this estate after the death of your honoured father (who, however, may live many years longer)' (I. xix). His wonderful crassness should not make us forget that the Bennet family, because of the entailed estate, cannot avoid contemplating Mr Bennet's death, and its consequences.

Death before old age was much more common for Jane Austen than it is for us. The wives of three of her brothers died in or following childbirth. Children also died, including her own month-old niece Elizabeth, daughter of her brother Charles, in 1814. In the second half of the eighteenth century, almost a quarter of children died before the age of ten, more than half of these in the first year of their lives.[10] Inevitably, mortality rates were much higher among the poor, but infant deaths were still common among the genteel classes. Mrs William Deedes, sister-in-law to the novelist's brother Edward, had nineteen children, of whom four died in infancy. The earliest of Austen's surviving letters, from January 1796, ends with an almost passing instance of infant mortality: 'I am sorry for the Beaches' loss of their little girl, especially as it is the one so much like me' (*Letters*, 1). The mother concerned, Henrietta-Maria Hicks-Beach, had nine children, four of whom died in infancy.[11] Perhaps the most shocking sentence that Austen ever wrote is about the death of an infant. 'Mrs Hall of Sherbourn was brought to bed yesterday of a dead child, some weeks before she expected, owing to a fright.—I suppose she happened unawares to look at her husband' (*Letters*, 10). It would not have been imaginable if stillbirths had not been so common.

The deaths of children and babies feature often enough in Austen's letters to make you suspect that she has kept them out of her fiction. There are just two examples, both external to the novels in which they feature. In *Persuasion* there is Sir Walter Elliot's 'still-born son', ruthlessly recorded in his copy of the Baronetage, though never mentioned within the novel itself. The poignancy of this is all the more powerfully implicit, given the narrative implications. If this son had lived, Kellynch Hall would not be going the way of Mr Elliot. In *Mansfield Park*, Fanny Price, back in Portsmouth with her family, finds herself thinking about 'another sister, a very pretty little girl' who was about five when she left Portsmouth and 'who had died a few years afterwards' (III. vii). When the news of her death had reached Mansfield, she 'had for a short time been quite afflicted'. Susan and Betsey fight over a silver knife that the dying Mary had left to Susan, bringing her lost child to Mrs Price's mind. 'Poor little sweet creature! Well, she was taken away from evil to come.' Mrs Price has learned an acceptance of mortality that elsewhere borders on Malthusian unconcern. As letters arrive telling Fanny of Tom Bertram's dangerous illness, none of the Prices 'could be interested in so remote an evil as illness in a family above an hundred miles off; not even Mrs. Price, beyond a brief question or two' (III. xiii). Austen has to tell us that this indifference to deaths in other families is common enough.

> Mrs. Price did quite as much for Lady Bertram, as Lady Bertram would have done for Mrs. Price. Three or four Prices might have been swept away, any or all, except Fanny and William, and Lady Bertram would have thought little about it; or perhaps might have caught from Mrs. Norris's lips the cant of its being a very happy thing, and a great blessing to their poor dear sister Price to have them so well provided for.

People do die, and not just the very young. Sir Walter Elliot's wife Elizabeth has died, as his favourite book records, some sixteen or seventeen years after marriage, probably in her late thirties. All the more contemptible, then, that, suggesting that Anne put off her appointment with Mrs Smith, he says in a kind of jest, 'She is not so near her end, I presume, but that she may hope to see another day' (II. v). Mrs Clay's husband has died while she is still a 'young woman'. In *Persuasion*, Fanny Harville has died in her twenties, and the novel need offer no further explanation of the fact (I. xi). In *Emma*, we are told that Captain Weston's first wife dies after three years of marriage, in her mid-twenties; the event, though sad, is not treated as remarkable. Jane Fairfax's father dies in action, and her mother follows, 'sinking under consumption and grief soon afterwards' (II. ii). The evidence of Austen's letters is more informative than any mortality statistics, for it conveys just that sense of precariousness that lies behind her novels and is unknown to most modern readers. Writing to Cassandra from Bath in May 1801, Austen talks of her aunt's cough and her mother's cold, before suddenly recalling something graver. 'You will be sorry to hear that Marianne Mapleton's disorder has ended fatally; she was beleived [*sic*] out of danger on Sunday, but a sudden relapse carried her off the next day' (*Letters*, 37). The daughter of a Bath surgeon, Miss Mapleton was twenty-one or twenty-two. If such a death was not unusual, why then should Marianne Dashwood not sicken and die? Mr Bennet's joke about his daughter Jane's indisposition – 'if she should die' – would be pointless if her death were inconceivable (I. vii). 'People do not die of little trifling colds,' declares Mrs Bennet, but this is cavalier.

It is hard to know what to make of a certain casualness in Austen's own treatment of deaths in her letters. 'Mr Waller is dead, I see;—I cannot greive [*sic*] about it, nor perhaps can his Widow very much' (*Letters* 53). She says this to Cassandra in passing, in between a list of family engagements and news of harvesting on her brother Edward's estate. Cassandra must have known just the reasons for the widow's possible lack of grief, but we never will. Had Mr Waller, whom they knew in Southampton, been a wife-beater? Or just a dull dinner companion? On the death of Mrs Wyndham Knatchbull in

1807 she wrote, 'I had no idea that anybody liked her, & therefore felt nothing for any Survivor, but I am now feeling away
on her Husband's account, and think he had better marry
Miss Sharpe' (*Letters*, 50). Not taking deaths very seriously
was part of life. Thus the force of her comment on news of
the Battle of Albuera in 1811. 'How horrible it is to have so
many people killed!—And what a blessing that one cares for
none of them' (*Letters*, 74). There is a grimly comic honesty
in such remarks that should sensitise us to some of her characters' casualness about the deaths of those about whom they
do not care. In *Mansfield Park*, the Honourable John Yates
complains that his theatrical pleasures were interrupted by
the sudden death of Lord Ravenshaw's grandmother (I. xiii).
'It is impossible to help wishing, that the news could have
been suppressed for just the three days we wanted.' It 'was
suggested' – after all, she was 'only a grand-mother' and did
live 'two hundred miles off'.

Mary Crawford exhibits her deep, cold carelessness when,
misjudging Fanny as ever she does, she jokes in a letter about
the possibility of Tom Bertram's death – an eventuality that
would leave Edmund as the heir to the title and the estate. 'To
have such a fine young man cut off in the flower of his days
is most melancholy. Poor Sir Thomas will feel it dreadfully.
I really am quite agitated on the subject. Fanny, Fanny, I see
you smile, and look cunning, but upon my honour, I never
bribed a physician in my life' (III. xiv). She writes this when
she believes Tom's death likely and is acknowledging, in some
sophisticated way, the benefit that might come to her from
it. By a flourish of irony, she tries to recruit Fanny to her
own sense of the desirability of Tom's death. Soon she is
speculating about the consequences for Edmund, who would
be suddenly and desirably presented with 'wealth and consequence'. Mary Crawford treats cynically the precariousness

of life, a fact that presses on all Austen's characters. Her first readers were aware of this precariousness in a way that we must rediscover as we read. Very few people die in her stories, but all her novels are shadowed by death.

Why Is It Risky to
Go to the Seaside?

'I have been long perfectly convinced, though perhaps I
never told you so before, that the sea is very rarely of use
to any body. I am sure it almost killed me once.'

Emma, I. xii

If bad things do happen at the seaside, one of Austen's heroines is safe. Emma Woodhouse (unlike her father, quoted
above) has never seen the sea. We find this out when she intervenes to halt a dangerous-tending disagreement between
her father and her sister about the merits of sea bathing. 'I
must beg you not to talk of the sea. It makes me envious and
miserable;—I who have never seen it!' (I. xii) She is being
tactful, but she is also being truthful. It is a satisfying touch,
telling us something essential about Emma: all-powerful in
Highbury, but incapable of reaching out beyond it; fearless
in her little world, but timid about what might lie outside
its closely hemmed borders. By a carefully managed irony,
however, she cannot escape the seaside. She is the unknow-
ing witness, even the abettor, of an amorous relationship that
was born at the seaside. Early in the novel we hear, from Mr

Woodhouse, that Frank Churchill's much-vaunted letter to Mrs Weston congratulating her on her marriage to his father is written from Weymouth (I. ii). Much later, we hear from Miss Bates that Jane Fairfax has been in Weymouth (II. i). When Jane Fairfax arrives in Highbury and meets Emma, we are told that 'She and Mr. Frank Churchill had been at Weymouth at the same time. It was known that they were a little acquainted' (II. ii). During his first visit to Hartfield after his arrival, Frank Churchill says that he is obliged to pay a visit to the Bates household (he pretends to have trouble remembering the name) because of his acquaintance with 'a lady'. Mr Weston guilelessly seconds his purpose. 'True, true, you are acquainted with Miss Fairfax; I remember you knew her at Weymouth, and a fine girl she is. Call upon her, by all means' (II. v). His son seems to hesitate – 'another day would do as well; but there was that degree of acquaintance at Weymouth which—' – before his father eggs him on.

If you search an e-text of *Emma*, it is possible to follow the seventeen mentions of Weymouth scattered through the novel and find a sure trail. Reconstructing events, you can see that even while Emma was contriving her fantasy courtship of Harriet Smith by Mr Elton, a true *amour* was being pursued on the Dorset coast. Emma's ignorance of what it might be like by the sea takes on an added significance. She does indeed know nothing of this zone of love. Every mention of the place name should be, to the Regency reader, a clue to a likely romance. For is love not more likely by the sea? In Austen's novels, seaside resorts are places for flirtations and engagements, attachments and elopements, love and sex. The seaside is naturally the place for honeymoons. In *Sense and Sensibility* Lucy Steele marries Robert Ferrars and they go on honeymoon to Dawlish in Devon. In *Mansfield Park* Mr Rushworth and Maria go on their honeymoon to Brighton

– 'almost as gay in winter as in summer' (II. iii). And to cap it all, Emma and Mr Knightley, once engaged, plan a 'fortnight's absence in a tour to the sea-side' following their marriage (III. xix). The resort is unspecified, suggesting that they have only got as far as agreeing that the seaside must be the thing. You might say that once Emma has really discovered love she is bound, at last, for the seaside. It will be by the sea that she and Mr Knightley begin a sexual relationship.

This last, projected trip to the sea should be enough to suggest that seaside resorts were not inherently disreputable destinations in Austen's fiction. It would be wrong to think that these towns, increasingly dedicated to the leisure of their genteel and affluent visitors, were necessarily suspect places in the early nineteenth century. Thanks to the patronage of the Prince Regent, Brighton, it is true, acquired a certain louche reputation that it has never quite lost. Other resorts, however, were highly respectable. Many readers would have known that Weymouth was the favourite resort of George III and his family. They visited for the first time in 1789, stayed more than two months, and came regularly until 1805.[1] The King's presence in the town was a major feature of its public life: he ceremonially bathed, promenaded on the seafront, and attended events at the assembly rooms. The King's brother, the Duke of Gloucester, first came to Weymouth in 1765 and by the 1780s had built a grand house on the front; it was eventually purchased by the King.[2] It is important that Jane Fairfax has contracted her secret engagement at a respectable resort (if she and Frank Churchill had become attached at Brighton the implications would have been more worrying). Charlotte Palmer in *Sense and Sensibility* has, before her marriage, been husband-hunting in Weymouth: she is empty-headed, but Austen would not have let her go where her morals were in danger.

'Weymouth is altogether a shocking place I perceive, without recommendation of any kind,' Jane Austen wrote to Cassandra in September 1804 (*Letters*, 39). But this was a joke in reply to her sister's report that ice was unobtainable in the town – a lament later put into the mouth of Mrs Elton in *Emma* (II. xvi). Jane was in Lyme Regis with her parents while Cassandra had travelled down the coast to Weymouth with their brother Henry. There she had evidently hoped to see the royal family board their yacht, the *Royal Sovereign*, a little spectacle for the patriotic tourist. Mr Knightley does number Weymouth among 'the idlest haunts in the kingdom', but his disapproval is unreliable: the canny reader will see that it is one of those glimpses of his jealousy that we are allowed in the first volume of *Emma*.[3] 'We hear of him for ever at some watering-place or other. A little while ago, he was at Weymouth' (I. xviii). So it must be a dubious place. Mr Knightley's moral judgement comes when Emma is teasing him about his disapproval of Frank Churchill's conduct, 'taking the other side of the question from her real opinion'. Mr Knightley is riled, in advance of his competitor actually appearing. In this brilliant, redundant dialogue Emma is unconsciously exciting Mr Knightley to more and more eloquent denunciations of Frank Churchill's conduct. 'You seem determined to think ill of him,' she accurately observes. 'Me!—not at all,' he replies, 'rather displeased.' He is determined to think ill of Weymouth too.

Jealous Mr Knightley is not the only Austen character to voice disapproval of seaside resorts. Shortly before she died, Austen had begun work on a novel named after such a place. *Sanditon* opens with the blameless Heywood family encountering a man who calls himself 'Mr. Parker of Sanditon' and waxes enthusiastic about this 'young and rising Bathing-place, certainly the favourite spot of all that are to be found along the coast of Sussex' (Ch. 1). The 'well-looking Hale, Gentlemanlike' Mr Heywood observes that 'Every five years, one hears of some new place or other starting up by the Sea, and growing the fashion'. He is convinced that they are 'Bad things for the country'. His declaration discourages Mr Parker not a jot. Sanditon has none of the drawbacks, he assures his new acquaintance, of 'your large, overgrown Places like Brighton, or Worthing, or East Bourne'. Sanditon is the exception to his antipathy. And perhaps Mr Heywood's jaundiced views are not so very strong, for they do not stop him allowing his daughter to go on a trip to Sanditon with the proud Mr Parker. By the late eighteenth century, the annual seaside holiday had become a badge of genteel status.[4] Austen herself had often holidayed by the sea and had stayed in several of the resorts visited by her characters. She spent the summer of 1801 in Sidmouth, with her parents and sister. (It was in Sidmouth, according to Cassandra Austen, that her sister met an alluring gentleman who died before he could seek her out again).[5] In 1802 they took their holiday in Dawlish, while in both 1803 and 1804 they stayed in Lyme Regis. In 1805 she went to Folkestone and to Worthing.[6] There were no further seaside jaunts, it is true, but she hardly had personal reasons for thinking maritime towns sinful.

The sense of the seaside town as a dangerous place is, however, insistent in her fiction. If you were to gather the examples of risky behaviour by the sea, you might suppose that the author did have a poor view of the seaside. Louisa Musgrove's self-precipitation from the Cobb in Lyme Regis is but the last of a series of foolish or bad actions. Lydia Bennet elopes with Wickham when the two of them encounter each other in Brighton. The near-seduction of Mr Darcy's sister Georgiana is staged in a seaside resort: with the help of the perfidious ex-governess Mrs Younge, Wickham has lured her to Ramsgate, where, we infer, she is at his mercy. Only her brother's last-minute arrival thwarts him. In *Mansfield Park*, feckless Tom Bertram is a haunter of seaside resorts. On his return from Antigua, he does not come straight home to his mother and siblings (as he dutifully should), but goes to Weymouth (I. xii). With his father still in the West Indies, he should, as the eldest son, be returning to oversee the estate, but the lure of the shore is too strong. In Weymouth he meets the foolish, expensive Hon. John Yates (I. xiii). Yates leaves Weymouth only for 'a large party assembled for gaiety', and comes away from this to Mansfield with his dangerous scheme for amateur theatricals. Later in the novel Julia Bertram accompanies Mr and Mrs Rushworth to Brighton where she meets up with Mr Yates. In easy but devilish chat in front of Fanny, the Crawfords muse on Mr Yates's presence in the resort. 'Mr. Yates, I presume, is not far off,' says Henry (II. v). His sister brushes him off with 'I do not imagine he figures much in the letters to Mansfield Park; do you, Miss Price?' – which makes her brother's guess sound worse: Julia must be consorting with her admirer secretly. Julia's eventual elopement with Mr Yates proves their hints well founded.

Austen lets us imagine the seaside town as a place of licence. We wonder why Mr Elliot, who should be mourning his wife, has been at Sidmouth (I. xii). Rum people gravitate to the seafront. There is a wonderful cameo of the bad behaviour that becomes possible in such a place in an incidental piece of dialogue in *Mansfield Park*. Thomas Bertram is boastfully describing his evidently flirtatious behaviour with the younger Miss Sneyd, whoever she be. 'I went down to Ramsgate for a week with a friend last September—just after my return from the West Indies—my friend Sneyd . . . his father and mother and sisters were there, all new to me' (I. v). On arrival in Ramsgate, he and Sneyd find 'Mrs. and the two Miss Sneyds . . . out on the pier . . . with others of their acquaintance'. 'Mrs. Sneyd was surrounded by men,' he recalls. 'Surrounded by men' is an extraordinary phrase, expressing Tom Bertram's indiscretion even as it implies Mrs Sneyd's welcoming enjoyment of male attentions. Her preoccupation allows Tom to 'attach' himself to one of her daughters, and to walk 'by her side all the way home'. The young lady is apparently 'perfectly easy in her manners, and as ready to talk as to listen'. The point of the story for the teller is that he addressed himself to the younger daughter and thus offended the elder daughter. Inadvertently he provides a little picture of unsettling seaside gaiety, where promenading allows for all sorts of freedom.

Thoughts of the untoward things that might have happened to characters by the sea are in the heads of some of Austen's characters. It is a choice irony that Emma cannot see the relationship between Jane Fairfax and Frank Churchill because she has already started building on her fantasy of a relationship between Jane and her friend's new husband, Mr Dixon. Two young people of the opposite sex meeting at the seaside are liable to temptation, she seems to feel. What is there to do but take pleasure together? On a stroll into Highbury to survey the Crown Inn as a possible venue for a ball, Emma asks Frank Churchill whether he saw Jane Fairfax often in Weymouth. 'Were you often in the same society?' (II. vi). 'At this moment they were approaching Ford's, and he hastily exclaimed, "Ha! this must be the very shop that every body attends every day of their lives, as my father informs me."' He needs some blather about shopping to cover his discomposure, before he eventually returns to Emma's questions and is able to say calmly, 'I met her frequently at Weymouth' (II. vi). He knew the Campbells 'a little in town', and once at the resort 'we were very much in the same set'. Here is an epitome of what going to the seaside involves: visitors from London drawn together – for what? Emma, thinking of what Jane Fairfax might have been up to, supposes some very bad behaviour beside the sea. She hatches 'an ingenious and animating suspicion': an *amour* between Jane and the husband of the young woman, once Miss Campbell, with whom she has been brought up (II. i). There must be an 'attachment' between Jane Fairfax and Mr Dixon (II. ii). Perhaps it is 'simple, single, successless love on her side alone'. Or perhaps 'Mr. Dixon . . . had been very near changing one friend for the other'. What could be more likely, given the location? Miss Bates fuels the fantasy by telling Emma of the 'service' Mr Dixon 'rendered Jane at Weymouth, when they were out in that party on the water, and she, by the sudden whirling round of something or other among the sails, would have been dashed into the sea at once, and actually was all but gone' (II. i). The alert Mr Dixon, we hear, 'caught hold of her habit' and saved her from falling overboard. We presume that she cannot swim, and that, in all her clothing, she would soon disappear into the depths. Emma is happily imagining that with every seaside opportunity for flirtation, and the stimulus of this sudden act of preservation, illicit romance must have blossomed.

Frank Churchill takes the hint from Emma and supports her scandalous fantasy as a way of concealing his own attachment. When she tells him about the near-accident, he confesses that he was a member of that party of pleasure in the boat. Surely, Emma suggests, he must have noticed something between Jane and her saviour. 'I, simple I, saw nothing but the fact, that Miss Fairfax was nearly dashed from the vessel and that Mr. Dixon caught her.—It was the work of a moment' (II. viii). 'Simple I' should alert us, just where Emma is diverted: beneath this is all the implicit feeling of a man in love. Of course he notices nothing between Jane and Mr Dixon! He recalls the shock of it, and we are invited to imagine that this effect on him, rather than Jane Fairfax's gratitude to Mr Dixon, might have hastened a declaration of affection. Emma's theories are all as misconceived as ever, but her hunch that something amorous has taken place on the front and out in the bay is not wrong. At the seaside, it seems, people are freed from the usual restraints. At the seaside, we infer, there is no sense of established relationships or habitual forms of behaviour. No wonder that family story about Jane Austen, in her late twenties, meeting a man who was smitten by her but who died before he could pursue his interest, had a seaside setting.

Brighton, which Jane Austen does not ever seem to have visited, was the seaside town with the most vivid reputation. Nothing excites Lydia Bennet like the thought of it. 'In Lydia's imagination, a visit to Brighton comprised every possibility of earthly happiness. She saw with the creative eye of fancy, the streets of that gay bathing place covered with officers' (II. xviii). Brighton had become a fashionable bathing place in the mid-eighteenth century under the influence of local resident Dr Richard Russell, author of the hugely influential *Dissertation Concerning the Use of Sea Water in the Diseases of the Glands* (1753).[7] By the end of the eighteenth century, under the rather different influence of the Prince Regent, 'a shift took place from therapeutic aims to hedonistic ones'.[8] Kitty and Lydia's mother finds it easy to share their excitement at the thought of Brighton. Their first scheme is to get Mr Bennet to take them for the summer, his wife expressing her longing for the place more achingly than anyone. He will not abandon his library, but is willing to let his youngest daughter go to Brighton to parade as a 'common flirt' (II. xviii). A young woman travelling there without her family does need to be chaperoned, and this is Mrs Forster's job. But

Mrs Forster is 'a very young woman, and very lately married'. Presumably, being so compatible with Lydia, she is herself only in her teens, and no safeguard against the dangers of the raffish resort. Lydia and Wickham have every opportunity to develop a mutual attraction and arrange their elopement. Brighton makes it easy. After her marriage, Lydia, utterly unbowed, even recommends the place to her mother for her sisters. 'They must all go to Brighton. That is the place to get husbands' (III. ix).

Austen also had something particular against Ramsgate, where her sailor brother Francis was stationed in 1803–4. In a letter to Cassandra in 1813 she writes of a friend who has decided to move to Ramsgate and exclaims 'Bad Taste!' (*Letters*, 92). She then adds, 'He is very fond of the Sea however;—some Taste in that.' This is the contradiction that intrigues Austen and that makes the seaside such a fascinating place. As well as being a zone of licence and even licentiousness, it is inspiriting, heady, liberating. Whenever we get to see the sea – in *Mansfield Park*, in *Persuasion* and in *Sanditon* – the narrative breathes its pleasure in the prospect. Even among the absurdities of Sanditon, Charlotte Heywood is able to delight in the sea. Gazing from the window of her room in Trafalgar House soon after her arrival, she looks past 'the miscellaneous foreground of unfinished Buildings . . . to the Sea, dancing and sparkling in Sunshine and Freshness' (Ch. 4). Being by the sea can be delightful, but it is a kind of intoxication. Edward Ferrars engages himself to Lucy Steele in Plymouth: does he take seafront strolls with her? When Fanny Price walks with Mr Crawford and her sister on the Portsmouth ramparts on a mild March day, with the shadows chasing across the sea, 'dancing in its glee and dashing against the ramparts with so fine a sound', she feels its 'combination of charms' (III. xi). So much so that she is made 'almost careless of the circumstances under which she felt them' – those circumstances being the attentions of her would-be suitor, with whom she is arm in arm. She is tired from the walking and needs his support – and she is charmed by 'the loveliness of the day' and therefore the more susceptible to his attentions. Her sea-born 'tender reveries' give him the chance 'to look in her face without detection', noticing that she is 'as bewitching as ever' but, thanks to her family home, 'less blooming' than she should be.

You go to the seaside for your health, so it becomes a place for the ill.

Henry Crawford knows what the sea can do, for he has his sister write a letter beginning with happy recollection of 'the balmy air, the sparkling sea, and your sweet looks and conversation', all blended in 'the most delicious harmony' (III. xii). We know that this is well-nigh dictated, because near the end of the letter she is telling Fanny to leave Portsmouth: 'Those vile sea breezes are the ruin of beauty and health.' Her aunt 'felt affected, if within ten miles of the sea'. This suggests an impossible sensitivity, but presumably her aunt's hatred of her seafaring husband gave her this special aversion. It is a nicely peculiar expression of feeling, as Austen's contemporaries were used to thinking of the seaside as a kind of tonic. Sea bathing was one of the prescriptions in the fashionable doctor's armoury. In a letter of August 1805 Austen tells her sister that their eleven-year-old nephew Edward (eldest son of their brother Edward) is ill and that Dr Wilmot is to be consulted: 'If Sea-Bathing should be recommended' he will stay with them in Worthing (*Letters*, 45). The novelist expresses no scepticism about this proposed treatment, even though enthusiasm for sea bathing in her novels is made to seem absurd. 'A little sea-bathing would set me up forever,'

declares Mrs Bennet idiotically in *Pride and Prejudice*, seconding Lydia's wish to be in Brighton (II. xviii). Kitty claims
that her aunt Mrs Philips has told her that bathing in the sea
'would do *me* a great deal of good'. For these two, the supposedly health-giving influences of the sea would be the excuse
for a pleasure trip. For Emma Woodhouse's sister Isabella
the influences are real. Mr and Mrs John Knightley have not
visited Highbury during the summer because the holiday 'had
been given to sea-bathing for the children' (I. xi). She and her
father, fellow hypochondriacs, energetically debate the relative merits of Southend and Cromer and the good or bad
effects of sea air (I. xii). Mr Wingfield (her apothecary) is
supposed to recommend it; Mr Perry is supposed to doubt
its efficacy. The daughter's celebration of the delights of
Southend (where Austen's brother Charles lived for a time) is
the less convincing for her assurance that they 'never found
the least inconvenience from the mud' (I. xii). Mr Woodhouse
thinks 'the sea is very rarely of use to any body. I am sure it
almost killed me once.' Yet, despite the sea's near-fatal prop-
erties, Mr Woodhouse is prepared to contemplate one resort.
'You should have gone to Cromer, my dear, if you went any
where.' Why? Because Mr Perry has been there and thus told
his rich, weak-headed patient that it is 'the best of all the sea-
bathing places'.

The superstitious faith in the efficacy of the seaside is
at its most extreme in the opening of *Sanditon*, where Mr
Parker, who has just sprained his ankle when his coach over-
turned, assures his wife that, once back at home, 'we have our
remedy at hand you know.—A little of our own Bracing Sea
Air will soon set me on my feet again' (Ch. 1). The enthusiasm of Mr Parker is imitated in the narration. 'Nobody
could catch cold by the Sea, Nobody wanted Appetite by the
Sea, Nobody wanted Spirits, Nobody wanted Strength' (Ch.

2). The fortunes of Sanditon seem founded on its capacity to attract invalids and hypochondriacs. As Tony Tanner puts it, 'The invention and promotion of Sanditon is inseparable from the invention and promotion of sickness.'[9] You go to the seaside for your health, so it becomes a place for the ill. As Mr Parker delights in saying, 'Never was there a place more palpably designed by Nature for the resort of the Invalid' (Ch. 1). Sea air and sea bathing are 'healing, softing, relaxing—fortifying and bracing—seemingly just as was wanted'. Mr Parker's faith in the curative powers of air and bathing knows no limit. 'The sea air and sea bathing together were nearly infallible, one or the other of them being a match for every disorder of the stomach, the lungs or the blood' (Ch. 2). Yet all this talk of health is not such nonsense after all. A late afternoon stroll and a morning walk by the sea are apparently enough to transform Anne, whose 'very pretty features' reappear, 'having the bloom and freshness of youth restored by the fine wind which had been blowing on her complexion, and by the animation of eye which it had also produced' (I. xii). Both the unknown 'gentleman' walking down to the beach, and Captain Wentworth himself, seem to notice.

Lyme, though, has a special status, being granted a strangely sub-travelogue descriptive paragraph by the author, who strays well away from what her characters can observe to detail the charms of the surrounding countryside. 'Charmouth, with its high grounds and extensive sweeps of country, and still more its sweet retired bay . . . the woody varieties of the cheerful village of Up Lyme . . . Pinny, with its green chasms between romantic rocks . . .' (I. xi). The touristic prose expresses some need to do justice to the allure of this place, where Anne is to be rekindled but where excitement is also to produce such folly. For this is not the seaside of assemblies and *flâneurs* and relationships in flux, where elopements and engagements are always likely. This is the seaside of visceral excitement or melancholy, of rocks and cliffs and chasms, such as are documented in Austen's peculiar paragraph. It is a place where the visitors spend time 'wondering and admiring' and it is just the place for Captain Benwick to walk and recite Byron or Scott to himself. In the other novels the seaside resort is a place of parade; in autumn and winter, Lyme is a place of 'retirement' for the Harvilles and Captain Benwick. There is a time to go to the seaside. Those who go out of season find a very different place. (Think of Mrs Croft, having to spend a winter in Deal while her husband was at sea – the only time in her life 'that I ever fancied myself unwell' (I. viii).)

'The young people were all wild to see Lyme' (I. xi). 'Wild' is a word for the Musgrove girls: earlier in the novel they are 'wild for dancing' (I. vi). It is the sea that draws them, for the place is off the beaten track and largely (in November) shut up. Once they have arrived and booked in at their hotel, 'the next thing to be done was unquestionably to walk directly down to the sea'. It is likely that Austen herself had taken a November holiday in Lyme in 1803, in her late twenties, and would have had memories of the place out of season.[10] She visited again the next summer, when she danced in the assembly rooms and bathed in the sea (*Letters*, 39). She walked for an hour on the Cobb with Miss Armstrong, a family friend. Her experiences might be behind Mary Musgrove's enjoyment of her stay in Lyme, supposedly justified by Louisa's injury. Pretending to remain in the town to help look after her sister-in-law, Mary 'had found more to enjoy than to suffer' (II. ii). She breathlessly tells Anne and Lady Russell that, 'She had been taken to Charmouth too, and she had bathed, and gone to church, and there were a great many more people to look at in the church at Lyme than at Uppercross.' Church attendance is made a seaside recreation. Bathing – it is November – might well mean in Lyme's indoor baths (Jefford's), built in 1804.

For Anne, the sea exerts a kind of spell. On their morning in Lyme, she and Henrietta Musgrove walk down to the sands before breakfast 'to watch the flowing of the tide' (I. xii). 'They praised the morning; gloried in the sea; sympathized in the delight of the fresh-feeling breeze—and were silent.' By the sea Anne comes back to life, 'the bloom and freshness of youth restored'. She comes back to what we might call sexual life. No wonder that Mr Elliot can ingratiate himself by talking to her of Lyme and agreeing in her 'lively' wish to visit it again (II. iv). With great meaning, Anne later tells Captain Wentworth, 'I should very much like to see Lyme again . . . So much novelty and beauty!' (II. viii). It is what happened to her there that draws Anne back to the place in her mind and conversation. Bad things happen at the seaside because it is a place of licence. In Austen's first four novels, it is distant from the main events and beyond the knowledge of the heroine. We have to imagine what goes on there. In *Persuasion*, we finally travel to the sea and find that licence can also be a kind of liberation.

SEVEN

Why Is the Weather Important?

'. . . though you will never own being affected by weather, I think every body feels a north-east wind.'

Emma, III. xiv

There is weather in English fiction before Austen, but she is the first novelist to mark the small changes in the weather that anyone might notice on any ordinary day. Partly this is circumstantial precision: the weather has to be minutely observed because each Austen novel follows a tightly defined chronology. As we pass in *Emma* from Christmas to midsummer, as *Persuasion* takes us from autumn in Somerset to winter in Bath, the patterns of the weather change too. Meteorology clues us in to the passing of the year. But it is more than this. Austen likes to make her plots turn on the weather. Having arranged her characters and defined their situations, having planned her love stories and hatched the misunderstandings that might impede them, she lets the weather shape events. It is her way of admitting chance into her narratives.

Look at any single episode in which the weather shapes some important encounter and you might hardly notice the role that Austen gives it. But note the pattern of other such weather-produced accidents, and you can see a design. Take the moment in *Persuasion* where Anne Elliot meets Captain Wentworth in Bath. She has just found out about Louisa Musgrove's engagement to Captain Benwick; Captain Wentworth, she realises, is 'unshackled and free' (II. vi). There is hope. It starts raining and she takes shelter in a shop with her companions, her sister Elizabeth, Mrs Clay and Mr Elliot. Through the shop window she suddenly sees Captain Wentworth in the street (II. vii). In a state of confusion she finds herself moving towards the door 'to see if it rained' – as if the weather was really what was on her mind. Then Captain Wentworth himself enters the shop. 'He was more obviously struck and confused by the sight of her, than she had ever observed before; he looked quite red.' They converse falteringly, while the rain creates a fuss and a bustle in which Lady Dalrymple's carriage is made available to Elizabeth and Mrs Clay, and Mr Elliot goes back and forth making arrangements. Suddenly brought together, Captain Wentworth and Anne hardly notice all the business – until Mr Elliot returns to whisk her off. Captain Wentworth has just been showing her his new umbrella, but is denied the chance to put it to gallant use. A little West Country rain creates the drama of the episode, in which Captain Wentworth has to take second place to Mr Elliot. Nothing like the weather to bring matters to a crisis.

Sense and Sensibility is kicked into life by a misjudgement about the weather: Marianne goes walking on the Devon hills with her younger sister Margaret, convincing herself that 'the partial sunshine of a showery sky' bodes well' (I. ix). 'Marianne's declaration that the day would be lastingly fair' is, of course, folly, revealed when 'a driving rain set full in their face'. Fleeing for home, Marianne trips and is rescued by the handsome Willoughby. It might seem a fortunate accident, the beginning of a romance, but at the root of this episode is Marianne's determination to delude herself about the weather. The plot of *Pride and Prejudice* is also made early to depend on the weather. When Jane is invited to visit Netherfield, Mrs Bennet famously requires that the horses that would pull the Bennet coach be unavailable. They must be being used on the farm. So Jane must travel on horseback 'because it seems likely to rain' (I. vii). Some amateur forecasting settles Jane's fate: she will have to stay the night, giving her all the more chance to win Mr Bingley's heart. And Mrs Bennet is not wrong; it does indeed rain hard. She duly takes the 'credit' for the climatic conditions, although the consequences are rather beyond her control: Jane catches 'a violent cold' and is confined to her bed.

Emma is probably the most weather-dependent of all Austen's novels. So often mentioned and so frequent an influence is weather in *Emma* that earth scientist Euan Nisbet was moved to make a meteorological analysis of its patterns in *Nature* magazine. '*Emma* is weather. Meteorology shapes the novel'.[1] In the very first chapter, Emma recalls for Mr Knightley's benefit how the match between the Westons was first suggested to her when she and Miss Taylor were caught in a light 'mizzle' on a walk through Highbury and Mr Weston had 'darted away with so much gallantry, and borrowed two umbrellas for us from Farmer Mitchell's'. This was Mr Weston's first sign of romantic inclination, according to Emma. And the evidence is that Emma, who spends the novel being so wrong about so much, was right about this. Would-be lovers love to make the weather their collaborator. Emma finds this to her cost when a slight snowfall flusters the guests into a hurried departure from the Westons' dinner party, and she finds herself entrapped in a carriage with a suddenly, drunkenly amorous Mr Elton. Later, in another encounter forced by the weather, heavy rain makes Harriet take shelter in Ford's shop, and thus occasions her awkward, emotional meeting with Robert Martin and his sister (II. iii). Harriet's feelings for Robert Martin are clearly reawakened.

Exposure to the weather was a basic fact of the author's life. 'Our Pond is brimful & our roads are dirty & our walls are damp, & we sit wishing every bad day may be the last', Austen wrote from Chawton in March 1816 (*Letters*, 137). Those who walk, particularly women, are always wondering about the weather. Miss Bates clucks about the possibility of rain on behalf of her weather-susceptible niece. 'Jane, you had better go home directly—I would not have you out in a shower!' (II. iii). Always walking, pale and strained, Jane Fairfax's vulnerability to the weather is no mere neurosis. She is truly exposed to the elements. But when it comes to letter collection, she is dauntless. Mr John Knightley, who has been out with his two boys, hopes that she was not caught out in the rain and she pretends not: 'it did not absolutely rain when I set out' (II. xvi). He teases her, having seen her setting out just as the rain was beginning, and assures her that when she is older she will never think a letter 'worth going through the rain for'. His teasing produces the nearest to a *cri de coeur* that we ever hear from Jane Fairfax, as she says that he has 'every body dearest' to him 'always at hand', while she 'probably, never shall again'. The post office, where letters wait for collection, 'must always have the power to draw me out, in worse weather than today'. Utterly constrained by her circumstances, the weather is one constraint she will not obey. But the tense expressiveness of this exchange is soon overtaken by much less significant weather-talk, as her walk in the rain becomes the topic first for Mr Woodhouse ('Young ladies should take care of themselves') and then Mrs Elton ('You sad girl, how could you do such a thing?').

The point of the exchange is that Jane Fairfax is indeed vulnerable, so the first-time reader should infer that she has some strong reason for persisting in her walking. We might think Mr Woodhouse rather readily frightened by the Surrey climate, but Austen makes a point of having Mrs Weston give advice, 'kindly and persuasively': 'The spring I always think requires more than common care.' Equally susceptible to the weather, and liable to be exposed to it, is Fanny Price in *Mansfield Park*. On a broiling July day she is twice sent by Mrs Norris on errands to her house in the village and is thoroughly 'knocked up' as a result (I. iii). Her vulnerability to the weather is a symptom of her greater defencelessness: she must follow her aunt's uncharitable orders. A volume later she has again been sent out on an errand by her aunt Norris when she is spotted from the parsonage, sheltering from the rain under a tree. Dr Grant appears with an umbrella and she finds that she must enter the house, to the relief of Miss Crawford 'who had just been contemplating the dismal rain in a very desponding state of mind' (II. iv). Fanny soon wishes to leave, so she and Mary Crawford engage in a debate about the state of the weather. Fanny says that the weather is now fair, but Miss Crawford demurs. 'I know a black cloud when I see it; and you must not set forward while it is so threatening.' It is the beginning of Miss Crawford's attempts to win Fanny round, to seduce her. She requires the weather to support her case, and throws in the offer of some harp music if she will stay.

Jane Austen's own letters to her sister invariably include accounts of what the weather has been like where she is, in Hampshire or Kent or London. It seems that such reports are expected, perhaps that it would be peculiar not to include some mention of recent weather. We should realise how determining the weather can be. 'How lucky we were in our weather

yesterday!—This wet morning makes one more sensible of it,'
wrote Austen in May 1813 (*Letters*, 84). She was lucky on this
particular day because she had been on an outing to the Hog's
Back in Surrey, travelling in a curricle – an open carriage – but
the sense of having a life shaped by the weather is common
and constant in her letters. Most often it is the sense of being
hampered by the weather, as in a letter to her nephew Edward
in July 1816 where she complains of unseasonal days of rain
that have kept her indoors. 'It is really too bad, & has been
too bad for a long time, much worse than anybody *can* bear,
& I begin to think it will never be fine again' (*Letters*, 142).
She adds a joke about her subjection to the climate. 'This is a
finesse of mine, for I have often observed that if one writes
about the Weather, it is generally completely changed before
the Letter is read.'

Like the author, Elizabeth Bennet is attentive to the weather,
for she is liberated by being out of doors. She visits her sick
sister by walking across the fields in what the Bingley sisters
call 'dirty weather', though this is a telling inaccuracy on the
part of two cosseted ladies (I. vii). On Elizabeth's visit to the
Collins marital home in the early spring, the weather is 'so
fine for the time of year' that she has the 'great enjoyment'
of frequent walks (II. vii). She loves to walk, while her sisters
need to walk in order to get to the local town. To the Bennet
girls the weather matters very much. In the period before the
Netherfield ball, they spend four or five days imprisoned in
their house because 'there was such a succession of rain as
prevented their walking to Meryton once. No aunt, no officers,
no news could be sought after' (I. xvii). Such is rural life, without the use of a coach at least. In *Persuasion* Mary Musgrove
is bitter about the imprisoning effect of winter weather in
Somerset. As she writes in a letter to Anne, 'What dreadful
weather we have had! It may not be felt in Bath, with your

nice pavements; but in the country it is of some consequence. I have not had a creature call on me since the second week in January' (II. vi). Even in Bath, where Mary thinks the weather makes no difference, a woman cannot go out on her own if it is raining much. When Anne is looking forward to meeting the Musgrove party, and especially Captain Wentworth, at the White Hart, the weather heightens her anxiety by preventing her for some time from attempting the walk (II. xi). In *Emma*, in contrast, the heroine is delighted to be trapped by the weather in the wake of the Mr Elton debacle. Immobilised for 'many days' by snow and rain, she can communicate with Harriet only 'by note' (I. xvi). Only men can scorn the weather, in special circumstances, like Mr Knightley riding back from London 'through the rain' to see Emma and declare himself (III. xiii). But men can be confined too, like Tom Bertram, trying to explain away the theatricals to his father in *Mansfield Park*: 'We have had such incessant rains almost since October began, that we have been nearly confined to the house for days together' (II. i). In *Sense and Sensibility*, the grumpy Mr Palmer finds the restrictive influence of bad weather a reason for his own grumpiness. 'Such weather makes every thing and every body disgusting. Dullness is as much produced within doors as without, by rain. It makes one detest all one's acquaintance. What the devil does Sir John mean by not having a billiard room in his house? How few people know what comfort is! Sir John is as stupid as the weather' (I. xx).

With everyone so susceptible to the weather, talking about the weather is not evidently banal. Marianne Dashwood is scornful of those who talk only of 'the weather and the roads' (*Sense and Sensibility*, I. x), but we need not share her scorn. The weather is the first topic of conversation between Elizabeth Bennet and Wickham, by no means unresourceful conversationalists (I. xvi). The weather can indeed be the refuge of the conversationally limited; so Lady Middleton in *Sense and Sensibility* can only talk about her children and the weather. Yet the first of these topics is made to seem the less truly communicative. The most intelligent of Austen's characters talk about the weather. When Edward Ferrars arrives unannounced near the end of *Sense and Sensibility*, Elinor, unable to express any of her true feelings or apprehensions, 'sat down again and talked of the weather' (III. xii). 'When Elinor had ceased to rejoice in the dryness of the season, a very awful pause took place.' In *Persuasion*, when Anne nervously engages in conversation with Captain Wentworth at the concert in Bath, wholly uncertain about his feelings towards her, they start with the weather (II. viii). In *Emma*, when Mrs Weston finds herself in a conversation with Mr Knightley about the likelihood of Emma marrying, she is relieved (because of her own hopes for her stepson as a possible husband) when he makes the 'quiet transition' to 'What does Weston think of the weather; shall we have rain?' (I. v).

Mr Weston himself talks about the weather in a rather peculiar way. When his son cancels his expected visit to Highbury, he consoles himself that a later visit will be better: 'better time of year; better weather' (I. xviii). All manner of things will be well. When his son later writes to announce his imminent arrival, Mr Weston duly invokes the weather to show that all is indeed for the best. 'I was always glad he did not come at Christmas; now we are going to have just the right weather for him, fine, dry, settled weather' (II. v). Listening to this, you should realise that there is invariably something a little misjudging about whatever Mr Weston says. You can recall his comment during the Randalls' dinner party, where he responds to Mr Woodhouse's panic at news of snow with the acknowledgement that 'he had known it to be snowing some time, but had not said a word, lest it should make Mr Woodhouse uncomfortable' (I. xv). In fact he gives an extra twist to Mr Woodhouse's anxiety by professing the hope that all the roads will be blocked so that his guests are compelled to stay. Mr Weston is sanguine, contented, optimistic, but though these are likeable characteristics, he is therefore often wrong-headed. He is at it again when news comes that Mrs Churchill is moving to Richmond. The time of year couldn't be better for Frank's constant visits, 'weather genial and pleasant, always inviting one out, and never too hot for exercise' (II. xviii). He is forever making the weather the mirror of his hopes, and always making out that everything is for the best. Anybody who makes the weather serve their hopes is to be suspected.

The weather is reality, and the novelist expects us to notice those who try to fit it to their purposes.

'The weather is mended, which I attribute to my writing about it,' wrote Austen in a letter to her sister in 1808 (*Letters,* 55). When you talk rubbish about the weather you are indeed not to be trusted. On the outing to Box Hill, Frank Churchill says that he was 'cross' on the day of the Donwell strawberry picking because 'The heat overcame me' (III. vii). 'It is hotter today,' points out Emma, to which Frank nonsensically replies, 'Not to my feelings.' He resorts to nonsense about the weather because he is covering the tracks of his lovers' quarrel with Jane Fairfax. Some people talk credibly about the weather, and some incredibly. The weather is reality, and the novelist expects us to notice those who try to fit it to their purposes. In *Mansfield Park* Mrs Norris indulges the meteorological ill will that has ever tempted the envious or the malign. Nettled by Fanny's invitation to dine with the Grants, she wishes bad weather upon her niece. 'And if it should rain, which I think exceedingly likely, for I never saw it more threatening for a wet evening in my life—you must manage as well as you can' (II. v). She tells her niece that she must not expect the Bertram carriage to be sent for, 'so you must make up your mind to what may happen'. She wishes on Fanny not just a soaking, but an evening of worrying about the weather – until Sir Thomas dispels all anxiety by telling her that his coach will take and return her.

Deluded and self-deluding, Marianne Dashwood is a great one for requiring the weather to conform to her desires. Her self-deceptive hopes of the weather, which led to that initial meeting with Willoughby, persist. In London she cannot understand why Willoughby has not written or called, until Mrs Jennings remarks that Sir John will not like to leave Devon if 'this open weather holds' (II.v). Marianne seizes on the thought gratefully: all keen huntsmen will be staying in the country. And then she naturally begins projecting her wishes on to the weather: 'it cannot be expected to last long . . . Frosts will soon set in, and in all probability with severity. In another day or two, perhaps; this extreme mildness can hardly last longer—nay, perhaps it may freeze to-night!' Marianne's talk of the weather comically epitomises her folly, for she speaks as if there were some reason for her wishes to come to pass – as if what is merely her desire were some fact in the external world. She is 'happy in the mildness of the weather, and still happier in her expectation of a frost'. Suddenly she is transformed into a keen, though hopelessly biased, meteorologist, 'busy in observing the direction of the wind, watching the variations of the sky and imagining an alteration in the air'. We know that there is some more human and disturbing explanation of his silence, but Marianne will have only the elements to blame. One delusion (the weather is the reason) becomes another (the weather is changing to bring him to her). We, like Elinor, are 'alternately diverted and pained'.

Her folly continues. At Cleveland she likes to wander in the grounds 'in free and luxurious solitude', and on her first day the morning is 'fine and dry' and she can indulge herself. However, 'Marianne, in her plan of employment abroad, had not calculated for any change of weather during their stay at Cleveland' (even though it is April).

> With great surprise therefore, did she find herself prevented by a settled rain from going out again after dinner. She had depended on a twilight walk to the Grecian temple, and perhaps all over the grounds, and an evening merely cold or damp would not have deterred her from it; but an heavy and settled rain even *she* could not fancy dry or pleasant weather for walking (III. vi).

It is striking that only when she is penitent and recuperating, near the end of the novel, does she begin talking of the weather rationally (III. x). She will take walks with Elinor, she says, 'When the weather is settled, and I have recovered my strength'.

Yet the weather will not influence all alike. When hot weather comes to *Mansfield Park*, everyone (except Fanny) is out riding and determined to be pleased, 'the heat only supplying inconvenience enough to be talked of with pleasure' (I. vii). Fanny, meanwhile, roasted by Mrs Norris, is reduced to headaches and tearfulness. In *Emma* the hot June weather of the Donwell strawberry party is perceived differently by different characters. Mr Woodhouse is indoors with a fire; Mrs Elton is bringing on heatstroke with all her talking and strawberry picking; Emma finds the day delicious. Frank Churchill arrives late with a catalogue of complaints about the weather.

> The heat was excessive; he had never suffered any thing like it—almost wished he had staid at home—nothing killed him like heat—he could bear any degree of cold, etc., but heat was intolerable—and he sat down, at the greatest possible distance from the slight remains of Mr. Woodhouse's fire, looking very deplorable. (III. vi)

As ever with him, this is a blind. He is agitated because he has fallen out with Jane Fairfax, whom he has met in the road walking home to Highbury. 'I am glad I have done being in love with him. I should not like a man who is so soon discomposed by a hot morning,' thinks Emma, foolishly – for she has not been in love with him and it is not the hot morning that has rumpled him. He is merely fixing his discontent on the weather. 'You will all be going soon I suppose; the whole party breaking up. I met *one* as I came—Madness in such weather!—absolute madness!' The weather has nothing really to do with his feelings.

The poets of Austen's lifetime were happy to use the pathetic fallacy. 'O there is blessing in this gentle breeze . . .' begins the greatest poem of the Romantic era, Wordsworth's *The Prelude*. The elements conspire to assure the poet that Nature restores and strengthens and delights him. We come near such discovery of human feelings reflected in the elements in *Persuasion*, where Anne is prone to find the fading autumn light of the first half of the novel an index of her own melancholy. As she waits on her own at Uppercross for Lady Russell's carriage to fetch her from her sister's house she muses on the likely (as she thinks it) betrothal of Captain Wentworth and Louisa Musgrove. She has an hour for such reflections, 'on a dark November day, a small thick rain almost blotting out the very few objects ever to be discerned from the windows' (II. i). This autumnal novel uses touches of weather which we hardly notice at first but which suggest the heroine's melancholy. When Anne arrives with Lady Russell in Bath, a place she dislikes, we get a 'dim view of the extensive buildings, smoking in rain' (II. ii). Anne's companion is alive to the prospect of her 'winter pleasures'; our heroine sees things differently.

The nearest to a pathetic fallacy that Austen truly hazards comes in *Emma* : 'The weather added what it could of gloom' (III. xii). Emma has found out about Frank Churchill's engagement to Jane Fairfax and is contemplating the possible pairing of Mr Knightley and Harriet Smith. The world is narrowing. 'A cold stormy rain set in' – unseasonal for July. 'The weather affected Mr. Woodhouse', requiring Emma ceaselessly to be attentive to him in order to keep him 'tolerably comfortable'. The evening of rain lengthens out like the long prospect of her future days with only her father for company. We should not merely think that Mr Woodhouse is foolish for letting the grim weather get to him. Commenting on recent 'terrible' weather in a letter to Martha Lloyd, Austen described its effect on Mrs Austen. 'My Mother slept through a good deal of Sunday, but still it was impossible not to be disordered by such a sky, & even yesterday she was but poorly' (*Letters*, 82). That 'impossible' does not sound sarcastic: grim weather was naturally grim for the spirits, and where a person was easily indisposed (Mr Woodhouse or Mrs Austen) it could easily make them 'poorly'. 'The weather continued much the same all the following morning; and the same loneliness, and the same melancholy, seemed to reign at Hartfield' (III. xiii). But then it shifts: 'the wind changed into a softer quarter; the clouds were carried off; the sun appeared; it was summer again' (III. xiii). Emma can escape into the shrubbery at Hartfield. The weather has liberated her from her gloom and self-absorption – and from her father. She has her 'spirits freshened' by the

welcome fine weather and soon finds herself joined by Mr
Knightley. 'He meant to walk with her, she found.' At the critical moment in their conversation, where he offers a revelation and she declines to know it, they reach the house and
she decides to 'take another turn' around the garden. A new,
benign climate blesses their exchange, and he gets the chance
to tell her not that he wishes to marry Harriet – which was
her fear – but that he loves her. It is the walk in the sudden
fine weather that allows for Mr Knightley's proposal, apparently unpremeditated before he discovers the occasion. The
shrewd reader will regard the final betrothal of Emma and
Mr Knightley as inevitable, from the moment we know that
he is the only person ever to find fault with her. But the best
comedy recruits chance, and the lucky change of weather
in *Emma* is there to let us imagine how it might have been
otherwise.

EIGHT

Do We Ever See the Lower Classes?

'The man who fetches our letters every morning (one of our men, I forget his name) shall inquire for yours too and bring them to you.'

Emma, II. xvi

It is usual to observe that Jane Austen's novels have no room for the labouring classes. Defenders will say that she is simply limiting herself to the world and the genteel classes that she knew; critics will suggest that the exclusion from her fiction of all except gentlemen and ladies shows a certain narrowness of the imagination, for she was certainly surrounded by members of the labouring classes. In Chawton when she arrived, the majority of the 400 or so inhabitants were forestry or agricultural workers.[1] The charge of the critics is worth a careful answer, since Austen herself invites the reader to be unsettled by one of her own characters' absolute negligence of the lower orders. Henry Crawford in *Mansfield Park* has inherited a rich Norfolk estate. When he is trying to woo Fanny Price in Portsmouth, he talks of how he has been doing good on behalf of industrious families there. 'He had introduced himself to some tenants whom he had never seen before; he had begun making acquaintance with cottages whose very existence, though on his own estate, had been hitherto unknown to him' (III. x). His account is 'well aimed'. 'To be the friend of the poor and oppressed!' The exclamation mark gives us the force of Fanny's unspoken response. Yet his account also implies the carelessness of his landlordism before now and the invisibility to him of those beneath his social horizon (even if they are paying him rent).

Some of her characters acknowledge poverty. It is the arch-snob Emma Woodhouse who pays 'a charitable visit' to 'a poor sick family' in *Emma* (I. x). The account of the visit seems suspended between endorsement and satire: Emma is 'very compassionate' and has 'no romantic expectations of extraordinary virtue' – even if she does afterwards embark on some sermonising to Harriet. Yet there is no doubt of the 'wretchedness' of what she has seen. She has given money as well as counsel, and soon a child comes from the cottage with a pitcher to get broth from Hartfield. Later, when walking with Harriet and trying to divert her protégée's mind from thoughts of Mr Elton, she talks of 'what the poor must suffer in winter' (II. i). The rich are expected to relieve the poor. In *Persuasion*, Anne Elliot is ashamed to know that, with the Crofts installed in Kellynch Hall instead of her father and sister, 'the poor' are sure of 'the best attention and relief' (II. i). Having returned to Kellynch from Uppercross to stay with Lady Russell, Anne herself engages in more than one 'visit of charity in the village' (I. ii).

What is poverty? There is Mrs Smith in *Persuasion*: 'She was a widow, and poor' (II. v). She rents two rooms in a cheap part of Bath. Unable to walk, she relies on a servant (Mary) whom she shares with all the other occupants of her lodgings. She has to be rung for. Mrs Smith's very poverty seems to put her on a conversational level with those to whom Austen's characters do not usually talk. When Anne visits her after the concert, she already knows much about the gathering 'through the short cut of a laundress and a waiter' (II. ix). Suddenly you catch a world of chat and information passing beneath the hearing of genteel characters. 'Did you observe the woman who opened the door to you, when you called yesterday?' she asks Anne (II. ix). Anne of course noticed 'no one in particular' – when in fact it was Nurse Rooke, who observed her closely, knowing much that was said about Mr Elliot's relationship with her. Yet Mrs Smith's status, which has made her the conversational companion of members of the lower classes, is temporary. Her circumstances have been reduced by her husband's improvidence and Mr Elliot's nefariousness, and like some character from Victorian fiction, she is restored to deserving affluence at the end of the novel.

Another character reduced from gentility is Miss Bates in *Emma*. Mr Knightley explicitly says 'She is poor' (III. vii), but she and her ageing mother, living in a couple of upstairs rooms, themselves employ one maid-of-all-work, Patty, who cooks and cleans. *Emma* is a novel which lets you feel the embarrassment – or Hobbesian carelessness – of those who are luckily rich and are living close to those who are unluckily poor. Austen inserts some entirely unnecessary evidence of poverty in Highbury into one of Miss Bates's rambling monologues. She is trying to remember when she first heard that her niece had accepted Mrs Elton's arrangement of a governess's post, and recollects Mr Elton being called out of the room by 'old John Abdy's son' (III. viii). We find out from Miss Bates, ever particular, that the old man is a bedridden former clerk to the vicar (her father), and that she visits him. His son, an ostler at the Crown, is after parish relief for him, and must persuade Mr Elton into dispensing it.

The crucial distinction is between those who employ servants, and those who do not. Almost all the named characters
who belong to the latter category in Austen's novels are themselves servants; to her first readers, as habituated to the presence of servants as the novelist, they would not have been
invisible at all. Indeed, her novels rely on the readers 'seeing'
these servants in a way that we have forgotten to do. Her characters are wise not to forget that they are often observed by
servants. Colonel Brandon recalls how his planned elopement
with Eliza, the woman he loved who was promised in marriage
to his brother, was scotched by a servant. 'The treachery, or
the folly, of my cousin's maid betrayed us' (II. ix). It is a foolish person who does not shape conversation to take account
of the presence of servants. In *Pride and Prejudice*, Elizabeth
and the Gardiners are relieved when Mrs Bennet withdraws
to her room in the wake of Lydia's elopement, 'for they knew
that she had not prudence enough to hold her tongue before
the servants, while they waited at table' (III. v). Hearing
the account of her mother's reactions when the news about
Lydia was first broken, Elizabeth cries out that every servant must have known 'the whole story before the end of the
day'. And when the servants know, so does the world. They
are self-interested monitors, who will not necessarily protect
those whom they watch. Lady Catherine de Bourgh boasts
of having sent two servants with her niece to Ramsgate ('I
am excessively attentive to all these things'), but they do not
manage to prevent the planned elopment (I. xiv). In fact, the
scheme is facilitated by a diabolical servant, Mrs Younge, the
former governess to Miss Darcy

The reader who supposes that Austen's fictional servants
form a class of devoted, silent attendants will miss many
tricks. The fact that servants are also a problem is behind Mr
Bennet's remark to his just-engaged daughter Jane that she

and Bingley are 'so easy, that every servant will cheat you' (III. xiii). Servants have their own interests. It would have been odd for Austen's novels not to imagine difficulties with servants, for her own letters are full of them. Writing to her niece Anna in 1814, Aunt Jane pauses from detailed advice about her would-be novel to tell her important news. 'Your Aunt Frank's Housemaid has just given her warning, but whether she is worth your having, or w^d take your place I know not . . . She leaves your Aunt, because she cannot agree with her fellow servants. She is in love with the Man—& her head seems rather turned' (*Letters*, 108). She goes on to detail her relations and previous service. Her letters some-times hint at the shifting balance of power between servants and their less affluent employers. 'Mary's promised maid has jilted her, & hired herself elsewhere' (*Letters*, 24). Mary is her sister-in-law, evidently outbid for the services of a maid who knows her market value. The dismissal of servants is significant news. 'Mrs Digweed parts with both Hannah & old Cook, the former will not give up her Lover, who is a Man of bad Character, the Latter is guilty only of being unequal to anything' (*Letters*, 145).

Fellowship with servants is a warning sign. In *Sense and Sensibility*, cheerful, vulgar Mrs Jennings, mother of a minor aristocrat, is happy enough to travel with 'her maid' and 'take comfort' in her 'gossip' rather than enjoy the company of the Dashwood sisters (III. x). In *Mansfield Park*, it is a nice touch that Tom Bertram, recently returned to England from a year in the West Indies, writes to the gamekeeper before he writes to his brother (I. xii). Back in the household, he crassly insists on talking to Fanny and others about one of the horses 'and the opinion of the groom, from whom he had just parted' (I. xii). His sisters recruit their servants to their own cruelties. When the ten-year-old Fanny arrives at the great house of her aunt and uncle, they are the supporting cast to Maria's and Julia's unkindness. 'Her elder cousins mortified her by reflections on her size, and abashed her by noticing her shyness: Miss Lee wondered at her ignorance, and the maid-servants sneered at her clothes' (I. ii).

It is a nice piece of sociological realism on Austen's part that the character who complains the most about servants in her novels is the impecunious 'slattern' Mrs Price in *Mansfield Park* (III. viii). Within minutes of Fanny arriving after an eight-year absence, her mother is moaning about the failings of Rebecca, complaints with which her daughter Susan readily falls in (III. vii). Soon Rebecca herself is squabbling with eleven-year-old Sam over carrying Fanny's trunk. Fanny discovers that Rebecca is 'the upper servant', there also being 'an attendant girl' of 'inferior appearance' called Sally (III. vii). When Mrs Price does think to ask about the lives of her sisters at Mansfield Park, it is a route to her favourite topic of discontent. 'How did her sister Bertram manage about her servants? Was she as much plagued as herself to get tolerable servants?' (III. vii) Then she is away, into a disquisition: 'the shocking character of all the Portsmouth servants, of whom she believed her own two were the very worst, engrossed her completely'. She has taught not only fourteen-year-old Susan but even five-year-old Betsey to complain endlessly about Rebecca. 'I am sure the place is easy enough,' observes Mrs Price, giving us an indication why the spatial and economic proximity of servants to their employers is a likely cause of mutual disgruntlement. Rebecca is 'never where she ought to be', which is not the narrator's information but a report of the constant complaint. Even in these cramped lodgings, she cannot ever be in the right place. It is her ordeal rather than her fault. 'Whatever was wanted, was halloo'd for, and the servants halloo'd out their excuses from the kitchen' (III. viii).

Rebecca is a fright, as we know when Fanny sighs with relief that Mr Crawford has not sampled 'Rebecca's cookery and Rebecca's waiting' (III. x). Fanny has to survive on surreptitiously purchased biscuits and buns, for she is not equal to 'Rebecca's puddings, and Rebecca's hashes', served on 'half-cleaned plates' with 'not half-cleaned knives and forks' (III. xi). When Mrs Price is walking out with her family on a Sunday, her greatest possible torment is to see 'Rebecca pass by with a flower in her hat' (III. xi). This is the one day when she has no pretence of power over her and the thought that she has a better life is just too aggravating. When Mrs Price goes for her weekly walk on the ramparts she meets acquaintances for news and 'talked over the badness of the Portsmouth servants'. It is almost the only topic on which she is able to fix her mind. When she is first told of her niece Maria's presumed adultery, she barely has time to hope that it is not true, 'it would be so very shocking!', before she starts noticing that Rebecca has not cleaned the carpet and recruiting young Betsey in her laments (III. xv). Austen's first readers, themselves reliant on servants, would have been able to relish the background drama of Mrs Price's exasperation at her servants.

For the more privileged, there is the pleasure of complaining about other people's servants. In *Emma* Mrs Elton condemns 'Donwell servants, who are all, I have often observed, extremely awkward and remiss.—I am sure I would not have such a creature as his Harry stand at our sideboard for any consideration. And as for Mrs. Hodges, Wright holds her very cheap indeed.—She promised Wright a receipt, and never sent it' (III. xvi). In *Persuasion*, Mary Musgrove complains to Anne that her mother-in-law's upper house-maid and laundry-maid 'are gadding about the village, all day long. I meet them wherever I go' (I. vi). Her own servant Jemima has told her that 'they are always tempting her to take a walk with them', but luckily, according to Mary, Jemima is 'the trustiest, steadiest creature in the world'. The character who thinks that their own servant is wonderful belongs with the character who thinks that all their servants are useless. For of course Mrs Musgrove tells Anne that the aforementioned Jemima, Mary's nursery-maid, 'is always upon the gad'. 'I can declare, she is such a fine-dressing lady, that she is enough to ruin any servants she comes near.' She invites Anne to report 'any thing amiss' that she observes herself. By allowing these confident confidences to mirror each other so exactly, the novel invites us to imagine both employers beguiled by their own servants – critics who are really dupes.

The reader is equally invited to recoil from the character who is unpleasant to servants. General Tilney in *Northanger Abbey* gets angry with his servant, William, for not opening a door for Catherine when she rushes in to their Bath apartment. If Catherine had not intervened, he might have lost 'the favour of his master for ever, if not his place' – even though he is entirely blameless (I. xiii). The General's anger is always just under the surface in the novel, and here we are asked to suspect how he might regularly vent his fury on his servants. In *Sense and Sensibility* a whole political economy of employer–servant relations is satirically implied by Mrs John Dashwood's recollection of her mother being 'clogged' by the requirement in her husband's will to pay annuities to three 'old superannuated servants' (I. ii). 'Twice every year, these annuities were to be paid; and then there was the trouble of getting it to them; and then one of them was said to have died, and afterwards it turned out to be no such thing.' The detail mentioning how wearisome it was even to have to convey the funds is beautiful. Even better is the farce of wishfulness implied by the rumour of the death of one of these

hapless ex-retainers, sparking the evident disappointment of
the family when he or she was discovered to be living still.
It was 'unkind' of her father to require the payment, judges
a woman who has all the kindness of a Goneril. The utterly
mean-spirited Mrs Ferrars is legally obliged to pay the annuities, and we are left in no doubt that she would otherwise
have given the former servants nothing. In which case, the
unfortunate ex-employees would almost certainly have had to
eke out their final years on poor relief.[2] Being considerate to
ex-servants is always virtuous, and in *Sense and Sensibility* the
virtue is rather obviously rewarded. Colonel Brandon manages
to find his sister-in-law Eliza, an impoverished fallen woman,
because of his paternalistic care. 'Regard for a former servant
of my own, who had since fallen into misfortune, carried me
to visit him in a spunging-house, where he was confined for
debt; and there, in the same house, under a similar confinement, was my unfortunate sister' (II. ix).

A sure sign that Lady Denham in *Sanditon* is (as the heroine
thinks) 'very, very mean' is her pride in not paying her servants more (Ch. 7). Other Austen characters like to be above
the economic system that binds their servants to them. Lady
Bertram is amazed and relieved to find that, in her husband's
absence, Edmund is capable of 'settling with the servants' (I.
iv). We are left to imagine how irksome such everyday negotiations would be for her. In contrast, her sister Mrs Norris
loves to talk about talking to servants. Her excuse for sending
Fanny on endless errands in the heat of the day is that she
has been doing just this. 'I was talking to Mr. Green at that
very time about your mother's dairymaid, by *her* desire, and
had promised John Groom to write to Mrs. Jefferies about his
son, and the poor fellow was waiting for me half an hour' (I.
vii) She is too busy bossing the servants to get a servant to
do the errands. This is officiousness and the mere exercise

of power, of course. When Sir Thomas returns unexpectedly from Antigua, she pesters him to eat something, for if he asked for food 'she might have gone to the house-keeper with troublesome directions, and insulted the footmen with injunctions of despatch' (II. i).

Austen's monsters are invariably attentive to the lower
orders, for thus they exercise their self-importance.

There are plenty of servants in *Mansfield* Park and, hardly noticed by the other characters but noticed by the attentive reader, Mrs Norris is invariably in among them. The very fact that she is keen to call servants by name is a sign of her interfering bent. When bustling over the arrival of tea she suggests that Lady Bertram 'hurry Baddeley a little, he seems behind hand to-night' (I. i). She refers to the inferior coachmen as Stephen and Charles (II. ii). She has a special interest in servants. On the visit to Sotherton we find that she has 'fallen in with the housekeeper' (I. ix) and on the return journey she talks of how 'good old Mrs. Whitaker' has well nigh forced a cream cheese upon her (I. x). She later calls her 'a treasure', apparently on the grounds that she never allows wine at the servants' table and has sacked two housemaids 'for wearing white gowns'. (White was the most fashionably elegant colour for a woman's dress, and therefore presumptuous in a mere servant.[3]) A woman after her own heart. In her company she meets the benighted Sotherton gardener, and has soon 'set him right as to his grandson's illness, convinced him it was an ague, and presented him a charm for it' (I. x). She has never, of course, seen the ailing grandson. That 'convinced him' is the perfect touch, letting you imagine the force of Mrs Norris's assertion and the helpless need of the elderly retainer to concur. And what about the charm? Does Mrs Norris carry a supply of these? Naturally she gets a plant out of him, for he must see the kind of person that she is. Although this man never speaks and is never named, you glimpse how his life must be spent falling in with the inclinations of his betters.

Mrs Norris's professed solicitousness for the servants should encourage a contrary reading. Back at Mansfield, where she is 'cross because the house-keeper would have her own way with the supper', she is, in reality, in a war for power with the senior servants (II. ix).Vaunting herself to her brother-in-law for her encouragement of the connection with the Rushworths, she narrates the sufferings of the 'poor old coachman', who has been afflicted with 'the rheumatism which I had been doctoring him for, ever since Michaelmas' (II. ii). And then, decisively, 'I cured him at last.' Leaving the dinner at the Parsonage, she chivvies Fanny, 'Quick, quick. I cannot bear to keep good old Wilcox waiting. You should always remember the coachman and horses' (II. vii). In fact she is only interested in bullying her niece. All the small examples of her talk about servants are there to let you imagine the quotidian meddling and bullying that these servants must endure. They are not her servants, of course. Mansfield Park has a large retinue of retainers who dine in their own Hall. They are not paid by Mrs Norris, they are just her potential victims. Christopher Jackson is favoured by Sir Thomas, so it is no suprise when Mrs Norris tells us that 'the Jacksons are very encroaching, I have always said so' (I. xv). She is boasting of having intercepted the hapless ten-year-old Dick Jackson on his way to the Servants' Hall with a couple of pieces of wood for his father. She calls the Jackson parents 'Mother' and 'Father', with a kind of officious familiarity that is her special tone. By her own account, she speaks sharply to their ten-year-old son, 'a great lubberly fellow', and sends him off, perhaps in tears (he 'looked very silly' in response to her harshness).

Austen's monsters are invariably attentive to the lower orders, for thus they exercise their self-importance. The Collinses' housemaids have to suffer the admonishments of Lady Catherine de Bourgh whenever she calls (II. vii). The local cottagers have to suffer her attentions when she arrives to 'scold them into harmony and plenty'. Mrs Elton brandishes her servants in conversation, unnecessarily telling Emma how Wright (presumably her housekeeper) will always dish up enough to allow Jane Fairfax a portion. Later she offers to have Jane Fairfax's letters fetched from the post office for her by 'the man who fetches our letters every morning (one of our men, I forget his name)' (II. xvi). Her amnesia is itself a boast. Talking of her servants is her way of showing off: 'it is a kindness to employ our men'. Clearly any intelligent servant would do well to avoid unnecessary encounters with either of these two, but we are expected to notice that even employers who think of themselves as considerate can be oppressive. In the background of *Emma* is the little drama of Mr Woodhouse's relations with his servants, all the more resonant because this rich and sedentary man imagines himself the kindest of masters. His is an ordinary kind of hypocrisy. He provides his carriage and his coachman James to carry Mrs and Miss Bates and Mrs Goddard back and forth frequently from their homes to Hartfield, though if the trips had been 'only once a year', the narrator tells us, he would have worried about his servant and his horses (I. iii). He is serving his own pleasures, naturally, as Miss Bates and Mrs Goddard are his powerless, recruited companions. At the Coles' party, we find out from Emma that she would like to have the Woodhouse coach used sometimes by friends like the Bateses, but she cannot think of it because of Mr

Woodhouse's concerns for James. Mr Knightley concurs (II. viii). As soon as Mr Woodhouse's own gentle selfishness is not being indulged, he starts worrying about his servant. He is always mentioning James – 'James will take you very safely' – as if being coachman in the lanes of Surrey were a dangerous posting (II. vii). He worries away about James, though when it snows it is Mr Knightley who goes out to talk to both coachmen to find out their opinions of the ease of a return journey (I. xv).

Austen slyly lets you glimpse the irksomeness of life as one of Mr Woodhouse's servants in his very praise of their virtues. Discovering that Emma has sent the Bateses a hindquarter of pork, Mr Woodhouse discourses on the dangers of eating this meat, unless 'very thoroughly boiled, just as Serle boils our's' (II. iii). Serle, the invisible Hartfield cook, features in Mr Woodhouse's conversation as a prodigy of culinary skill. 'Serle understands boiling an egg better than any body. I would not recommend an egg boiled by any body else' (I. iii). This fragment of dialogue is a little miracle of absurdity, suggesting something of Serle's skills at managing her employer's expectations (Serle's gender is never specified, but only peculiarly grand or fashionable households usually employed expensive male cooks). We know that life in the Hartfield kitchen must be determined by Mr Woodhouse's endless fussiness, but perhaps that Serle has simply become skilled at pretending to pander to her master's nervous demands. The subtext of all Mr Woodhouse's kind remarks about his servants is that they have to put up with all his fussing. We have to infer this from his own comments, as when he delivers his 'great opinion' of James's daughter Hannah, recently appointed as a maid to the Westons (I. i). 'Whenever I see her, she always curtseys and asks me how I do, in a very pretty manner; and when you have had her here to do needlework, I observe she always turns the lock of the door the right way and never bangs it. I am sure she will be an excellent servant.' His praise manages to be both weak-minded and imperious. In his implied dealings with servants we can imagine what Austen calls his 'gentle selfishness' – a choice oxymoron for his self-pleasing exhibition of consideration for others. His ordinary expectations are probably high. Austen allows us the little detail of his ordering Emma's maid, the cook and the butler to wait up for her when she goes out to the Coles'.

There are plenty of servants to go round at Hartfield. Mr Woodhouse must have at least six or seven: a butler, a cook, a coachman, at least one gardener, a lady's maid, a kitchen maid, another general maid, perhaps another manservant who doubles as an extra coachman – and all for himself and his daughter. The number of servants you employ is a sign of your status, as when we hear in *Emma* of the rise of the Coles, resented by our heroine. 'With their wealth, their views increased; their want of a larger house, their inclination for more company. They added to their house, to their number of servants, to their expenses of every sort' (II. vii). Further down the social scale, the Martins 'have no indoors man', Harriet Smith tells Emma, though 'Mrs. Martin talks of taking a boy another year' (I. iv). This is Harriet awkwardly trying to puff the Martins' social standing and succeeding in doing the opposite. When Mr and Mrs John Dashwood stage a London dinner in *Sense and Sensibility*, the servants are part of the show. 'The dinner was a grand one, the servants were numerous, and everything bespoke the Mistress's inclination for shew, and the Master's ability to support it' (II. xii). In Bath, the Elliots rent a house in Camden Place, out of the fashionable swim. They can just manage a flourish of servants. When Mr Elliot visits on Anne's first evening in Bath, he is admitted 'with all the state which a butler and foot-boy could give' (II. ii). But when Elizabeth contemplates inviting the Musgrove party for dinner, she cannot bear their witnessing 'the difference of style, the reduction of servants, which a dinner must betray' (II. x). So instead she asks them 'for an evening', avoiding the need for serving and waiting at table that would reveal the small numbers of their servants.

Austen's readers would have known what a modest number of servants was. When the Dashwoods move to Devon, Elinor's wisdom 'limited' them to three servants, who are duly whistled off from Sussex (I. v). These three are presumed to have some loyalty to the Dashwoods, being 'speedily provided from amongst those who had formed their establishment at Norland' ('speedily' implying ready volunteers). Talking to Elinor, Mrs Jennings later begins to imagine a modestly happy existence for Edward and Lucy, on perhaps five hundred a year, in 'such another cottage as yours—or a little bigger—with two maids and two men' (III. i). And she begins to allot her own maid Betty's 'out of place' sister to them. When she hears that Edward has been disinherited she rapidly alters her calculations. 'Two maids and two men indeed!—as I talked of t'other day.—No, no, they must get a stout girl of all works.—Betty's sister would never do for them *now*' (III. ii). At the end of the eighteenth century, it would have been normal for a member of the country gentry of modest means to employ four or five servants. The Rev. William Gilpin, on £700 per year, had four permanent servants.[*] As the Austens planned their move to Bath in January 1801, Jane told her sister, 'My Mother looks forward with as much certainty as you can do, to our keeping two Maids—my father is the only one not in the secret' (*Letters*, 29). This would have meant having four servants in total. But several households in Austen have many more. At

Mansfield Park there seem to be hordes. Fanny is saved from the advances of Mr Crawford one evening by the appearance of Baddely (the butler) with tea, heading a 'procession' of 'cake-bearers' and those carrying the tea-board and the urn. The Bennets have a housekeeper (Hill), a butler (III. vii), a cook and two housemaids (III. viii). There are probably more: a manservant, a gardener, a kitchen maid. Northanger Abbey is full of servants (remember that the General is proud of his 'offices'). Catherine Morland, having sneaked into Mrs Tilney's room, hears footsteps. 'To be found there, even by a servant, would be unpleasant . . .' (II. ix). Later, upset by the letter in which her brother tells her how Isabella has jilted him, she cannot retreat to her own room because 'the house-maids were busy in it' (II. x). Surely the ubiquitous servants are the 'voluntary spies' Henry invokes (II. ix).

We can imagine how they talk about what they see and hear. Only occasionally are their voices recorded: the old coachman in *Mansfield Park*, praising Mary Crawford's 'good heart for riding' and remembering Fanny's fearfulness (I. vii); the butler Baddeley politely contradicting Mrs Norris, with 'a half-smile' that speaks his delight in having to do so (III. i). We should, however, guess at the talk of servants. In *Persuasion*, one clue as to the identity of the unknown 'gentleman' at the inn in Lyme is the fact that his servant has been chatting to the waiter about his master's prospects: 'he did not mention no particular family; but he said his master was a very rich gentleman, and would be a baronight some day' (II. xii). The fortunes of servants depend on those of their masters and mistresses – and the waiter's blissful mispronunciation turns the rank of which Sir Walter is so vain into the slurred calcu-lation of one of the lower orders. Baronet – Knight – some such thing: only the promise of increased wages and better premises is likely to matter.

In the persons of servants, the lower orders are ever-present in Austen's fiction. The novelist expects the reader to 'see' them (often the male servants will be dressed in livery). As Elizabeth Bennet acknowledges with pain, family troubles take place in a domestic theatre with an audience of servants. 'What praise is more valuable than the praise of an intelligent servant?' asks the narrator of *Pride and Prejudice*, in effect echoing Elizabeth's thought (III. i). There is nothing like the verdict of a servant, for the servants see everything, and we as readers should see them watching and listening.

NINE

Which Important Characters Never Speak in the Novels?

He had a pleasing face and a melancholy air, just as he ought to have, and drew back from conversation.

Persuasion, I. xii

'*Oratio imago animi.* – Language most shows a man: Speak, that I may see thee', wrote the dramatist Ben Jonson, elaborating a Latin idiom.[1] The great novelists of the nineteenth century, including Jane Austen, learned to make us discern a character through his or her speech. The rather few critics who have written on speech in Austen's fiction have discovered how each of her speakers seems to have their own idiolect – a way of speaking that is individually distinctive.[2] In the art of creating idiolects the novelist is like the dramatist, but in the presentation of conversation the novelist has an extra resource: she can report dialogue without quoting it. In any particular scene a character might be speaking without his or her words actually being given to us. Austen, one of the greatest of all writers of dialogue, also developed a technique that is not usually noticed: the selective denial of quoted speech to particular characters.

Sometimes this denial is like a little joke that must have delighted the author exactly because it is difficult to spot. Such seems to be the case with Captain Benwick, the grieving poetry-lover in *Persuasion*. On her visit to Lyme with Captain Wentworth and the Musgroves, Anne Elliot spends much of her time deep in talk with this mournful naval officer, yet not a word that he speaks is ever quoted. We are given a good idea of their topics of literary conversation, we are invited to imagine him plangently reciting lines from the poems of Scott and Byron 'which imaged a broken heart, or a mind destroyed by wretchedness', but we are never allowed actually to hear him speak (I. xi). Captain Benwick belongs to a special class of Austen's characters: those who may play an important part in the story, may often be present on the page, may even be talking a good deal – but do not enter the novel's recorded dialogue. The effect is extraordinary, and surely affects readers who are not necessarily conscious of Benwick's speechlessness. The fact that we never hear him speak means that he never quite achieves singularity. We are left with the suspicion that he is performing by rote. The author's buried joke is that all his outpouring amounts to no real expression of individual feeling or opinion.

And outpouring it seems to be. Anne Elliot and the Musgroves have already been told Captain Benwick's sad history by Captain Wentworth before they meet him at Lyme. He is still distraught at the death of Fanny Harville, to whom he was engaged. When he is first encountered, he is described as a young man with 'a pleasing face and a melancholy air', who 'drew back from conversation' (I. xi). Yet his avoidance of conversation does not mean that he does not want to talk. *Au contraire.* On her first evening in Lyme, Anne gets Captain Benwick for company and finds that, though he is 'shy', he eventually has plenty to say– notably about his 'taste in reading' (I. xi). In fact, 'he did not seem reserved', and soon he is talking about poetry and repeating the appropriate chunks of Scott and Byron that he has got by heart. He has found out the lines that seem to dignify his own feelings. Anne spends most of the evening with him (not without motive: she is keen to avoid the conversation of Captain Wentworth). But, being full of quotations himself, he says nothing that the author thinks worth quoting.

The next day Captain Benwick seeks Anne out and he is soon talking again, disputing over books (I. xii). Captain Harville is grateful to her for 'making that poor fellow talk so much'. He has been silently brooding over his books, it seems, while 'shut up' with the unbookish Harvilles. Now Anne has done the 'good deed' of a thoroughgoing therapist and given him the chance to talk. The sense is delicately given that Anne is becoming rather the victim of this silent man who has so quickly discovered the consolation of talk. As the party walks along the Cobb for a last time before leaving, 'Anne found Captain Benwick again drawing near her.' Of course he is going to talk and recite some more, but Austen is not going to tax the reader with what he says. Her heroine's response is charitable rather than delighted: 'she gladly gave him all her attention as long as attention was possible'. Not enough attention for any of his words to lodge.

When Charles Musgrove returns from Lyme and tells Anne about Captain Benwick, it is about him talking. '"Oh! He talks of you," cried Charles, "in such terms . . . His head is full of some books that he is reading upon your recommendation, and he wants to talk to you about them . . . I overheard him telling Henrietta all about it"' (II. ii). He keeps being talked about as talking, but his own words are kept from us. Charles vaguely remembers something he might have said about Anne – 'Elegance, sweetness, beauty' – but not any actual statement. He will never actually speak to us. The 'poor fellow' is sad, no doubt of it, but by declining, among all his effusions, to give us his own words, Austen animates our doubts about all his feelings. It is funny and it is narratively cunning, for Captain Benwick's rapid tumble into an engagement with Louisa Musgrove will provoke Anne's dispute with Captain Harville about the retentiveness of men's and women's feelings, prompting Captain Wentworth to his declaration. We should already know from the absence in the novel of Benwick's own speech that there has been something self-pleasing in his discussion of the poetry of feeling. After his engagement to Louisa becomes official, Charles Musgrove describes him sitting next to his inamorata, 'reading verses, or whispering to her, all day long' (II. x). His conversation is more like a private flow of discourse. He has to be dragged into exchanges with other men. Charles Musgrove observes, 'when one can but get him to talk, he has plenty to say', but we will have to take his word for it.

There is sometimes something comical in Austen's refusal to let a minor character be heard. Mr Musgrove in *Persuasion* is often present but never gets a word in – in contrast to the loquacious Mrs Musgrove. Benevolent and affluent, he is led by the inclinations of his wife and daughters. Comparably in *Pride and Prejudice*, Miss de Bourgh, Lady Catherine's daughter, hardly has the right to be given any words of her own. During her stay in Kent, whenever Elizabeth meets Lady Catherine, Miss de Bourgh is always of the company, yet she is incapable of contributing anything to the dialogue. Lady Catherine's daughter 'spoke very little', we are told, but in fact she speaks to us not at all: she is made entirely silent by the novel. Austen contrives a deliberate impression of her nothingness that is comic because the young woman is otherwise so privileged, and because her mother is so persuaded of her accomplishments. When Elizabeth joins her table for cards she finds it 'superlatively stupid', with talk about the game that is simply too tedious to relate (II. vi). When Elizabeth and Maria Lucas take their final leave before returning to Hertfordshire, she 'exerted herself so far as to curtsey and hold out her hand to both' (II. xv). She is, of course, the stooge to her endlessly talking, endlessly commanding mother, and we can feel as we read that she has been stunned into non-expression.

The other unspeaking young woman in the book is Georgiana Darcy. When she is first introduced by her brother, Elizabeth sees that she is 'exceedingly shy' and finds it difficult 'to obtain even a word from her beyond a monosyllable' (III. ii). When we next meet her she is attended by those baleful sisters Miss Bingley and Mrs Hurst, who are watching over her exchanges with Elizabeth, and she therefore has the more reason for restraint. Like Miss de Bourgh she has a paid companion, a genteel lady called Mrs Annesley, who is employed to do some of the talking for her. Elizabeth thinks that Miss Darcy looks 'as if she wished for courage' to join in the conversation, and sometimes she does 'venture a short sentence, when there was least danger of its being heard' (III. iii). The impression of her reticence is strongly conveyed by Austen's decision never to quote her. When her brother appears, Miss Darcy 'exerted herself much more to talk', but who knows what she said? Miss Bingley mentions the militia, hoping to mortify Elizabeth with memories of Wickham, while unaware of Miss Darcy's 'meditated elopement' with him. Elizabeth is a match for this thrust, covering for Miss Darcy's embarrassment. 'Georgiana also recovered in time, though not enough to be able to speak any more.' Her wordlessness is her timidity, but something else too. The reminder that she was close to being deceived into elopement with Wickham is also a further explanation of her speechlessness.

Her awkwardness, we are told, proceeds 'from shyness and the fear of doing wrong' and she is painfully aware that she has indeed come perilously close to 'doing wrong'. Her near-seduction by Wickham has robbed her of the capacity to speak for herself.

Pride and Prejudice has a high proportion of dialogue, so the non-contribution of these characters to the conversations that swirl around them should be noticeable to the other characters. In contrast, there are silent characters in Austen whose silence is a fact for the reader but not for the other characters. These are characters whose silence the novelist has elaborately arranged. A rival to Captain Benwick as a kind of authorial joke is Mr Perry, the local apothecary in *Emma*. Never has a character had so much of their speech reported by other characters without any of it ever being quoted by the author. Mr Woodhouse is endlessly citing his judgements, and his dialogue is punctuated with 'Perry said . . . Perry tells me . . .' There is nothing that Mr Woodhouse likes to tell any companion more than what Mr Perry has supposedly said – but in the novel Mr Perry actually says nothing. It is as if this absence from dialogue mimics ths successful quack's wise practice, which must be to go along with whatever such a wealthy hypochondriac wants to believe. Who knows whether Mr Perry has said most of the things that Mr Woodhouse attributes to him? The novelist keeps him from speaking, imitating his own canny reticence. Mr Perry's silence (despite all those reports of his sentiments) must have tickled his creator. It is what allows you to imagine his life – and even his thoughts – as the well-remunerated stooge of the Highbury gentry. They have come to rely on him, and to reward him financially for their reliance. He is their echo. When Harriet Smith becomes interested in riddles, Mr Woodhouse even consults 'his good friend Perry' in search of an example, though the apothecary 'did not at present recollect any thing of the riddle kind' (I. ix). Mr Woodhouse is slavish in his reliance, but it is not only he who reports what Mr Perry has said; everyone else in Highbury seems to repeat Mr Perry's comments. Mr Perry is naturally the origin of much village gossip, being constantly on the move from one person's house to the next. When Harriet Smith, for instance, gives Emma her account of Mr Elton's mission to London to have Emma's picture of her framed, the apothecary is her original source. Harriet has been told by Miss Nash, head-teacher at Mrs Goddard's school, who has heard about it from Mr Perry. In Harriet's account, Mr Perry is as loquacious as ever. He has met Mr Elton on the road and, realising that he was going to miss their whist club for the sake of this romantic errand, 'had remonstrated with him about it, and told him how shabby it was in him . . . and tried very much to persuade him to put off his journey' (I. viii).

Everybody hears Mr Perry talking except the reader. Even when he is actually present his speech is kept from us. In the one chapter told from Mr Knightley's point of view (III. v), two parties, consisting of most of the novel's main characters, meet and walk up to Hartfield to visit Mr Woodhouse. 'As they were turning into the grounds, Mr. Perry passed by on horseback. The gentlemen spoke of his horse.' It is a crucial encounter, leading to Frank Churchill's 'blunder' in mentioning the likelihood of Mr Perry 'setting up his carriage'. Mr Perry is riding a horse, but is evidently making so much money from the hypochondriacs of Highbury that he can accede to his wife's desire for a carriage. Frank Churchill is *au fait* with this development because of his secret communication with Jane Fairfax, and is therefore in difficulties when asked by Mrs Weston how he knows. Mr Perry, the local go-between, is as important as ever in this episode, yet we are not going to hear if he really has a voice of his own. Only once do we get close to hearing him, when he comes to Hartfield after having called on Jane Fairfax, who is ailing because she has broken off her engagement with Frank Churchill. Mr Perry tells Emma that his new patient's health 'seemed for the moment completely deranged', and that 'Her spirits seemed overcome' (III. ix). Even here Austen is determined to keep us from his actual speech, giving us his diagnosis in elaborately reported mode. On another occasion we seem to get a preserved specimen of his actual advice, when Emma is trying to answer her father's anxiety about the health-damaging consequences of the forthcoming ball at the Crown. He need not worry because Mrs Weston will be in charge of arrangements, 'Our own dear Mrs Weston, who is carefulness itself' (II. xi). Grasping for evidence of her former governess's care for people's health, she asks her father to recall what Mr' Perry said 'so many years ago' when she had measles. 'If *Miss Taylor* undertakes to wrap Miss Emma up, you need not have any fears, sir' (II. xi). This is not him speaking, but it purports to be a quotation remembered down the years – and, if it is such, what a blissfully idiotic sentiment it is! As if wrapping up were a cure for measles, that common killer of children in the nineteenth century, and as if Miss Taylor's wrapping-up skills were uniquely infallible.

The other important example of speechlessness in *Emma* is equally carefully arranged by the novelist, though not such a source of mischievous pleasure. It is Robert Martin, loving suitor and (despite Emma's stupid endeavours) destined husband of Harriet Smith. Soon after we and Emma have first been told about Robert Martin by the obviously enamoured Harriet, he meets Emma and Harriet out walking in Highbury. He is himself on foot, so there is the opportunity for conversation. The novel imitates Emma's own unfriendly distance from him, as she walks a few yards ahead 'while they talked together' (I. iv). The exchange between himself and Harriet has to be brief, 'as Miss Woodhouse must not be kept waiting' – unwilling to allow their intimacy to prosper, Emma has made it evident that her friend must leave. Having curtailed their conversation, which was clearly a pleasure to both of them, she embarks on her critique, which includes a slur on 'the uncouthness of a voice, which I heard to be unmodulated as I stood there'. What is this 'uncouthness'? Is there anything real in Emma's description? Are we to guess that Robert Martin might have a regional accent? We cannot know. Emma compares his manner 'of speaking; of being silent' unfavourably with Mr Weston and Mr Elton. Harriet accepts the implied denigration, but a reader who knows Mr Weston's tactless geniality and Mr Elton's hypocritical *politesse* will doubt that he so obviously comes off second best.

What he says remains for us to guess at. Austen cannot let us hear him, just as Emma cannot allow truth or goodwill to enter her estimate. The silencing of both Robert Martin and one of his sisters, whom we also later meet, is a consequence of seeing the people and events of the novel so much through Emma's eyes. Emma does not want to hear them as the people they are, rather than the characters she has invented. The Martins as a family remain deprived of speech by the novel because Austen is wryly loyal to Emma's determination that they be considered unworthy of her companion's attention. Naturally Austen is not following her heroine's prejudices, but exposing them. The technique allows her to expose these prejudices not just to the reader but to the heroine herself. The perfection of this is when Austen has Harriet report her first encounter with Robert Martin and his sister Elizabeth after she has rejected his offer of marriage (II. iii). Arriving highly 'agitated' at Hartfield, she tells Emma that she was taking shelter in Ford's shop when the Martins entered. In her longest speech of the whole novel, Harriet describes, 'unchecked' by Emma, the confusing encounter, in which both sister and brother speak to her, hesitantly but kindly. All of the speech is Harriet's: flustered, foolish, inarticulate, yet entirely truthful. We cannot know what Robert Martin has said – 'so he came and spoke and I answered' – but even Emma, listening, recognises the signs of 'real feeling'. Harriet adds that as she set off he came out of the shop to warn her that the likeliest route back to Hartfield was half-flooded. It is a subtle touch, demonstrating a kind of awkward tenderness, especially given his awareness that Harriet must be returning to the house of her manipulator.

Mr Knightley reports his conversations with Robert Martin in reliable detail but he never quotes him. Marilyn Butler calls Robert Martin Mr Knightley's 'wholly silent alter ego' – silent because he 'acts, and simply is, with the solidity that comes from well-defined involvement with a physical world'.[3] Yet he is not really silent; it is the novel that keeps him so, in compliance with its heroine's inclination. Finally, with Emma engaged to Mr Knightley, she accepts Harriet's forthcoming marriage to Robert Martin with thankful relief. 'It would be a great pleasure to know Robert Martin' (III. xviii). He has not been allowed to speak because Emma has excluded him from social acceptance. He has been unknowable because Emma has foolishly preferred him that way. But in the future she will be able to hear him and speak to him.

> *Declining to quote a character is a kind of*
> *diminution of him or her.*

Speechlessness is not always as complete as Robert Martin's or Mr Perry's. Mrs Philips in *Pride and Prejudice*, Mrs

Bennet's sister, looks as though she will be another such, until she belatedly and farcically struggles into the novel's dialogue. Until very late in the proceedings, Austen relishes her speechless garrulousness. For two chapters of the first volume of the novel, when she entertains the Bennet girls at her house in Meryton on two consecutive days, with Mr Collins, Mr Wickham and Mr Denny, she is present throughout, and constantly talking, but nothing she says is quoted (I. xv–xvi). The paradox is delicious, for she makes quite a noise. On the first occasion, Mr Denny and Mr Wickham decline to accompany the Bennet *filles* into Mr Philips's house when invited by Lydia, 'in spite of Mrs Philips throwing up the parlour window, and loudly seconding the invitation'. She is very loud, but has nothing to say. On the second occasion, what she talks about is reported to us, but not a word quoted. The joke of Mrs Philips's absence from the novel's dialogue is that she is a dedicated talker (she is, after all, Mrs Bennet's sister). Listening to Mr Collins's endless description of 'the grandeur of Lady Catherine and her mansion' (I. xvi) – which we are mercifully spared – we see her 'resolving to retail it all among her neighbours as soon as she could'. She is a specialiser in gossip. After Lydia's fall from virtue, she visits the Bennets frequently, ostensibly to cheer them up, but in fact to report 'some fresh instance of Wickham's extravagance or irregularity' (III. vi). Once her sister has told her of Jane's engagement to Mr Bingley, '*she* ventured, without any permission, to do the same by all her neighbours in Meryton' (III. xiii).

But then Austen springs a little surprise. Having barred Mrs Philips from direct speech for so long, she finally lets her enter the novel's dialogue. She is allowed to tell her sister a piece of gossip that she has heard from Mrs Nicholls, the housekeeper at Netherfield, when she spots her in the street in Meryton and goes out of her house to accost her (III. xi). Mrs Bennet has just reminded her sister that 'we agreed long ago never to mention a word about it' ('it' being Mr Bingley's relationship with Jane Bennet). The reminder is quite enough to loosen Mrs Philips's tongue: 'You may depend upon it . . .' What follows is a choice morsel of news about the number of ducks that Mrs Nicholls has ordered from the butcher for her impending house guests. This is the quintessence of Mrs Philips's contribution to conversation. In order to get this comic effect, Austen has made her one of the special family of her characters allowed to speak in our hearing just once. She belongs with her opposite, Mrs Bates in *Emma*, who does sometimes speak but whose actual words always have to give way to the flow of speech from 'her more active, talking daughter' (I. i). Just once she is forced to speak so that we too can hear her. When Emma penitently visits the Bates household after the disastrous Box Hill trip, Miss Bates, to whom she has spoken so cruelly, has bustled into the adjoining room with Jane Fairfax (III. viii). We imagine that she is trying to calm her niece, who has just agreed to a position as governess and is certainly in no frame of mind to be entertaining such a visitor. So Mrs Bates speaks because she has to, hardly covering the painful confusion of family affairs. 'I am afraid Jane is not very well . . . but I do not know; they *tell* me she is well. I dare say my daughter will be here presently . . .'

The sour, mean Mrs Ferrars in *Sense and Sensibility* is 'not a woman of many words; for, unlike people in general, she proportioned them to the number of her ideas' (II. xii). Disdainful of Elinor, she says nothing to her and Austen repays the compliment by declining to quote her. Only at the end of Mrs John Dashwood's London dinner party, where we first meet her, do we get a couple of utterances that epitomise her. Shown the screen that Elinor has painted she manages a neglectful 'Hum . . . very pretty', and when Marianne asks why her hostess is celebrating Miss Morton's painting skills over Elinor's, she retorts 'Miss Morton is Lord Morton's daughter.' As if this were to say everything necessary about the regard one should have for such a person. Declining to quote a character is a kind of diminution of him or her. We and Elizabeth spend many hours in the company of Mr Bingley's brother-in-law Mr Hurst in *Pride and Prejudice*, without there being any word of his worth transcribing. Yet Austen cannot quite leave him silent. He manages one whole sentence and then a couple of words. When Elizabeth, staying at Netherfield, prefers a book to joining in a game of loo he is provoked to utterance. 'Do you prefer reading to cards? . . . that is rather singular' (I. viii). At last he is roused to real feeling. Later, when Jane is sufficiently recovered to appear in the drawing room to be greeted by everyone, he manages a throttled 'very glad' (I. xi). It is the merest semblance of politeness.

More complicated and unsettling is the speechlessness of Dr Grant for much of *Mansfield Park*. He is often present, and he is often talking. He likes to do so. He is a man of the world who is pleased to discourse on politics with Mr Crawford, or money with Edmund Bertram (II. v). When Tom Bertram wants to cover for a conversational faux pas, he relies on Dr Grant's readiness to opine on momentous matters. 'A strange business this in America, Dr. Grant! What is your opinion?' (I. xii) He is invariably described as involved in conversation. 'Dr. Grant laughingly congratulated Miss Crawford . . . Dr. Grant was in the vestibule, and as they stopt to speak to him . . . leaving Dr. Grant and Mrs. Norris to dispute over their last play . . . observed by Sir Thomas, who was standing in chat with Dr. Grant . . .' Yet his actual words are carefully avoided, even on occasions when every other character present has some of his or her speech quoted. Slowly we gain the impression of a man who is not worth quoting, not because he is dull and stupid, like Mr Hurst, but because his self-concern excludes him from the plot. *Mansfield Park* is a novel where so much conversation, thanks to the Crawfords, is a matter of manoeuvre and manipulation. Dr Grant's absence from direct speech confirms his unconcern about the flirtation and amorous rivalry being staged around him. We have this confirmed on the two occasions when we are allowed to hear his actual words, for when he is quoted it is on food. Early in the novel he tells Mrs Norris over dinner that the apricot tree that she planted in the Parsonage garden (which she remembers cost seven shillings) produces worthless fruit. They no more have the flavour of 'a moor park apricot' than 'these potatoes' (I. vi). Mrs Grant must quickly placate the outraged Mrs Norris. He speaks directly again for the only time, to his wife, on the subject of what Edmund and Fanny might have to eat for dinner with them. 'A friendly meeting, and not a fine dinner, is all we have in view. A turkey, or a goose, or a leg of mutton, or whatever you and your cook chuse to give us' (II. iv). It is the *faux* carelessness of a man who always thinks keenly of food.

Austen enjoys the effect of making a speechless character speak, but she does the opposite too: she silences a character who once had plenty to say, Fanny Price's younger sister Susan in *Mansfield Park*. When Fanny returns to her family home in Portsmouth, she finds it, as has often been noticed, a place of cacophony. One of the voices belongs to Susan, whom Fanny first hears answering back when admonished by her mother. "'I was upstairs, mama, moving my things," said Susan, in a fearless, self-defending tone, which startled Fanny. "You know you had but just settled that my sister Fanny and I should have the other room; and I could not get Rebecca to give me any help"' (III. vii). Fanny finds her sister quite ready to defend her corner, later arguing over the possession of a knife left to her by another sister who died. But then Fanny and Susan become intimate and something peculiar happens: Susan never speaks again. She is absorbed into quietness. One of Austen's greatest skills is the fashioning of appropriate habits of speech for her characters; one of her nicest tricks is to stop her characters from speaking.

TEN

What Games Do Characters Play?

'What shall I do, Sir Thomas? Whist and speculation; which will amuse me most?'

Mansfield Park, II. vii

Jane Austen makes her characters play games because, we might say, this was one aspect of the social world she knew. She made her characters play the games – especially the card games – that she played herself. Yet she is up to something else as well. Her books do not just feature games because, in her day, these filled the long evenings in provincial England. In her novels, games serve a novelist's purposes. Because most of her first readers would have been able to recognise the particular games that are mentioned, they would have been able to see the arrangements of space and the conversational groupings that the games produced. For the first purpose of games in her novels is to divide and dispose her characters. Card playing joins people and separates them. Describing a sociable evening in Kent to her sister, Austen reported that '. . . one Card Table was formed, the rest of us sat & talked' (*Letters*, 55). Some play cards, and some do not; or some play one game, and some another. In a different letter, Austen describes how fourteen sat down to dinner at Ashe Rectory, home of the Lefroy family, in November 1800. After the meal 'There was a whist & casino table, & six outsiders' (the whist and casino games each taking four players) (*Letters*, 27). The outsiders have to entertain themselves. 'Rice & Lucy made love, Mat: Robinson fell asleep, James and Mrs Augusta alternately read Dr Jenner's pamphlet on the cow pox, & I bestowed my company by turns on all'.

Austen's humorous picture of herself drifting from one conversational partner to another while half her fellow guests are fixed to their card tables is reminiscent of Elizabeth Bennet's behaviour during an evening of cards at Netherfield. In *Pride and Prejudice*, the Austen novel that most frequently sits its characters down to cards, the first game is one in which all the characters present play, except for Elizabeth, who is thereby free to tease. She is staying with the Bingleys because Jane is ill, and is summoned from her sister's sick-room for evening coffee. Entering the drawing room she finds 'the whole party' – Mr Darcy, Mr Bingley, his two sisters and his brother-in-law Mr Hurst – 'at loo' (I. viii). She is invited to join the game (loo must have at least five players, and can have more), 'but suspecting them to be playing high she declined'. Loo, the wise reader would know, had acquired an ill repute as the ruin of keen players. There is a pool of money – or chips – to pay out the winners of tricks, but any player who chooses to stay in and does not win a trick is 'looed', and must pay a forfeit into the pool for the next round. In some versions of the game, the forfeit is limited; in Unlimited Loo, the forfeit is equivalent to the amount currently in the pool. This can lead to the size of the pool, and subsequent forfeits, multiplying hugely. Clearly Elizabeth senses that her hosts might be playing just this version of the game, suitable only for those without any money worries.

Elizabeth says that she will 'amuse herself' with a book, prompting some hostile responses.

> Mr. Hurst looked at her with astonishment.
>
> 'Do you prefer reading to cards?' said he; 'that is rather singular.'
>
> 'Miss Eliza Bennet,' said Miss Bingley, 'despises cards. She is a great reader, and has no pleasure in anything else.'

With characteristic ill manners, Miss Bingley accuses Elizabeth of bookish sniffiness about cards. In fact, our heroine plays cards on several occasions in the novel. Her hidden concern about the amounts of money being wagered leaves her the one mobile character in the scene. Everyone except Elizabeth is fixed around the card table. The conversational exchange that follows is shaped by this fact, and Elizabeth's freedom to drift around the room, to move away from the 'party' or to join it, enables her to express her mischievous freedom in dialogue. The Bingleys talk while they play, and when the subject turns to Pemberley, Mr Darcy's home, Elizabeth finds her attention tugged away from her book and she crosses to the players: 'she drew near the card-table, and stationed herself between Mr. Bingley and his eldest sister, to observe the game'. Observing the game is her pretext. Soon conversation moves from Mr Darcy's sister Georgiana to the common extent of female 'accomplishments', and Elizabeth joins in teasing dispute with Darcy about his lofty expectations of young women. It is a famous little exchange, in which the mutual attraction of the speakers is expressed by their ostensible opposition – and all the more brilliantly for Elizabeth's apparent ignorance of her own motives. (Why does the mention of Pemberley drag her away from her reading?) Everyone but Elizabeth must talk with half a mind on their cards, while she darts her ripostes among them.

Mr Hurst call them to order, 'with bitter complaints of their inattention to what was going forward'. Conversation is stopped, and Elizabeth soon leaves the room. For her, watching play is no entertainment to compare with playful dialogue. Not so Mrs Hurst, Bingley's sister. The next day, when her brother and her husband are playing the two-handed game of piquet, she dutifully sits 'observing their game' (I. x). This game splits the two men off from Darcy and Miss Bingley, the former attempting to write a letter while the latter tries to insinuate her attentions. Without cards, Mr Hurst is without resources. In the evening, when his 'petition' to play again is rejected ('Mr. Darcy did not wish for cards'), he has 'nothing to do, but to stretch himself on one of the sophas and go to sleep' (I. xi). Cards are the only refuge of the conversationally null. In *Sense and Sensibility*, Lady Middleton is always wanting to play cards, being incapable of conversation. When her husband goes off to his club in Exeter, Elinor, Marianne and Margaret are invited for dinner to preserve her 'from the frightful solitude which had threatened her' (II. i). After tea, the card table is brought in and Lady Middleton proposes 'a rubber of Casino'. Marianne declines in uncivil fashion – 'you know I detest cards' – and goes off to play the piano. Elinor wants to speak in confidence to Lucy Steele, who has at their last meeting revealed her secret engagement to Edward Ferrars. Lucy is, ingratiatingly, completing the filigree basket she is making for Lady Middleton's daughter, so Elinor proposes to 'cut out' of the card game to help Lucy with her basket. Casino allowing for a variable number of players, the reduction to four (Lady Middleton, Mrs Jennings, the elder Miss Steele and Margaret Dashwood) is easily accommodated, while the game separates the rest of the company from Elinor and Lucy (the piano music helping to cover their *sotto voce* exchange).

When Elinor and Marianne attend Lady Middleton to a large, smart London party, she soon sits down to casino, freeing the sisters from the nothingness of her conversation, but also allowing Marianne to experience the shock of meeting Willoughby without having her as a spectator (II. vi). At parties and balls, card games are for those who will not dance. At the ball at the Crown in *Emma*, the heroine is disappointed to see Mr Knightley in the company of 'the husbands, and fathers, and whist players', removed from physical display. These men pretend to take an interest in the dancing just until 'their rubbers were made up' (III. ii). Whist is what men do when they are no longer young or attractive – when they are unsexed. Emma's scorn of cards is rather different from Marianne's. Marianne prides herself on transcending triviality; Emma, who elsewhere enjoys games, regards cards as the unimaginative time-filling of her fellow villagers. Visiting the Bateses for the first time in the novel, Emma intends to avoid the topic of Mr Elton as much as she can, and instead 'to wander at large amongst all the Mistresses and Misses of Highbury and their card-parties' (II. i). In her mind – which is where this sentence is placed – card parties are equally the empty distraction of Highbury women and the empty substance of Miss Bates's usual chat. Highbury seems addicted to cards. At the Crown Inn, the former ballroom is now used only 'to accommodate a whist club established among the gentlemen and half-gentlemen of the place' (II. vi). Such a club existed in Austen's early unfinished novel draft *The Watsons*, where the wealthy Mr Edwards belongs to 'a quiet little Whist club that meets three times a week at the White Hart'.[1] Here too it is clearly the respectable time-filling activity of dull men in a provincial town or village. Meanwhile the women in *Emma* visit each other's homes for those card parties. 'We were just going to cards,' says Miss Bates of a typical Highbury afternoon, to mark the time when a triumphant Mrs Elton arrives to announce Jane Fairfax's acceptance of the governess's post (III. viii). Newly arrived in the village, Mrs Elton needs to signal her superiority at these gatherings, and does so not by refusing to join them but by being shocked by 'there being no ice in the Highbury card parties' (II. xvi).

In *Persuasion*, Anne Elliot's lack of enthusiasm for card games is made to seem a symptom of her integrity and her inwardness. She makes a big show, for Captain Wentworth's sake, of her lack of interest in the evening card party at Camden Place, where Mr Elliot will be a guest: 'I am no card-player' (II. x). But it is not merely show. Captain Wentworth recalls his intimate knowledge of her eight years earlier: 'You did not use to like cards; but time makes many changes.' Her attitude to card games weirdly becomes the test of her consistency as a character. '"I am not so much changed," cried Anne', as if a new-found liking for card games would indi-cate a falling into conventional role playing. Her avoidance of card games is a sign of her distance from the novel's other characters: even her friend and admirer Lady Russell is a card player. Yet it is a matter of self-image rather than of Austen's attribution. By the time of her sister Elizabeth's 'card-party', Anne, engaged once again to Captain Wentworth, is too happy to worry that it is 'a commonplace business, too numerous for intimacy, too small for variety' (II. xi). Perhaps she is prepared to play cards after all.

Austen herself cannot have thought it all so pointless. In her letters she specifically mentions playing brag, casino, commerce, cribbage, quadrille, speculation, vingt-un and whist. When she writes to her sister she sometimes specifies her own successes at the card table (e.g. *Letters*, 45) or reports the triumphs of others (*Letters*, 56). Playing well is pleasurable, and playing badly is irritating. On one occasion she complains that her teenage nephew Edward 'acquitted himself to admiration in every particular except selling his Deals at Vingt-un' (*Letters*, 149). He is almost perfect, but smooth play at vingt-un is a real social skill that he has not quite acquired. So we should not assume that we need share Emma's scorn. Mr Perry is naturally aggrieved when he finds that Mr Elton intends to skip the next gathering of the Highbury whist club at a moment's notice (I. viii). He is off to London on his mission to get Emma's portrait of Harriet framed. What will they do? He is 'their best player' (a fact that might itself suggest the vicar's powers of calculation). Harriet and Emma are delighted to hear that he has given up his card game for his gallant undertaking, but they should instead see this selfishness as another sign that he is not a man to be trusted.

Whist is usually played for money in Austen's novels. We are invited to notice which games involve gambling and which do not, whilst realising that playing for modest sums of money was normal for Austen and should not seem inherently bad. At the first ball in *Mansfield Park*, Mrs Norris tries to get Tom Bertram to join a rubber of whist where they are playing for half-crowns (2s 6d), but tempts him by suggesting that he and Dr Grant might like to play for half-guineas (10s 6d). Characteristically, she convicts herself of impropriety and him of a love of gambling. After the abortive outing to Bristol in *Northanger Abbey*, Isabella Thorpe finds solace in 'a pool of commerce' with James Morland and her brother (I. xi). This does not reveal her character because the game is played for money, but because it involves bartering and bargaining. The object is to 'make your hand' by exchanging some of your own cards with those on the table, or by 'buying' an extra card. Being all about trading what you have for what you think might be better, it is just the game for her – an imitation of the business of her life. It is a game that Austen herself played with her friends the Digweeds (*Letters*, 27) and with an unidentified admirer of her sister dubbed 'Le Chevalier', while on holiday in Lyme (*Letters*, 39). Commerce is mentioned again as being played in the Austen household – evidently for money (*Letters*, 56). Indeed, when Austen finds that a visit to Mrs Maitland in Southampton has become 'a thorough party', with 'a quadrille & a Commerce Table', she has to back out. 'There were two pools at Commerce, but I would not play more than one, for the Stake was three shillings, & I cannot afford to lose that, twice in an evening' (*Letters*, 57).

It is respectable enough to play cards for money it seems. When Mr Collins accompanies the Bennet sisters to their aunt's house in Meryton, he declares himself inexpert but glad to play, as the game is appropriate for someone 'in my situation of life' (I. xvi). A few pages later he has lost every point (quite an achievement) and the total of five shillings, and is solemnly assuring Mrs Philips 'that he considered the money as a mere trifle'. While he is playing whist there is a 'nice comfortable noisy game of lottery tickets' for the rest of the company (I. xv). This seems to be played for 'fish' – tokens of winnings rather than real money. 'Mr. Wickham did not play at whist', leaving him free to tell his lies about Darcy to Elizabeth, safely separated from the whist players and cocooned by the hubbub of the lottery game. Lydia is engrossed in the latter and has conveniently ceased to pay him any attention. Mr Wickham seems to be playing too, but has the 'leisure' to converse with Elizabeth. The reluctance to play whist is nicely contrived given what we later find out about his real appetites. When he takes Lydia with him to London he leaves Brighton with gambling debts of 'more than a thousand pounds' (III. vi). 'A gamester!' cries Jane. He must have glanced at the Meryton whist game with an expert's cold eye. On the walk back to Longbourn, Lydia can talk of nothing but 'the fish she had lost and the fish she had won', marking her out as just the likeliest future partner for Wickham.

So even when everyone plays at something, cards can separate groups out from each other. Later in *Pride and Prejudice*, at Rosings there are cards after dinner and tea with Lady Catherine de Bourgh. Lady Catherine, Sir William Lucas and Mr and Mrs Collins play quadrille, so Elizabeth is condemned 'to play at cassino' at a separate table with Maria Lucas, Miss de Bourgh (who has chosen the game) and her companion Mrs Jenkinson (II. vi). After the preceding pages of gloriously antagonistic exchanges between Elizabeth and Lady Catherine, we are now condemned to novelistic silence. 'Their table was superlatively stupid. Scarcely a syllable was uttered that did not relate to the game.' A great deal is said at the other table, but as Elizabeth is no longer part of the talk, it is not worth quoting. Cards at Rosings are a kind of tyranny: Lady Catherine and her daughter decide on the games, which go on 'as long as they chose'. In *Mansfield Park* it is the self-indulging Dr Grant who dictates terms. After dinner and tea at the Parsonage, the whist table is 'formed really for the amusement of Dr. Grant, by his attentive wife, though it was not supposed to be so' (II. v). The presumption seems to be that Fanny will not play, while Mary Crawford is 'too much vexed' by discussion of Edmund's future living to be involved and turns to her harp. The players must be the Grants, Henry Crawford and Edmund Bertram; with

Edmund separated from Mary Crawford the drama drains from the scene.

*Some games are for clever people, and some are
for the empty-headed.*

A little later in *Mansfield Park*, the Parsonage is the setting for another after-dinner card game, the most carefully choreographed in all Austen's fiction. Fanny and her recently arrived brother William accompany the Bertrams to dinner with the Grants. After dinner there is to be a whist table again, with enough people left over for 'a round game' (a game accommodating any number of players). Sir Thomas takes to whist with Mrs Norris and the Grants; the others play speculation (II. vii). As ever, the novelist's purpose is to separate some players from others. Sir Thomas and Mrs Norris are evidently absorbed in their play: they win a game by the odd trick, 'by Sir Thomas's capital play and her own, against Dr. and Mrs. Grant's great hands'. This is Mrs Norris's triumphant self-vaunting, mingled with her sycophancy to her brother-in-law. Whist is the perfect chance to combine her aggression and her pretence of allegiance to her sister's rich family, and it is the chance to win some money. Meanwhile, unnoticed by these players, the remaining characters play a game that elaborately enacts the different competitors' undeclared wishes.

Speculation is a complicated game that is no longer familiar to us. It might have been a private joke to make Mary Crawford the self-thwarting conqueror of the speculation table in *Mansfield Park*, for it was a game that the author herself championed in her family. When Edward Austen's bereaved sons Edward and George travelled from school in Winchester to stay with Aunt Jane and her mother in Southampton, after the death of their mother in October 1808, they had to be diverted from grief, as she told her sister Cassandra. 'We do not want amusements; bilbocatch, at which George is indefatigable, spillikins. Paper ships, riddles, conundrums, and cards, with watching the flow and ebb of the river, and now and then a stroll out, keep us well employed' (*Letters*, 60). Speculation worked best. 'I introduced *speculation*, and it was so much approved that we hardly knew how to leave off' (*Letters*, 60). Two months later, when the boys had returned to their father in Kent and had Cassandra staying with them, Jane Austen was writing to her sister saying, 'I hope Speculation is generally liked' (*Letters*, 64). Evidently Cassandra wrote back saying that they preferred brag: 'it mortifies me deeply, because Speculation was under my patronage' (*Letters*, 64). 'When one comes to reason upon it, it cannot stand its ground against Speculation.' She even composed some doggerel verses in praise of speculation to be conveyed to her nephew Edward (*Letters*, 65).

It was a relatively new game, which Austen had to explain to her nephews just as the Crawfords had to explain it to Fanny and the entirely uncomprehending Lady Bertram. In *The Watsons*, composed in 1805, Mrs Watson testifies to its fashionable standing in her suburban world: '*Speculation* is the only round game at Croydon now'.[2] Dickens mentions it in *Nicholas Nickleby* (1839), where it is made analogous with the financial risk-taking that ruins Nicholas's father. 'Speculation is a round game; the players see little or nothing of their cards at first starting; gains MAY be great—and so may losses.'[3] The joke of the analogy suggests the author's confidence that readers will know of the card game. Fanny has no previous experience of it, but quickly grasps its principles – well enough to try to play for her brother to win. In her playing of the game we see a paradox of her character distilled: she is an ingénue who quickly perceives the subtleties that more worldly characters miss. Every player emerges in character. In particular, the game is a carefully arranged vignette of the Crawfords' schemes and efforts at manipulation. The comic summary of this is Lady Bertram's: 'I am never to see my cards; and Mr. Crawford does all the rest' (II. vii). He is the arch-manipulator, while his sister is the restive gambler, staking more on victory than it can ever be worth. In speculation, players may bid to buy what they suppose might be a winning card in the possession of another player. So a player may 'buy' a card that does not win, or may pay more for a card than it gains.

It is not exactly a proper competition at all, as Mr Crawford intervenes to prevent Fanny selling her queen to her brother William for a low price and to try to ensure that she will win. 'The game will be yours, turning to her again—it will certainly be yours': this is more insistence than prediction. Henry Crawford is ingratiating himself with Fanny; Mary Crawford is testing herself against Edmund. The point of the game for the novelist is that it allows two simultaneous activities (for those with the wits): playing and talking. We keep noticing this because the dialogue calls attention to it via the instructions that Crawford gives in parentheses to Lady Bertram; he can keep two activities in his mind, where she can hardly manage one. He is playing the game and, for his sister's benefit, asking Edmund about his future home at Thornton Lacey. Mary Crawford is playing – and listening. The card game and the topic of Edmund's future are intimately connected, though the Bertrams cannot see this. Indeed, in little flashes of audacity the Crawfords glancingly declare themselves. 'I never do wrong without gaining by it,' says Henry (about losing his way); 'No cold prudence for me,' announces Mary (of her play). Everything really is a game for them, and all the better if they can flaunt their schemes in front of those whom they deceive.

Speculation is the electricity that courses through the company, and seems a good word too for the activity of the reader – for the engagement of not just our interest but our intelligence. Austen herself uses the word for what is going on the minds of her characters. Sir Thomas tells Henry Crawford of Edmund's aspirations to dedicate himself to his duties as a parish priest, considerably irking the listening Mary Crawford. 'All the agreeable of *her* speculation was over for that hour. It was time to have done with cards if sermons prevailed, and she was glad to find it necessary to come to a conclusion and be able to refresh her spirits by a change of place and neighbour.' Her speculation, about the possibility of marriage to Edmund, has been rather thwarted than encouraged. 'If I lose the game, it shall not be from not striving for it,' she announces, as if she really is saying something about herself rather than the game. Yet it is the treatment of all her social exchanges as subtle game-playing that robs her of any final triumph. 'The game was hers, and only did not pay her for what she had given to secure it.' Speculation, which she and her brother are using for their manipulative purposes, becomes a metaphor for what she loses by being so manipulative. She wins by paying more than she can gain.

Some games are for clever people, and some are for the empty-headed. In *Emma*, the clever and the empty-headed play together. Mr Woodhouse loves games – his piquet with Mrs Goddard (II. vii) and, especially, his backgammon. Backgammon is just right for him, relying enough on chance to offer him the occasional opportunity of victory, especially if the other player is guileful enough to help him win. No wonder it is also the game that Mr Bennet plays with Mr Collins (*Pride and Prejudice*, I. xv). We learn from Miss

Bates that during the Highbury balls Mr Woodhouse passes the evening with 'a vast deal of chat, and backgammon' with Mrs Bates (III. ii). When, late in the novel, a chastened Emma looks back to the trip to Box Hill, considering it as a morning 'totally bare of rational satisfaction', she thinks that 'a whole evening of backgammon with her father was felicity to it' (III. viii). Here at least she is doing something unselfish, 'giving up the sweetest hours of the twenty-four to his comfort'. The hours and hours of backgammon with Mr Woodhouse lie in wait for her if she really is committed to avoiding marriage, as she claims.

This image of an almost eternal backgammon game with Mr Woodhouse is all the more powerful because of Emma's native love of intriguing play. *Emma* is a novel in which game playing is exciting enough to seem dangerous. 'A most dangerous game' is just the phrase that Mr Knightley chooses to describe Frank Churchill's flirtation with Emma, designed to distract her from his attachment to Jane Fairfax. Game playing is an activity into which Mr Elton, 'invited to contribute any really good enigmas, charades, or conundrums that he might recollect', is disastrously recruited (I. ix). Perceiving the game-playing ethos of Highbury, he submits his notorious puzzle (a 'charade', in the vocabulary of the day). Harriet duly fails to understand it; more dangerously, Emma duly misinterprets it. In a letter of 1816 Austen describes friends 'taking kindly to our Charades, & other Games', and she and her family enjoyed just the word games to which Mr Elton takes with such alacrity (*Letters*, 145).[4] Harriet has enjoyed 'merry evening games' with the Martins, but her games with Emma will be rather more hazardous. Emma likes to treat life as a game or puzzle. 'She is a riddle, quite a riddle!' she says to herself about Jane Fairfax, amazed that she should be willing to spend time with Mrs Elton (II. xv). Emma draws other characters into games; even her slow-witted father tries to join in the business of charades. On Box Hill Mr Weston foolishly tries to please Emma with his fatuous word game, the answer to which is a pun on her name, before Frank Churchill, 'ordered by Miss Woodhouse', proposes the game of clever utterances that end in such ill feeling (III. vii). At the novel's heart is the anagram game played at Hartfield, in which messages are being sent by Frank Churchill to Jane Fairfax, and misdirecting signals being sent by him to Emma. The game is Frank Churchill's idea – 'We had great amusement with those letters one morning. I want to puzzle you again' – but Emma is 'pleased' with the suggestion (III. v). In fact, Frank Churchill is playing a 'deeper game' than Emma knows. The judgement is Mr Knightley's, for the whole game chapter is narrated from his point of view. He sees the players and watchers round that table – Emma, Frank Churchill, Jane Fairfax, Miss Bates, Harriet Smith, Mr and Mrs Weston, Mr Woodhouse – and sees how little most of them understand of what is going on in play. As ever, the game brings characters together precisely in order to divide them.

ELEVEN

Is There Any Sex in Jane Austen?

'We both know that he has been profligate in every sense
of the word . . .'

Pride and Prejudice, III. v

Keith Nearing, the twenty-year-old protagonist of Martin
Amis's novel *The Pregnant Widow*, spends a summer at a
luxurious Italian castle having somewhat unenthusiastic sex
with his girlfriend, Lily, dreaming of having sex with his
girlfriend's friend, Sheherazade, and reading his way through
the English Novel. One week is spent on Jane Austen, the
sexual implications of whose plots become the matter of his
pillow talk. With the apparent licence of his creator, he tells
Lily about the sex that actually takes place between the lines
of these supposedly prim books. At the end of *Northanger
Abbey*, according to Keith, Frederick Tilney beds Isabella
Thorpe. 'She persuades herself that he's somehow going to
marry her. After.'[1] 'So she's ruined. She's lost,' suggests Lily.
'Utterly,' confirms Keith. Later he goes on to other Austen
novels. '*Mansfield Park*'s got *two* fucks. Henry Crawford fucks
Maria Bertram. And Mr Yates fucks her sister Julia. And he's
an Honourable.'[2] Amis's novel doubles as an *hommage* to the

Great Tradition of English fiction, and Keith's curt summaries are declarations that Austen's novels are not the proper and passionless affairs that some have thought.

There *are* characters who have sex in Austen's novels, but not all these ones. Catherine Morland's brother James is jilted by her 'friend' Isabella Thorpe, who thinks Captain Frederick Tilney a more alluring prospect. Henry and Eleanor Tilney tell Catherine, however, that Frederick would be unlikely to marry an impecunious girl like Isabella. And sure enough he soon abandons her to flirt for a couple of days with one Charlotte Davis, before going back to his regiment. Isabella returns from Bath to Putney, writing Catherine a letter that is designed to prepare the ground for a revival of her relationship with James. Catherine now realises that Isabella is 'a vain coquette' (II. xii), but she does not for a moment think her 'ruined'. Henry Tilney confirms that his brother undertook the flirtation 'for mischief's sake', but expresses none of the dismay that would have been excited by a sexual liaison. If they have had sex, the author knows nothing of it. As for Julia Bertram, she does elope with the Hon. John Yates – to Scotland, where she can marry her paramour without parental consent. She has certainly slept with him by the end of the novel, but as a wife with her husband.

Amis's novel is alert to the sexual coding to be found in Austen – what it means when Catherine Morland's figure gains in 'consequence'; why the word 'stout' might be used of Lydia Bennet – but it also follows a trend of both recent film adaptations and some recent academic criticism, discovering more sex implicit in Austen than narrative logic allows. Keith Nearing's inaccuracy is a fault precisely because Austen does require her reader to think about sex. She requires us, for instance, to think about Lydia Bennet having had sex, repeatedly and, we must infer, enjoyably. Lydia has lived with Wickham for almost a month before their marriage. When Mr Darcy discovers the couple cohabiting he talks to Lydia and tries 'to persuade her to quit her present disgraceful situation', but she is having none of it (III. x). According to the letter written to Elizabeth by her uncle, Mr Gardiner, 'She was sure they should be married some time or other, and it did not much signify when.' The Wickhams arrive at Longbourn on their wedding day, already knowing each other intimately. Elizabeth notes that Lydia is 'exceedingly fond' of her new husband (III. ix). Not only is she sexually unabashed, she is, it seems, sexually gratified. Mr Collins solemnly regrets 'that their living together before the marriage took place, should be so generally known' (III. xv). He and the foolish Mary Bennet adopt a language of moral absolutism about this. The 'lesson' Mary finds is 'that loss of virtue in a female is irretrievable—that one false step involves her in endless ruin' (III. v). Elizabeth reacts with 'amazement', but not because she has never heard such sentiments before: the novels of Samuel Richardson, which, according to her brother Henry, Jane Austen so admired, proceed on exactly Mary's assumption.[3] The eponymous heroine of *Pamela* (subtitled 'Virtue Rewarded') took her 'virtue' to be synonymous with her virginity. 'Arm yourself, my dear Child, for the worst; and resolve to lose your Life sooner than your Virtue,' writes her father when he hears of her master's seductive advances.[4] Elizabeth is presumably 'amazed' because her sister so smugly parrots the formulae of novelists and conduct book writers. It is on a par with Mr Collins's 'The death of your daughter would have been a blessing in comparison of this' (III. vi).

Lydia's sexual adventures naturally become the stuff of local gossip. The narrator comments drily on responses in the 'neighbourhood' at the news of Lydia's planned marriage. 'To be sure, it would have been more for the advantage of conversation had Miss Lydia Bennet come upon the town; or, as the happiest alternative, been secluded from the world, in some distant farmhouse' (III. viii). Local *schadenfreude*, that is to say, would have been best satisfied by Lydia becoming a prostitute, as she might have done in a Victorian novel. Lydia is highly unusual in the fiction of her day and earlier in going to bed with a man before marriage and emerging unbowed. Her punishment of being sent to live in Newcastle is mild by the standards of other novels. Her youth – she is sixteen less than two months before her elopement – makes her immunity the more striking. But though she escapes unbowed, Austen cannot resist telling you about the future of the Wickhams' relationship. 'His affection for her soon sunk into indifference; her's lasted a little longer' (III. xix). 'Affection' here surely means something like sexual interest. Passion's trance passes rapidly, as it does in *Mansfield Park*: Mrs Rushworth has been willing to go off with Mr Crawford because 'she loved him', but he has ceased to be interested after 'a very few months' (III. vii).

> She was not to be prevailed on to leave Mr. Crawford. She hoped to marry him, and they continued together till she was obliged to be convinced that such hope was vain, and till the disappointment and wretchedness arising from the conviction rendered her temper so bad, and her feelings for him so like hatred, as to make them for a while each other's punishment, and then induce a voluntary separation.

Mrs Rushworth's first sexual passions are, we infer, the more powerful because she can compare Henry Crawford's caresses with those of her unappealing husband. Sexual intoxication ends with the repeated inflicting of that 'mutual punishment' which, we have just heard, she will suffer interminably in her adulteress's imprisonment with Mrs Norris. The author is doing plenty of punishing, and imposing just the exile 'an establishment . . . remote and private' – that the denizens of Meryton might have liked for Lydia Bennet.

After eloping, Wickham and Lydia go to stay in London lodgings recommended by the corrupted Mrs Younge, presumably calling themselves man and wife. For those who wish to stay close to home, having illicit sex would not be easy. In *Northanger Abbey* Henry Tilney corrects Catherine's Gothic fantasy about his father having murdered his mother by reminding her of the 'voluntary spies' who surround them (II. ix): these must mostly have been servants, constant observers of their masters' and mistresses' improprieties. Surveying his case histories of divorce from the late seventeenth to the mid-nineteenth centuries, as detailed in court records, Lawrence Stone draws one unambiguous lesson: 'All stories of female adultery in high society prove that it was virtually impossible for persons surrounded day and night by servants who waited on them hand and foot to conduct a love-affair without it becoming known below stairs.'[5] In *Mansfield Park* it is a servant who knows just what has been going on between Henry Crawford and Mrs Rushworth, and who sharpens the crisis. Sir Thomas's friend Mr Harding tries to make it possible for Mrs Rushworth to return to the marital home, but it is not easy. 'The maid-servant of Mrs. Rushworth, senior, threatened alarmingly' (III. xvi). Clearly she is threatening to make public her knowledge of the relationship, and is in a position to give an account considerably more lurid than what has already been offered in the newspapers. She 'had exposure in her power'. When Mary Crawford talks to Edmund of the 'folly' of her brother and his sister, she shakes her head in a worldly way about Maria's cardinal error – 'her putting herself in the power of a servant'.

Usually, in order to seduce a genteel young woman in an Austen novel one must elope with her. In *Sense and Sensibility* we discover that Willoughby has eloped with the sixteen-year-old Eliza from Bath. She disappears for eight months before Colonel Brandon, her guardian, finds her: she has a baby, and she and her child are 'removed . . . into the country' (II. ix). Willoughby has since abandoned Marianne, but, Colonel Brandon muses, 'who can tell what were his designs on her?' In a confession scene with Elinor, late in the novel, Willoughby admits that he was once a 'libertine' but claims that he truly loved Marianne (III. viii). He persuades Elinor to think better of him than she did after hearing Colonel Brandon's story. Yet, while professing guilt, he cannot contemplate marrying the girl he has seduced and is free to forget her. Encoded in *Sense and Sensibility* is the suggestion that acceptance of gentlemen's sexual indiscretions was widespread. Mrs Jennings's stage whispers about Colonel Brandon's supposed 'natural daughter' acknowledge that, while 'young ladies' were supposed to be appalled by such a thing, it was a norm (I. xiii). (In the first edition of *Sense and Sensibility*, Austen tells us that 'Lady Middleton's delicacy was shocked' by the mention of 'so improper a subject', but this is excised from the revised second edition.[6]) Despite Elinor's resistance, Mrs Jennings persists in believing in the existence of Colonel Brandon's 'love-child' (II. viii). This phrase was a novel one in 1811 (the OED records the first use in English as 1805) and would have had a peculiar weight with the novel's first readers. Mrs Jennings finds all too readily a modish euphemism for a sexual indiscretion. The girl to whom she refers is in fact the illegitimate daughter of Colonel Brandon's now-dead sister-in-law. 'I called her a distant relation; but I am well aware that I have in general been suspected of a much nearer connection with her' (II. ix). He is too honourable to say anything publicly to scotch this rumour.

Austen's stories rely on an acknowledgement of men's sexual appetites, which explain why that 'truth universally acknowledged', an affluent bachelor's desire for a wife, is in fact true. There are several men in Austen's fiction who do 'want' a wife for reasons beyond financial calculation. Mr

Collins wants one; Charles Musgrove wanted one. The former might hope to please Lady Catherine de Bourgh, but surely has other reasons. The latter, having been turned down by Anne Elliot, rationally turned to her younger sister. Both men being proper in their different ways, and both being called 'young', we might surmise that a desire for sexual release motivated them, and that an early nineteenth-century reader would understand this. Similarly, Mr Elton, the Highbury vicar, is 'a young man living alone without liking it' (*Emma*, I. iii). That last phrase seems to carry a weight of already understood meaning. Only a wilfully innocent reader could think that he yearns for a wife just to choose his fabrics and argue with his cook. Austen's narratives sometimes depend upon our imagining male sexual needs. Catching us wondering how Mr Palmer in *Sense and Sensibility*, an intelligent if ill-natured man, could possibly have married a woman as idiotic as Charlotte Jennings, Austen lets Elinor reflect on the puzzle. 'His temper might perhaps be a little soured by finding, like many others of his sex, that through some unaccountable bias in favour of beauty, he was the husband of a very silly woman—but she knew that this kind of blunder was too common for any sensible man to be lastingly hurt by it' (I. xx). It is an extraordinary judgement, for Mr Palmer surely is 'lastingly' affected by his rash inclination: he is married to a fool for the rest of his days. Elinor's word for what he has done – 'blunder' – diminishes its consequences and implies that she has seen this happen often. His error has been his yen for 'beauty' – or we might say, his susceptibility to 'sex appeal'. At this stage of the novel, Charlotte Palmer is heavily pregnant with their first child (though he is scarcely able to talk to his wife, he does make love to her). Perhaps her advanced state of pregnancy means a temporary denial of sex. More reason for his peculiar grumpiness.

Why does Robert Ferrars marry Lucy Steele in *Sense and Sensibility*? All the evidence is for a process of sexual intoxication that she manages with great skill (III. xiv). He marries her 'speedily' because he wants her. Lucy has 'considerable beauty': it is the first thing we know about her (I. xxi). She trades on sexual allure (not mere bluff — we are explicitly told of the 'great happiness' of their honeymoon). Mr Bennet's choice of Mrs Bennet has also been sensually determined. In the first chapter of *Pride and Prejudice* his joke about his wife not accompanying his daughters to meet Mr Bingley lest he 'like you the best of the party' has a hint of ruefulness (I. i). As a young man he had been 'captivated by youth and beauty' (II. xix). Having made his mistake, he lives with it. 'Mr. Bennet was not of a disposition to seek comfort for the disappointment which his own imprudence had brought on, in any of those pleasures which too often console the unfortunate for their folly or their vice' (II. xix). This is suitably evasive. Some have taken it to mean that Mr Bennet did not take a mistress; it seems more likely to mean that he did not take to the bottle. After all, we can infer that Mr and Mrs Bennet have carried on an active sex life well into middle age as, 'for many years after Lydia's birth', Mrs Bennet is sure that they will eventually have a son (III. viii).

One wonders too about Mr John Knightley, who is clever and, like his brother, has 'penetration'. He is openly irritated by most of his wife's preoccupations and must perceive her foolishness. Why did he marry her? Presumably because of physical attraction; their five children after only seven years of marriage might be evidence of this. Similarly, we guess that Sir Thomas Bertram has chosen his wife for her sex appeal. And we joltingly realise that Henry Crawford has committed himself to marrying Fanny Price because of sexual longing. '"How the pleasing plague had stolen on him" he could not say' (*Mansfield Park*, II. xii). Rakish he might be, but he knows that he can only sleep with Fanny by becoming her husband. His sister confirms our sense of his yearning later in the same chapter when she observes, 'a wife you *loved* would be the happiest of women', before adding, with a flat acceptance of an inevitable logic, 'even when you ceased to love, she would yet find in you the liberality and good-breeding of a gentleman'. Here, as Austen expects the reader to notice, 'love' is synonymous with sexual appetite. Her brother cannot acknowledge the possibility of 'ceasing to love Fanny Price', but Mary Crawford's confident prediction invites us to understand the basis of his addiction. It also clearly implies that, at this stage, Henry will eventually begin looking elsewhere for his sexual pleasures.

If Austen's novels acknowledge men's sexual needs, it is hard to know what to think about some of the bachelors with whom her heroines are finally paired. Historians have found, in diaries and journals, the pains of sexual longing to which some gentlemen confessed, and to which some succumbed, visiting prostitutes or enjoying sexual relationships with servants.[7] Can we think that Colonel Brandon, Mr Knightley or Captain Wentworth are indeed virgins before their marriages? Or that Mr Weston has remained chaste during the long years between the death of his first wife and his second marriage? In this last case, Austen does want us to realise that Mr Weston's marriage to Miss Taylor is not just a matter of genteel companionship. The widower is sexually reborn. Mr and Mrs Weston marry in late September or early October and Mrs Weston is pregnant within a month (her baby is born in late July). Fertility is one indicator of an active sex life. The nine brothers and sisters that Austen gives to Catherine Morland in *Northanger Abbey*, and the thirteen siblings Charlotte Heywood has in *Sanditon*, are evidence of the robust marital affection of their parents. (They are also a good reason for allowing these heroines to leave the family home, with a chaperone, for some comic adventures.) In Fanny Price's family, in contrast, procreation betokens an unruly sex drive. Mr Price is invalided out of the navy, so always at home; the strong implication is that the unaffordable getting of children goes with his other unrestrained habits, notably his drinking. Jane Austen famously said in a letter to her niece Fanny that she would recommend to Mrs Deedes, her brother Edward's sister-in-law, who had just given birth to her eighteenth child, 'the simple regimen of separate rooms' (*Letters*, 151). It is an option that the Prices, in their cramped lodgings, do not have.

We should not assume that sex is always part of marriage. We are given reason to think that Dr Grant does not have a physical relationship with Mrs Grant. 'He had a wife about fifteen years his junior, but no children' (I. iii). His pleasure principle seems centred on food and drink. Watching the couples dancing at a ball, and seeing Mrs Grant with Mr Yates, Tom Bertram tells Fanny, 'between ourselves she, poor woman! must want a lover as much as any of them. A desperate dull life her's must be with the doctor' (I. xii). His 'sly face' tells us of *his* reading of the Grants' marriage. But who knows what goes between husband and wife? The final chapters of *Sense and Sensibility* and *Mansfield Park*, which notionally cover the first months of their heroines' marriages, allow both novelist and reader to avoid thinking about sex. We are on the way to the Victorian habit of jumping from courtship to epilogue, in which a group of merry children sport at the feet of a couple who were merely on the brink of consummation when we last saw them. There is just one instance where we seem provoked to ask what happens to a woman after marriage: the case of Charlotte Lucas. She writes regularly to Elizabeth after her move to Kent, and we hear that 'Charlotte's first letters were received with a good deal of eagerness' (II. iii). There is 'curiosity' to know all sorts of things, including 'how happy she would dare pronounce herself to be'. The sexual implication is both entirely absent and pressing here. Surely Elizabeth, surely even a modest nineteenth-century reader, thinks about the consummation of this union? Charlotte writes 'cheerfully' and mentions 'nothing which she could not praise'. We and Elizabeth, wondering how she can bear it, must think about what it is she has to bear. It is likely that Charlotte is pregnant before the end of the novel. Mr Bennet tells Elizabeth that, in his letter, Mr Collins has talked about 'his dear Charlotte's situation, and his expectation of a young olive-branch' (III. xv). The puzzling thing is the absence of any strong reaction from Elizabeth. Perhaps she has been less guilty than many a reader of suppressing an awareness of what marriage to Mr Collins involves. Charlotte has, after all, given her the grand tour of the Collins's parsonage, which presumably includes the newly married couple's bedroom. While Elizabeth shrewdly appreciates Charlotte's clever arrangement of domestic space to keep her husband away from her during the day, she knows she must have to join him at night.

In Austen, as in the eighteenth-century novels from which she learned, pre-marital sex happens because a young woman gets into the hands of a rakish man, not because two people simply cannot resist each other.

Naturally, none of Austen's heroines would have sex before marriage, but sex before marriage is not unimaginable to her. Her most naive characters know that it happens – even Jane Bennet, though she is determined to believe otherwise. 'My father and mother believe the worst, but I cannot think so ill of him' (III. iv). And it happened in Austen's world. In a letter of 1808 to her sister, she seems to be referring to the known fact that her distant cousin Fanny Austen is getting married after a sexual indiscretion with her husband-to-be. 'I am sorry she has behaved so ill. There is some comfort to *us* in her misconduct, that we have not a congratulatory Letter to write' (*Letters*, 55). This hints at a reality never encountered in her fiction: two self-possessed adults who simply cannot wait for marriage. In Austen, as in the eighteenth-century novels from which she learned, pre-marital sex happens because a young woman gets into the hands of a rakish man, not because two people simply cannot resist each other. There are would-be rakes about. Sir Edward Denham in *Sanditon* has read the novels of Samuel Richardson and has decided that he will 'seduce' Clara Brereton (Ch. 8). But this is comedy. 'Clara saw through him, and had not the least intention of being seduced.' She will not be a character in one of the novels he favours.

'She is lost forever,' says Elizabeth to Darcy, but it is not so (*Pride and Prejudice*, III. iv). Lydia is saved by marriage, into which Wickham is bribed. Sex before marriage, however, is different from sex outside marriage. Fanny Price thinks of her cousin Maria's adultery as 'this sin of the first magnitude' (III. xv). Lady Bertram, not usually a person for forceful judgements, acknowledges 'the loss of a daughter, and a disgrace never to be wiped off' (III. xvi). Duly divorced, Maria is sent off to some Sartrean hell of confinement in a distant county with Mrs Norris for company. In *Sense and Sensibility*, the adultery of Eliza, Colonel Brandon's sister-in-law, also leads to her husband divorcing her, but has to be narratively justified. She is victim rather than agent. 'My brother had no regard for her; his pleasures were not what they ought to have been, and from the first he treated her unkindly' (II. ix). We take the middle phrase to mean that he was sexually dissolute (Colonel Brandon is speaking to Elinor, so some polite euphemism is necessary). The implication is confirmed when, a few sentences later, we hear that he was 'a husband to provoke inconstancy'. Is it surprising that 'she should fall'?

Adultery was not unknown among Jane Austen's acquaintances. In 1801 she wrote to Cassandra about a ball at the Upper Rooms in Bath where she had seen the notorious Hon. Mary-Cassandra Twistleton, divorced by her naval husband two years earlier on the grounds of adultery. 'I am proud to say that I have a very good eye at an Adultress, for tho' repeatedly assured that another in the same party was the *She*, I fixed upon the right one from the first' (*Letters*, 36). Adultery may have been heinous in Austen's eyes, but it appears that a woman disgraced for this sin could still comport herself with pleasure at a smart social gathering. The evidence of Austen's correspondence is that sexual irregularity was thought of as an aristocratic habit, and that aristocrats seemed able to be shameless about it. Writing to her niece Fanny in March 1817, she commented on the notable engagement of Caroline, daughter of Lord Paget, to the Earl of March, heir to the Dukedom of Richmond. Lord and Lady Paget had been divorced after the former had eloped with Lady Charlotte Wellesley, sister-in-law of the Duke of Wellington. She had in turn been divorced by her husband, Sir Henry Wellesley. 'If I were the Duchess of Richmond, I should be very miserable about my son's choice. What can be expected from a Paget, born & brought up in the centre of conjugal Infidelity & Divorces?—I will *not* be interested about Lady Caroline. I abhor all the race of Pagets' (*Letters*, 153). The sexual imbroglios of high society were public entertainment. Writing to Cassandra, Austen responds to the 'sad story' of a married woman, Letitia-Mary Powlett, who had eloped with the 2nd Viscount Sackville. 'A hint of it, with Initials, was in yesterday's Courier' (*Letters*, 53). The aggrieved husband, Colonel Powlett, won £3,000 in damages from the philandering Viscount.[8] Mrs Rushworth's adultery with Henry Crawford is similarly revealed in the newspaper that Mr Price is reading in his Portsmouth parlour. It reports, with hardly concealed relish, the 'matrimonial *fracas* in the family of Mr. R. of Wimpole Street' (III. xv). Lots of 'fine ladies', observes Mr Price, are 'going to the devil now-a-days': his implication is that these are loose times, a satisfying condemnation of his dissolute social superiors from an irresponsible drunkard.

Jane Austen and her readers lived in an era of considerable sexual licence among the elite. Not just the Prince Regent, but his brothers the Duke of York, the Duke of Clarence (later William IV) and the Duke of Kent (Queen Victoria's father) were notable for their sexual irregularities. No newspaper reader of the time could have been unaware of the tone they set. Listening to the Crawfords in *Mansfield Park* we sometimes hear the accents of a libertine Regency sub-culture. Mary Crawford jests lightly about how her 'friend' Flora Ross has chosen 'that horrid Lord Stornaway' (presumably for his title), even though he is as foolish as Mr Rushworth and uglier – and comes 'with a blackguard character' (III. v). The last fact sounds like a hint of a sexual history, dismissed with the sophisticated tone of one who has seen these things before. Flora Ross becomes Lady Stornaway, and Mary Crawford dares tell Fanny that her husband seems now not 'so very ill-looking' as she had previously thought him. He has at least bestowed a title on her friend. The adulterous relationship between Maria Rushworth and Henry Crawford is brewed in the circle – under the eyes – of Lady Stornoway and her sister Mrs Fraser, Mary Crawford's London companions. We are reliably told by Edmund that the latter is 'a cold-hearted, vain woman, who has married entirely from convenience' (III. xiii). Mrs Rushworth then goes to stay in Twickenham with Mrs Aylmer, credited by Mary Crawford for sending her husband off to Bath to fetch his mother. 'The Aylmers are pleasant people; and her husband away, she can have nothing but enjoyment,' Mary Crawford has blithely told Fanny (III. xiv). There Henry Crawford has 'constant access' to her (III. xvi). A fashionable, loose-living social group is hinted at in these references to characters we never meet. We might remember Mary Crawford recalling, 'Three years ago the Admiral, my honoured uncle, bought a cottage at Twickenham for us all to spend our summers in; and my aunt and I went down to it quite in raptures' (I. vi). Twickenham – in reach of London yet out of its sight – is just the place to pursue liaisons. Mary Crawford has known just what was happening, mentioning in a letter to Fanny that her brother has been in Richmond and seen Mrs Rushworth. 'Now do not make yourself uneasy with any queer fancies, because he has been spending a few days at Richmond' (III. xiv).

In her sexual morals Mary Crawford is made a puzzle, both to Edmund Bertram and perhaps to some readers. She has left the house of her uncle, Admiral Crawford, because he is 'a man of vicious conduct' who, upon his wife's death, 'chose . . . to bring his mistress under his own roof' (I. iv). Edmund knows all about this, and credits Miss Crawford for being offended at his conduct (I. vii). Yet Austen makes Mary Crawford reveal her own loose morals in her jokes. Privately she teases her brother about being 'spoiled' by 'the admiral's lessons', half-acknowledging his own libertine inclinations (I. iv). When talking of admirals, her extraordinary jest to a solemn Edmund – 'Of *Rears*, and *Vices*, I saw enough. Now, do not be suspecting me of a pun, I entreat' (I. vi) – is a moment of sexual flippancy that suggests she is used to rather different company.[9] The milieu in which she has grown up has had its influence. Her brother later tells her that he will not consult his uncle about his plans to marry Fanny Price. 'The Admiral hated marriage, and thought it never pardonable in a young man of independent fortune' (II. xii). There are men out there who choose to cohabit or to keep a mistress, and some, like Admiral Crawford, have even invented a code to recommend their behaviour. Jane Austen knew men like this. In 1801 she wrote of her sister-in-law Eliza finding the manners of Lord Craven 'very pleasing indeed', before adding, 'The little flaw of having a Mistress now living with him at Ashdown Park, seems to be the only unpleasing circumstance about him' (*Letters*, 30). But then aristocrats are different. In another letter she reports that 'Ld Lucan has taken a mistress' (*Letters*, 50).

Given this trait of the social elite, it is ironical that Emma Woodhouse convinces herself that Harriet Smith must be 'a gentleman's daughter' (I. iv). When Robert Martin makes proper enquiries of Mrs Goddard, after he and Harriet have become engaged, she is found to be the daughter of a mere 'tradesman', who is rich enough to maintain her and 'decent enough to have always wished for concealment' (III. xix). Emma shares in that judgement of what is 'decent'. If a man gives way to his passions, he should have the decency to hide, as well as pay for, the consequences. This is the heroine's thought, acknowledging what all sorts of men get up to, but also the propriety of keeping it concealed. Emma, who denies her own desires for much of the novel, half-imagines a world of sexual appetites and illicit liaisons. Earlier in the novel, wondering why Mr Weston is dragging her to Randalls for a conference with Mrs Weston just after the announcement of Mrs Churchill's death, she dreams up disturbing revelations about Frank Churchill's adoptive father: 'Half a dozen natural children, perhaps—and poor Frank cut off!' (III. x). It is a self-amusing notion, but exaggerates a real possibility. It is Emma's habit to evade a truth by indulging in a fancy. As she does so, Austen is requiring the reader again to recognise what she has sometimes been accused of denying: that humans are driven by sexual appetites.

TWELVE

What Do Characters Say
When the Heroine Is Not There?

And Fanny, what was *she* doing and thinking all this while?
Mansfield Park, I. v

Charlotte Lucas's decision to marry Mr Collins is justly famous. Here, it seems, Jane Austen shows you what courtship and marriage really meant in the early nineteenth century. A respectable man needs a wife; a woman of 'small fortune' needs 'an establishment' (*Pride and Prejudice*, I. xxii). For those readers down the years who have looked for feminist inclinations in Austen's fiction, this is the evidence: a chasteningly unsentimental picture of the compromises that an intelligent woman has to make for material reasons. Yet Charlotte Lucas's decision is not memorable for reasons of sexual politics. Her acceptance of Mr Collins gets its power from a narrative trick: Austen's removal of the novel's heroine. Charlotte Lucas makes her life choice in one of the very few scenes in *Pride and Prejudice* from which Elizabeth Bennet is absent. In the embarrassing wake of Elizabeth's rejection of Mr Collins's proposal, her best friend has taken on the burden of conversing with him. Elizabeth is grateful to Charlotte, but she is not exactly being selfless. 'Charlotte's kindness extended farther than Elizabeth had any conception of; —its object was nothing else than to secure her from any return of Mr. Collins's addresses, by engaging them towards herself' (I. xxii). She knows her game. Suitably encouraged, Mr Collins is soon hastening over to Lucas Lodge to make his offer, and as he does so the narrative switches its attention to Charlotte and leaves the unsuspecting Elizabeth behind. There is Charlotte, expectant, watching for her suitor 'from an upper window' and setting out 'to meet him accidentally in the lane'. We do not get Mr Collins's words, or Charlotte's, but we do get her thoughts as she reflects with satisfaction on her decision. Austen has decided to let us see the world from Charlotte's point of view. Elizabeth's absence is emphasised by her friend's one reason for feeling some discomfort: 'The least agreeable circumstance in the business was the surprise it must occasion to Elizabeth Bennet.'

Austen's heroines are vivid to us because her novels are narrated from their points of view and suffused by their consciousnesses. Yet one of Austen's devices is to leave her heroine behind, to give us a glimpse of what the world is like in her absence. In all her novels except *Mansfield Park* this is done only occasionally, so that we receive a peculiar jolt when it happens. Charlotte Lucas's encounter in the lane with Mr Collins is only the third scene in *Pride and Prejudice* where Elizabeth is left behind. It has happened before, when Elizabeth is visiting Netherfield, where Jane is ill in bed. After dinner she retires to attend to her sister and we, surprisingly, stay in the drawing room where we hear Miss Bingley and Mrs Hurst deplore Elizabeth's walk across the fields and the Bennets' 'low connections' (I. viii). They are performing for Mr Darcy and Mr Bingley. We are suddenly to feel their determination to prevent either man's attachment to either Bennet sister, to realise what Jane and Elizabeth are up against. In a second, much briefer, exchange, we hear Miss Bingley needling Mr Darcy about the prospect of acquiring Mrs Bennet as a mother-in-law, but succeeding only in reminding him of Elizabeth's 'beautiful eyes' (I. x). The device of such an exchange is used again much later when Elizabeth is invited to Pemberley to visit Georgiana Darcy, who is accompanied by those malign Bingley sisters (III. iii). After Elizabeth's visit, we stay behind to hear Miss Bingley deride Elizabeth's supposed beauty for the benefit of Mr Darcy, who is finally forced to silence her by declaring Elizabeth 'one of the hand-somest women of my acquaintance'. This time the threat of Miss Bingley is utterly deflated. We see that Elizabeth still has her hold on Mr Darcy. Her absence means, however, that she does not know this as we do. She must discover their love for each other as a surprise.

The most continually present of Austen's heroines is the least knowing: Catherine Morland. Until the penultimate chapter of *Northanger Abbey*, she is there at every moment, in every line – with only a moment's exception. She first meets, dances with and talks to Henry Tilney in the third chapter of the novel. At the end of that chapter, Austen wonders face-tiously whether her heroine dreamed about him that night, before reassuring us that the sensible Mr Allen had discreetly looked into things.

How proper Mr. Tilney might be as a dreamer or a lover had not yet perhaps entered Mr. Allen's head, but that he was not objectionable as a common acquaintance for his young charge he was on inquiry satisfied; for he had early in the evening taken pains to know who her partner was, and had been assured of Mr. Tilney's being a clergyman, and of a very respectable family in Gloucestershire (I. iii).

The naive Catherine is not left to her own instincts. For a sentence we glimpse conversations that take place out of her hearing, but we do not actually leave her company until the penultimate chapter of the novel, just before Henry Tilney arrives unannounced at the Morlands' home. Suddenly Austen leaves Catherine to her own devices. Mrs Morland, worried about her daughter's 'loss of spirits', recommends an essay 'about young girls that have been spoilt for home by great acquaintance' and leaves the room to fetch the book in question.

> It was some time before she could find what she looked for; and other family matters occurring to detain her, a quarter of an hour had elapsed ere she returned downstairs with the volume from which so much was hoped. Her avocations above having shut out all noise but what she created herself, she knew not that a visitor had arrived within the last few minutes, till, on entering the room, the first object she beheld was a young man whom she had never seen before (II. xv).

In its quiet way it is an extraordinary abandonment of her heroine. We return downstairs to see the nervous young man and awkward young woman with Mrs Morland's eyes, and we suddenly know that betrothal is imminent. For at last Catherine has been trusted to live beyond the novelist's monitoring of her.

Northanger Abbey begins with Catherine – 'No one who had ever seen Catherine Morland in her infancy would have supposed her born to be an heroine' – but only one other Austen novel starts with the heroine: 'Emma Woodhouse, handsome, clever, and rich, with a comfortable home and happy disposition, seemed to unite some of the best blessings of existence; and had lived nearly twenty-one years in the world with very little to distress or vex her.' Emma bustles straight in to take over. All Austen's other novels begin at a tangent to their heroines. *Sense and Sensibility* starts a long way away from Elinor Dashwood, the first chapter giving a family history of the Dashwoods and the extraordinary second chapter consisting almost entirely of a conversation between John Dashwood and his wife in which they agree not to give his stepmother and half-sisters any money. In the third chapter, we find out about the attachment between Elinor and Edward Ferrars, in order to hear Marianne and her mother discuss Edward in Elinor's absence, Marianne declaring, 'His eyes want all that spirit, that fire, which at once announce virtue and intelligence. And besides all this, I am afraid, mama, he has no real taste' (I. iii). The novel appears to be dividing our interest between the two sisters. We accompany Marianne as she wanders around Norland saying farewell to its trees. Once arrived in Devon, we follow Marianne and Margaret on their foolish walk on the downs. Elinor is left behind as the two younger sisters relish 'the animating gales' and jointly pity 'the fears which had prevented their mother and Elinor from sharing such delightful sensations' (I. ix). Yet any impression that we are sharing our sympathies between Elinor and Marianne – between sense and sensibility – is soon corrected. Once we have tasted Marianne's folly we abandon her point of view, slowly occupying Elinor's pained consciousness.

If Catherine Morland is the most present of Austen's heroines, Fanny Price is the most absent. *Mansfield Park* is the one Austen novel in which conversations commonly take place without the heroine. There is a characteristic moment early in the novel when Edmund and his sister Julia arrive back, late on a summer evening, after dinner at the Parsonage with the Crawfords. They enter the drawing room, 'glowing and cheerful, the very reverse of what they found in the three ladies sitting there' (I. vii): Maria is reading sulkily, Lady Bertram is comatose and Mrs Norris is cross and uncommunicative. But where is Fanny? asks Edmund. Has she gone to bed? Mrs Norris does not know, but then Fanny's 'gentle voice' is heard from the other end of the big room. She was there all the time; the 'three ladies' were in fact four. The narrative merely behaved for a little while as though Fanny were absent, picking up the habit from the Bertrams. 'She does not fully participate in the world but as a result she sees things more clearly and accurately than those who do.'[1] Her non-participation is realised by Austen in a sequence of absences. From the first chapter, where Sir Thomas and Lady Bertram discuss with Mrs Norris the scheme for taking charge of one of Mrs Price's children, Fanny is subject to plans made in her absence. Whether Lady Bertram and Mrs Norris are deciding where she will live – 'Good heaven! what could I do with Fanny?' – or Sir Thomas is talking about having a ball for Fanny and her brother, she is often off stage while decisions are made on her behalf. Her fate is always to be decided by others.

The ease with which Fanny is ignored is emphasised by the number of exchanges that take place without her. These even include some featuring only men. It is often said that women are present in every scene in Austen's fiction, but this is not true.[2] There is a fleeting example of male-only exchange in *Pride and Prejudice*, where Mr Bingley comes to Longbourn to shoot with Mr Bennet (but in fact to propose to his daughter).

> Bingley was punctual to his appointment; and he and Mr. Bennet spent the morning together, as had been agreed on. The latter was much more agreeable than his companion expected. There was nothing of presumption or folly in Bingley that could

provoke his ridicule, or disgust him into silence; and he was more communicative, and less eccentric, than the other had ever seen him. (III. xiii).

This hint as to Mr Bennet's behaviour in rational male company takes us for a moment out of the world of his wife and daughters – but awkwardly, as if the author wanted to give another chance to a character whose paternal failings have been so thoroughly illuminated. In *Mansfield Park* the male-only scenes are much clearer and more important. The first is where Sir Thomas Bertram, unexpectedly returned from the West Indies, finds a strange young man, Mr Yates, rehearsing theatrical speeches in the billiard room of his own house (II. i). As they meet, Tom Bertram also enters the room, and attempts to appease his father's irritated feelings. The second scene without a woman occurs in the next chapter, when Edmund seeks out his father to give an account of 'the whole acting scheme'.

He was anxious, while vindicating himself, to say nothing unkind of the others: but there was only one amongst them whose conduct he could mention without some necessity of defence or palliation. 'We have all been more or less to blame,' said he, 'every one of us, excepting Fanny. Fanny is the only one who has judged rightly throughout; who has been consistent. *Her* feelings have been steadily against it from first to last. She never ceased to think of what was due to you. You will find Fanny everything you could wish.' (II. ii)

Much later in the novel we hear, in direct speech again, a snatch of conversation between Edmund and Sir Thomas on the subject of Fanny's resistance to Henry Crawford's proposal of marriage. 'I will speak to her, Sir; I will take the first opportunity of speaking to her alone' (III. iv). Sir Thomas responds by telling his son that Fanny is, at that moment, 'walking alone in the shrubbery'. Here are father and son, man-to-man, conspiring together to further the match, both utterly ignorant as to the major impediment: Fanny's love for Edmund. Later, in indirect speech, we have Edmund reporting back to his father that Mr Crawford had been 'too hasty' but that a 'return of affection' might eventually be hoped for. He believes himself 'perfectly acquainted' with Fanny's 'sentiments', and speaks confidently to Sir Thomas. And he is as ignorant of her true feelings as ever.

It is in *Mansfield Park* alone that Austen gives us these accumulated glimpses of men together, as if respecting the Bertrams' aristocratic delusion that all important decisions are made by a father and his sons. Another kind of scene in the novel, from which the Bertrams and Fanny are absent, shows us that power lies elsewhere. There is a sequence of five conversations at the Parsonage among the Crawfords and Mrs Grant that are cumulatively perhaps the most shocking exchanges in all Austen's fiction. The first occurs soon after the Crawfords have arrived. They have not yet met the Bertrams, but Mrs Grant has plans: '"Henry, you shall marry the youngest Miss Bertram, a nice, handsome, good-humoured, accomplished girl, who will make you very happy." Henry bowed and thanked her' (I. iv). Mary warns her sister that she is wasting her thoughts and efforts: 'He is the most horrible flirt that can be imagined. If your Miss Bertrams do not like to have their hearts broke, let them avoid Henry.' It is a pretty accurate prediction of what is to come. Henry assures Mrs Grant that he thinks highly of marriage, quoting *Paradise Lost* (the only Austen character to do so) with a mischievous emphasis: '"I consider the blessing of a wife as most justly described in those discreet lines of the poet—'Heaven's *last* best gift.'" "There, Mrs. Grant, you see how he dwells on one word, and only look at his smile. I assure you he is very detestable; the Admiral's lessons have quite spoiled him.'" There is something chilling in the jesting of brother and sister. Mary Crawford's mock-condemnation ('horrible', 'detestable') measures her distance from any real disapproval of his habitual behaviour.

There follow four more such exchanges, which structure the novel's plot. Their effect will be to make the Bertrams, including Fanny, seem unconscious players in the Crawfords' amusing game. Once the Bertrams and Crawfords have met, we go to the Parsonage again for more playful private talk. Does Henry really prefer Julia, asks Mary, 'for Miss Bertram is in general thought the handsomest' (I. v). 'So I should suppose. She has the advantage in every feature, and I prefer her countenance; but I like Julia best; Miss Bertram is certainly the handsomest, and I have found her the most agreeable, but I shall always like Julia best, because you order me.' Jesting is very quickly moving into something dangerous. Henry and Mary make clear that they already see that Maria does not care 'three straws' for Mr Rushworth, and that she is Henry's likely prey. Later, after the diversions of Sotherton and the negotiations over the taking of parts in the play, we go back to the Parsonage for an unmonitored conversation between Mary Crawford and Mrs Grant.

'I rather wonder Julia is not in love with Henry,' was her observation to Mary.

'I dare say she is,' replied Mary coldly. 'I imagine both sisters are.'

'Both! no, no, that must not be. Do not give him a hint of it. Think of Mr. Rushworth!'

'You had better tell Miss Bertram to think of Mr. Rushworth. It may do *her* some good.' (I. xvii)

Mary has well-evidenced scorn for Mr Rushworth and knows just how well Maria has been entangled.

> 'I would not give much for Mr. Rushworth's chance if Henry stept in before the articles were signed.'
>
> 'If you have such a suspicion, something must be done; and as soon as the play is all over, we will talk to him seriously and make him know his own mind; and if he means nothing, we will send him off, though he is Henry, for a time.'

Sir Thomas Bertram's return means that Mrs Grant's assertion will never be tested, though it hardly sounds as if, without Mary's backing, much could have come of it.

Mary speaks to her half-sister in cold candour: Henry has caught both the Bertram girls, and has meant to do so. Mary speaks as if she has seen this kind of thing before. The exchange is shocking because it takes place in Fanny's absence. If only she or the Bertrams could hear this! Fanny has observed Henry's flirtations with alarm, but her suspicions hardly go far enough. Even more chilling is the next Parsonage conversation, between Henry and Mary alone. 'Seeing the coast clear of the rest of the family', he asks his sister with a smile, 'And how do you think I mean to amuse myself, Mary, on the days that I do not hunt? . . . my plan is to make Fanny Price in love with me' (II. vi). Mary's reply is hardly good-hearted: 'Fanny Price! Nonsense! No, no. You ought to be satisfied with her two cousins.' To which her brother's rejoinder is devilish. 'But I cannot be satisfied without Fanny Price, without making a small hole in Fanny Price's heart.' Don't make her 'really unhappy,' says Mary. He has only a fortnight, so 'will not do her any harm'. He wants only to make her feel, when he leaves, 'that she shall be never happy again'. '"Moderation itself!" said Mary.'

Fanny's presence turns out to be a stronger charm than is allowed in her absence. In the final Parsonage conversation Henry Crawford takes his sister's arm and tells her that his plans have changed. 'I am quite determined, Mary. My mind is entirely made up. Will it astonish you? No: you must be aware that I am quite determined to marry Fanny Price' (II. xii). 'Lucky, lucky girl!' exclaims his sister, assuming that she will naturally comply. As ever, her fate seems to be being decided out of her hearing. *Mansfield Park* is a novel about its heroine's absence. When Fanny leaves Mansfield to go to Portsmouth, everything falls apart without her. We follow her, however, and in the whole of Volume III of the novel, there is not a scene or a dialogue from which she is absent – except, as fleetingly as could be, just after she has left, when we hear Lady Bertram's reply to Mrs Norris's opinion that Fanny will not be 'wanted or missed'. "'That may be, sister," was all Lady Bertram's reply. "I dare say you are very right; but I am sure I shall miss her very much"' (III. vi). With choice narrative irony, the only moment of Fanny's absence is an expression of sincere regret about that absence. The Bertrams have to learn what Lady Bertram, in her vapid, selfish way, has always known: that they cannot do without her.

> *Emma's brief absences let us glimpse a narrative*
> *of Mr Knightley's feelings, unfolding all the*
> *time alongside her own preoccupations.*

In *Emma*, the heroine's presence is so overweening that her absence, when it occurs, is a kind of shock. There are only four such scenes, all brief, in the whole novel. The first is in the fifth chapter, where we find Mr Knightley talking confidentially to Mrs Weston about Emma's fate.

'She always declares she will never marry, which, of course, means just nothing at all. But I have no idea that she has yet ever seen a man she cared for. It would not be a bad thing for her to be very much in love with a proper object. I should like to see Emma in love, and in some doubt of a return; it would do her good. But there is nobody hereabouts to attach her; and she goes so seldom from home.' (I. v)

Mrs Weston listens but conceals 'some favourite thoughts of her own and Mr Weston's on the subject'. Austen is inviting discerning readers to trick themselves. We can infer that the Westons have Frank Churchill in mind as a possible husband for Emma and we will care even more, as they do, about his impending appearance. Meanwhile Mr Knightley's rumination about the likelihood of Emma falling in love is a piece of calculated misdirection. Only on re-reading will we see that 'nobody hereabouts' draws attention to his own obtuseness about his deeper feelings for Emma. By taking place without the heroine, the exchange acquires a certain authority, and the misleading clues as to what is to come are made the stronger.

Emma is absent again only three times. The first of these absences is the most surprising, for it occurs when suddenly, in the third volume of the novel, the narration switches to Mr Knightley's point of view to report his suspicions about Frank Churchill.

Mr. Knightley began to suspect him of some inclination to trifle with Jane Fairfax. He could not understand it; but there were symptoms of intelligence between them—he thought so at least—symptoms of admiration on his side, which, having once observed, he could not persuade himself to think entirely void of meaning, however he might wish to escape any of Emma's errors of imagination. She was not present when the suspicion first

arose. He was dining with the Randalls family, and Jane, at the
Eltons'; and he had seen a look, more than a single look, at Miss
Fairfax, which, from the admirer of Miss Woodhouse, seemed
somewhat out of place. (III.v.)

We join him as he walks up to Hartfield and meets in the lane
Emma and Harriet, and then Frank Churchill, Miss Bates,
Jane Fairfax and the Westons. Emma is there, yet hardly
present: as they reach the gates to Hartfield Mr Perry passes
and Frank Churchill makes his blunder about knowing that
Mr Perry is to set up a carriage; 'Emma was out of hearing.'
Mr Knightley sees 'confusion suppressed or laughed away' in
Frank Churchill's face, but can't catch Jane Fairfax's response:
'she was indeed behind, and too busy with her shawl'. For the
rest of the chapter we watch Emma, Frank Churchill and Jane
Fairfax with Mr Knightley's eyes. He sees them play their
word game and detects 'disingenuousness and double dealing'.
In the very next chapter, Emma once more disappears, for
a comic conversation between Mr Knightley and Mrs Elton
in which the strawberry party at Donwell is suggested. We
are again given access to Mr Knightley's unspoken thoughts,
seeing that his plans are shaped by his wish 'to persuade Mr.
Woodhouse, as well as Emma, to join the party' (III. vi). But
more than this: Emma's absence is used to smuggle a new
suggestion about Mr Knightley's secret thoughts into the
narrative. Politely deflecting Mrs Elton's officious desires to
issue the invitations, he says that only one woman will ever
'invite what guests she pleases to Donwell'. "'—Mrs. Weston,
I suppose," interrupted Mrs. Elton, rather mortified. "No—
Mrs. Knightley;—and, till she is in being, I will manage such
matters myself.'"

Emma's absences are used to show the true folly of her
schemes: the secret understanding between Frank Churchill

and Jane Fairfax is not to be the complete surprise for the reader that it is for the heroine. But if this is the ostensible reason for these scenes, there is a deeper one too. Mr Knightley's suspicions, which arose that evening at the Eltons' when Emma 'was not present', have been ignited by the 'early dislike' that he has taken to Frank Churchill, 'for some reason best known to himself' (III. v). His hostile attention to Frank Churchill must be directed by jealousy. The deft irrelevance of his quip about some future 'Mrs Knightley' must be evidence of private thoughts about his own possible attachment. Emma's brief absences let us glimpse a narrative of Mr Knightley's feelings, unfolding all the time alongside her own preoccupations. There is one more such absence, a snatch of conversation when Mrs Weston, her baby on her knee, tells Mr Weston of Emma's engagement:

> the wonder of it was very soon nothing; and by the end of an hour he was not far from believing that he had always foreseen it.
>
> 'It is to be a secret, I conclude,' said he. 'These matters are always a secret, till it is found out that every body knows them. Only let me be told when I may speak out.—I wonder whether Jane has any suspicion.' (III. xvii)

It is the completion of a circle: in that first scene without Emma we glimpsed the Westons' schemes for her marriage to Frank Churchill; in this last one they discover how much better it is that she marry Mr Knightley. In this novel of secrets, their earlier hope that Emma would marry Frank will remain a secret.

Persuasion is arguably the Austen novel that most shares its heroine's experiences and feelings, yet in its opening chapters she only slowly becomes present to us. We come to her via her family's vanities and follies – 'she was only Anne'. She speaks for the first time in the third chapter, to express her admiration of the navy for reasons that are wholly unclear. A few pages later she speaks for only the second time, showing herself unaccountably well-informed about Admiral Croft's position in the navy and his war service. Only Mr Shepherd's forgetfulness at the end of the chapter about the name of Mrs Croft's brother – 'the gentleman who lived a few years back, at Monkford. Bless me! What was his name?' – forces an answer from Anne – '"You mean Mr. Wentworth, I suppose," said Anne' – an exchange that unleashes her feelings and forces her story on our attentions. Thus far the novel has been mimicking her family's neglect of her. After this opening there are only three moments in the novel when Anne is absent. The first comes just after Mary tells her that Captain Wentworth has found her 'so altered he should not have known you again' (I. vii). The narrative then switches to Captain Wentworth, to tell us that he had indeed 'used such words' and to show him discussing his interest in marriage with his sister.

> He had been most warmly attached to her, and had never seen a woman since whom he thought her equal; but, except from some natural sensation of curiosity, he had no desire of meeting her again. Her power with him was gone for ever.
>
> It was now his object to marry. (I. vii)

It is an audacious turning aside from the heroine. We briefly penetrate directly into Captain Wentworth's thoughts for the only time in the novel, in order to be told something about him that is entirely untrue: 'Her power with him was gone for ever.' It is self-delusion masquerading as narrative fact. He tells himself that Anne's power over him is 'gone for ever' because he would like to believe it to be true.

Anne is absent only twice more. In the first instance, we briefly see the Musgrove sisters at the window, looking out for Captain Wentworth, as Charles Hayter drones on about the Uppercross curacy (I. ix). It is a glimpse of the half-comic turmoil that Captain Wentworth is causing in the lives of the sisters, and of Charles Hayter, Henrietta's now displaced admirer. And finally there is the strange little scene much later in a shop (Molland's) in Bath. Anne has taken shelter from the rain with Elizabeth and Mrs Clay. Captain Wentworth enters with a party of others. They have some awkward conversation. Then Mr Elliot arrives to take Anne off. But we do not leave with her; we stay in the shop. The ladies of Captain Wentworth's party chat about Anne.

> '. . . One can guess what will happen there. He is always with them; half lives in the family, I believe. What a very good-looking man!'
>
> 'Yes, and Miss Atkinson, who dined with him once at the Wallises', says he is the most agreeable man she ever was in company with.'
>
> 'She is pretty, I think; Anne Elliot; very pretty when one comes to look at her. It is not the fashion to say so, but I confess I admire her more than her sister.'
>
> 'Oh! so do I.'
>
> 'And so do I. No comparison. But the men are all wild after Miss Elliot. Anne is too delicate for them.' (II. vii)

It is an unobtrusively brilliant use of dialogue. Nothing is said of Captain Wentworth's thoughts, but we listen to this exchange only because he is listening. In Anne's absence, we hear about her likely engagement to Mr Elliot with all Captain Wentworth's silent attention. We hear the verdict on her looks with all his silent interest. We feel his jealousy aroused and Anne's allure, her 'power over him', confirmed. It is appropriate that this happens once she has left the scene. For Austen often lets you understand her heroines by allowing you to glimpse things in their absence. Anne is removed so that we can feel her influence. It is fictional proof that we know someone best when we can see them in their absence, when we believe in them when they are not there.

THIRTEEN

How Much Money Is Enough?

'My father would be well pleased if the gentlemen were richer, but he has no other fault to find.'

Persuasion, II. x

The question of money is posed bluntly enough in *Sense and Sensibility*, when Elinor and Marianne Dashwood debate the importance or unimportance of wealth in the company of Edward Ferrars. Marianne reacts indignantly to Elinor's declaration that happiness has much to do with 'wealth': '"Elinor, for shame!" said Marianne, "money can only give happiness where there is nothing else to give it. Beyond a competence, it can afford no real satisfaction, as far as mere self is concerned"' (I. xvii). A 'competence' is the contemporary term for enough money, and Elinor takes up the word, smilingly suggesting that Marianne's 'competence' would be equivalent to her 'wealth'. The exchange that follows proves her right. Marianne's idea of a 'competence' is 'About eighteen hundred or two thousand a-year; not more than *that*.' The modern reader will know from trustworthy Elinor's response – '*Two* thousand a-year! *One* is my wealth!' – that Marianne has named a large sum; the first readers of the novel would have felt how very large it was – and therefore how very absurd Marianne was being. Defending herself against the implication that her demands are 'extravagant', Marianne herself mentions some of these. She hopes for 'a proper establishment of servants, a carriage, perhaps two, and hunters'.

Austen is always careful with her sums of money and particularly so in *Sense and Sensibility*, which has more talk of money than any other of her novels. Discussing the business of correcting proofs of this novel, she told Cassandra about her desire to correct some of the figures quoted. 'The *Incomes* remain as they were, but I will get them altered if I can' (*Letters*, 71). Presumably the sums of money remained the same as in an earlier version of the novel and no longer carried exactly the right implications. The opening chapters of *Sense and Sensibility* are painstakingly precise about money. Elinor and Marianne's father had 'only seven thousand pounds in his own disposal' (I. i). Their great-uncle leaves the three sisters 'a thousand pounds a-piece'. The total capital sum of £10,000 would give a total income of about £500 a year, which allows them their modest, harassed gentility. (Austen's first readers would have known what kind of income was represented by the capital sums specified in the novels, characters relying on returns of 5 per cent, the usual interest on investments in government funds.) In the second chapter, Mrs John Dashwood accurately calculates the Dashwoods' income. Yet the modern reader cannot know exactly what to think when she exclaims, 'Only conceive how comfortable they will be! Five hundred a-year! I am sure I cannot imagine how they will spend half of it' (I. ii). We do know by this stage of the dialogue that Mrs John Dashwood is meanness personified, and we catch the ring of absurdity when she completes her peroration by assuring her husband that 'as to your giving them more, it is quite absurd to think of it. They will be much more able to give *you* something.' We already know that John Dashwood has inherited an estate that gives him some £4,000 a year, in addition to his wife's money and an inheritance from his mother, so we can easily understand how her persuasion of her spouse has triumphed over truth and logic. But how adequate or inadequate is that £500?

In the very process of allowing himself to be persuaded out of allowing his sisters a regular income, John Dashwood concedes that they might easily find themselves under financial pressure. 'A present of fifty pounds, now and then, will prevent their ever being distressed for money,' he assures himself (I. ii). Historians caution against applying some blind multiplier to produce a modern equivalent of sums of money from the past, but it is not difficult to put numbers to some of the early nineteenth-century outlays that characterised degrees of affluence. We have helpful information from Austen's own family. After his retirement George Austen enjoyed an income of up to £600 per annum from his clerical livings and an annuity (*Letters*, 29); all this disappeared with his death. It paid for a rented house in Bath (the rent alone taking a quarter of his income) and three servants. Yet there is evidence that this income was only just sufficient: after three years the Austens moved from their house in Sydney Place to another in Green Park Buildings, an address that they had previously rejected. This might well have been an economy measure.[1] After Rev George Austen's death the Austen ladies had to live on £450 a year between them, much of it contributed by Jane Austen's brothers.[2] In a now notorious (because Mrs John Dashwood-like) letter to his brother Frank, Henry Austen explained unconvincingly how 'comfortable' this would make them.[3] In fact it reduced them to employing just one servant. In the summer months they had to become peripatetic, living with various relatives and friends in turn. The turn for the worse is instructive. We will find in Jane Austen's fiction, as in her life, £500–£600 per annum is the usual range of a 'competence' for a couple or a family unit. We might remember that John Dashwood, after his promise to his father on his deathbed, contemplates giving his half-sisters each a thousand pounds more. This would raise their joint annual income by £150 and move them into affluence. Naturally he decides against this.

An adequate income for a single person can be much less. Mr and Mrs Norris have 'very little less than a thousand a year' while Mr Norris is alive (I. i). After his death, Mrs Norris might be even more affluent. 'I hope, sister, things are not so very bad with you neither—considering. Sir Thomas says you will have six hundred a year,' says Lady Bertram (I. iii). 'Lady Bertram, I do not complain. I know I cannot live as I have done, but I must retrench where I can, and learn to be a better manager. I *have been* a liberal house-keeper enough, but I shall not be ashamed to practise economy now. My situation is as much altered as my income.' Mrs Norris savours the prospect of financial stringencies. 'It is unknown how much was consumed in our kitchen by odd comers and goers. At the White house, matters must be better looked after. I *must* live within my income, or I shall be miserable; and I own it would give me great satisfaction to be able to do rather more—to lay by a little at the end of the year.' The modern reader easily suspects the gist of this: that Mrs Norris's economies are her pleasure rather than her necessity. Austen's first readers would have known that this widow's income went well beyond her needs. Mrs Norris's affluence is all the greater when one considers that she is almost certainly living rent-free in 'a small house of Sir Thomas's in the village'.

Famously, Jane Austen names sums.

It makes me most uncomfortable to see
An English spinster of middle class
Describe the amorous effect of 'brass',
Reveal so frankly and with such sobriety
The economic basis of society.[4]

Austen's interest in money does not in itself single her out from other women novelists of her age. As Edward Copeland has shown in his brilliantly detailed study *Women Writing about Money*, 'The yearly income is an obsessive motif in women's fiction at the turn of the eighteenth century.'[5] What is extraordinary about Austen is not her candour but the precision with which she shows the influence of particular sums on particular people. Most of her major characters come with income tickets attached, not so much because the novelist wants us to notice how important money and the lack of money might be, as because she wants us to see her characters noticing these things. It is their understanding of money – and how they are bound to or separated from each other by money – that is at stake. There is a painfully revealing example in *Emma* where Miss Bates is telling Emma about Jane Fairfax's prospects as a governess to the Sucklings' friends the Smallridges. Having long fended off Mrs Elton's officious suggestions, she has relented and is going. 'To a Mrs. Smallridge—charming woman—most superior—to have the charge of her three little girls—delightful children' (III. viii). We should wince to hear Miss Bates parroting Mrs Elton's assurances (in truth, she has no idea whether Mrs Smallridge is 'charming' or not). We know that any friend of Selina Suckling is a poor prospect as an employer, and Emma knows this just as well as us. But we and Emma know too that Miss Bates must make herself believe in the desirability of this apparently inescapable option. Emma's feelings are troubled further when Miss Bates mentions her niece's proposed salary. 'It will be nothing but pleasure, a life of pleasure.—And her salary!—I really cannot venture to name her salary to you, Miss Woodhouse. Even you, used as you are to great sums, would hardly believe that so much could be given to a young person like Jane.' No sum is actually specified, but we can feel that Emma Woodhouse, 'handsome, clever, and rich', knows how modest it must be. Most governesses at this time earned between £20 and £30 a year, some as little as £12.[6] Jane Fairfax's proposed salary would certainly be an amount to embarrass a woman whose income from her capital is about £1,500 a year. If Miss Bates were not an assured innocent in her declarations, you might suspect satire: 'you, used as you are to great sums'. Nothing more needs to be said to exhibit the chasm about to open up between two young women who share much in the way of gentility, elegance and accomplishments. The exhibition is entirely dramatic: we are not told anything of how Emma feels about this cruel and merely lucky difference in their fortunes. We just see and feel her listening to Miss Bates with the knowledge of her own wealth heavy on her. We do not know exactly how much Miss Bates and her mother have to live on, but their ability to afford one all-purpose servant, Patty, suggests that it might be £100 per annum.[7] Austen would have expected a contemporary reader to have noticed her recoiling from the 'bad news' that their chimney needed sweeping and the real difference to their diet that the gift of Woodhouse pork and Knightley apples can make.

Perhaps Miss Bates does not know just how rich Miss Woodhouse is. If not, she is unusual. For the extraordinary thing is that everyone in Austen's fiction seems to know about everyone else's money. It is not so surprising that Mr Collins is able to tell Elizabeth Bennet, loftily, that he will make no demands on her father for a marriage portion, since he knows that 'one thousand pounds in the four per cents, which will not be yours until after your mother's decease, is all that you may ever be entitled to' (I. xix). He is just repeating common knowledge. In *Sense and Sensibility*, when John Dashwood asks Elinor what Colonel Brandon's fortune is, she does answer him and she does know: 'I believe about two thousand a-year' (II. xi). Elinor asks Mrs Jennings whether Miss Grey is 'very rich' and gets a definitive-sounding answer: 'Fifty thousand pounds, my dear' (II. viii). Elinor soon repeats the information to Colonel Brandon. Mrs Jennings also knows that Miss Grey is orphaned and has complete control over her fortune (and that she is disliked by her own guardians). *Mansfield Park* begins by informing us that 'about thirty years ago', Miss Maria Ward, 'with only seven thousand pounds', captivated Sir Thomas Bertram. 'All Huntingdon exclaimed on the greatness of the match', as if the financial details were common knowledge. (Miss Ward takes only a little more than Mrs Bennet into marriage.) Edmund Bertram, having his well-founded doubts about Mr Rushworth's capacities, says often to himself, 'If this man had not twelve thousand a year, he would be a very stupid fellow' (I. iv).

This is a world in which everyone knows – or thinks
they know – about everyone else's money.

If a novelist now were to tell us about somebody's income, it would be an authorial confidence. When Austen does so, she is giving us information that is available to her characters. When Wickham switches his attentions from Elizabeth to Miss King, it is because of her 'sudden acquisition of ten thousand pounds', a gain that seems entirely well-advertised (*Pride and Prejudice*, II. iii). Emma Woodhouse knows that

Mr Elton has proposed to her only because she is 'the heir-ess of thirty thousand pounds' (I. xvi) – and she can be sure that he knows her worth. Emma in her turn knows that Miss Campbell is due to inherit twelve thousand pounds, and absurdly assumes that this was Mr Dixon's only reason for marrying her, when he truly loved Jane Fairfax (II. ii). Incomes and inheritances are not confidential matters. Thus the extraordinary thing that Lady Catherine de Bourgh says to Elizabeth at their first meeting about girls learning to play the piano. 'The Miss Webbs all play, and their father has not so good an income as yours's' (II. vi). This is amazingly rude, but still sayable. Not only is the income of another family a discussable matter – just – but it is also a knowable matter. Lady Catherine has done her research. 'The topic itself was not hedged with the secrecy it possesses today. Letters and diaries sent along the news of other people's incomes almost as a duty.'[8] One of the most important original sources of information was the marriage settlement. Marriages among the landed and propertied involved legally binding settlements drawn up by lawyers (with no obligation to confidentiality).[9] Such agreements required explicit calculations of the worth of each party. When Dr and Mrs Grant move to Mansfield, Mrs Norris is appalled at their indulgence of culinary luxury. 'Inquire where she would, she could not find out that Mrs. Grant had ever had more than five thousand pounds' (I. iii). The amount of money she took into marriage is more or less public information. Mrs Norris, we are to infer, had the same seven thousand pounds on marriage as her younger sister Maria, now Lady Bertram.

In *Sense and Sensibility* Elinor bumps into her half-brother John Dashwood in a Piccadilly jeweller's shop and he gives her the outlines of a proposed marriage settlement between Edward Ferrars and the Hon. Miss Morton, 'only daughter of the late Lord Morton' (II. xi). The young lady has thirty thousand pounds; Edward's 'most excellent mother, Mrs. Ferrars, with the utmost liberality, will come forward, and settle on him a thousand a-year'. Social historians should hesitate before taking this as evidence of the openness with which settlements were discussed: John Dashwood is money-obsessed, and we can hear his love of lucre behind the empty doublings of 'most excellent' and 'utmost liberality'. (What he calls Mrs Ferrars's 'noble spirit' will later be aptly demonstrated when she disinherits her elder son for the sin of become engaged to a portionless young woman.) He surely should not be bandying such financial arrangements in a West End shop. Especially he should not be doing so when he knows that his sister was attached to the man whose proposed marriage he describes. His obtuseness and vulgarity are made worse by his announcement that Mrs Ferrars, his mother-in-law, has just given his wife 'bank-notes . . . to the amount of two hundred pounds' (almost half the annual income of Elinor, her mother, and her sisters). 'And extremely acceptable it is, for we must live at a great expense while we are here.' The stupidity of his avarice is all in that phrase 'extremely acceptable', used in talking to a sister who is so pushed for money that she has come to the shop to negotiate the sale of 'a few old-fashioned jewels of her mother'.

Talk of money in Austen is always dramatic, never just informative. We listen to John Dashwood's every inclination being warped by money. Yet he would not be able to have this conversation if marriage settlements were not broadcast. Sometimes the announcement of a marriage in a newspaper specified the amount of a dowry.[10] It is likely that a woman like Mrs Bennet would be quick to tell any interested or uninterested party of the conditions of her marriage settlement. Equally, the system of taxation made the incomes of the landed gentry widely known. Land Tax was levied annually and was based on a valuation of a person's estate. From 1799, income tax was assessed by local commissioners, often drawn from among the local landed gentry. Information about the income from estates like Henry Crawford's was therefore readily available and quickly circulated. 'Miss Julia and Mr. Crawford. Yes, indeed, a very pretty match,' says Mrs Rushworth to Mrs Norris. 'What is his property?' 'Four thousand a year' (I. xii). Some characters talk themselves of how much they are worth. In *Persuasion* Charles Musgrove tells Anne and Mary that 'from what he had once heard Captain Wentworth himself say, was very sure that he had not made less than twenty thousand pounds by the war. Here was a fortune at once; besides which, there would be the chance of what might be done in any future war' (I. ix). Captain Wentworth would be 'a capital match' for either of his sisters. At the opening of the final chapter, the figure is made more exact. 'Captain Wentworth, with five-and-twenty thousand pounds, and as high in his profession as merit and activity could place him, was no longer nobody' (II. xii). This too is information known by the characters as well as announced by the narrator: prize money won from capturing enemy ships was widely advertised.[11]

Of course, there can be mistakes. *Northanger Abbey* turns on the misreporting of a person's supposed wealth. It is because of John Thorpe that General Tilney believes Catherine to be rich. His treatment of our heroine is explained when Henry Tilney explains how John Thorpe had 'misled him' (II. xv). Consulted by the General, and imagining himself as Catherine's future husband, 'his vanity induced him to represent the family as yet more wealthy than his vanity and avarice had made him believe them'. Yet the very readiness with which the hard-hearted General Tilney believes this account suggests that he is used to reliable reports of other people's wealth. This is a world in which everyone knows, or thinks they know, about everyone else's money. Thorpe is a braggart whose own extravagance is bolstered by imagining everyone else to be immensely wealthy. The son of a widow, 'and a not very rich one', he has spent fifty guineas on a carriage (I. vii). He curses James Morland for not keeping a horse and gig, adding something in his 'loud and incoherent way' about 'its being a d— thing to be miserly', apparently believing, though Catherine hardly understands him, that the Morlands were 'people who rolled in money' (I. xi). He tends to believe that everyone is rich. He tells Catherine that General Tilney is 'A very fine fellow; as rich as a Jew' (I. xii). He has already said, 'Old Allen is as rich as a Jew—is not he?' (I. ix). And in a world where people rely on reports of each other's wealth, he is a dangerous character.

Not that the Morlands are poor. Having announced his engagement to Isabella Thorpe, James Morland is promised a living worth four hundred pounds per annum – plus the same again on his father's death. James is grateful but Isabella, on being 'heartily congratulated' by Catherine, is 'grave' with disappointment – clear enough to the reader, if not to her 'dear friend' (II. i). Mrs Thorpe calls four hundred a 'small income', and looks 'anxiously' at her daughter. The sum seems devised by the author to test Isabella and find her out. James Austen, Jane Austen's eldest brother, and his first wife, Anne Mathew, had married on £300 per annum.[12] But this was close to the borderline of gentility. Edward Ferrars is offered a living by Colonel Brandon that will fetch him something over £200 per year. The Colonel thinks that this will make him 'comfortable as a bachelor' but 'cannot enable him to marry' (III. iii). In a final reckoning, we hear that Elinor and Edward are to have this living, plus the annual interest on £3,000. This makes a total of £350 per annum – which is inadequate: 'they were neither of them quite enough in love to think that three hundred and fifty pounds a-year would supply them with the comforts of life' (III. xiii). Then Mrs Ferrars gives Edward £10,000 to match the amount that she gave his sister on marriage, and they are entirely comfortable. There is evidence that Fanny Price's mother has an income of about £400 per annum. Her sister, now Lady Bertram, brought £7,000 to her marriage to Sir Thomas, and we might infer that Fanny's mother would have been left the same amount. This would bring an income of £350 a year. Added to Mr Price's half-pay of up to £50 a year, this would give them an income sufficient for slightly threadbare gentility. But Mrs Price has many children, a drunken husband and no way with a domestic budget. Her daughter explicitly recognises that her appalling Aunt Norris might well have made the income adequate. The reader truly attuned to the value of money should know that the Price family could live a more comfortable life than they do.

What should be enough is not enough for Austen's extravagant characters. Willoughby in *Sense and Sensibility* has six or seven hundred a year, but 'lived at an expence to which that income could hardly be equal' (I. xiv). We are to realise that this income should be perfectly adequate for a genteel single man. When he hears that Edmund Bertram is due to get seven hundred a year from his living at Thornton Lacey, Henry Crawford thinks this is a decent amount, and is duly mocked by his sister, who wonders how he would feel if he were limited to seven hundred a year (II. v). Equally evident to the Regency reader would have been the wastefulness of Mr Bennet, a character always blamed less by us than by Austen's own heroine. His estate brings an income of £2,000 a year, which should be enough for a surplus to be put aside for dowries for all his daughters. He himself wished that 'instead of spending his whole income, he had laid by an annual sum for the better provision of his children, and of his wife, if she survived him' (III. viii).

The obscurity to present-day readers of monetary value in Austen means that some hints are likely to be lost. When Edmund Bertram objects to the probable expense of making a theatre in Mansfield Park, his brother Tom replies sarcastically, 'Yes, the expense of such an undertaking would be prodigious! . . . a whole twenty pounds.' (In fact it costs a good deal more.) This would have been the annual wage of a labouring man with a family, or perhaps of one of those servants recruited to erect the stage. Then there is the vulgarity of Mr Collins in *Pride and Prejudice* telling Mrs Philips that Lady Catherine's 'chimney-piece alone had cost eight hundred pounds' (I. xvi). This would have been the annual income of an affluent country gentleman. Later on in the novel, as Mr Collins walks across the park to Rosings with Elizabeth, Sir William Lucas and his daughter Maria, his companions are forced to listen to 'his enumeration of the windows in front of the house, and his relation of what the glazing altogether had originally cost Sir Lewis de Bourgh' (II. vi). Of course his knowledge must have come from Lady Catherine, and her money-obsessed boasts to her toadying auditor.

Certain markers of affluence might pass us by. No wonder, for instance, that so many characters talk and think about the ownership of carriages. The Austens themselves owned a carriage for a year or two in the late 1790s but then had to give it up.[13] Mrs Dashwood is persuaded by Elinor to sell their carriage: 'had she consulted only her own wishes, she would have kept it' (I. v). Edward Copeland quotes John Trusler's estimate in *The Economist* in the 1770s that an annual income of £800 would allow for the keeping of a carriage.[14] The inflation of the last decades of the eighteenth century would have taken this figure to about £1,000 a year, so we can see how foolish Mrs Dashwood was tempted to be. The plot of *Emma* turns on Mr Perry's planned purchase of a carriage; any genteel reader would have known just how affluent this must have declared him. And when Mrs Elton parades her provision of her carriage to ferry the Bates party to the ball at the Crown, she advertises her own membership of this economic elite.

Caring about love rather than money is admirable. When Catherine Morland declares, 'to marry for money I think the wickedest thing in existence', her hyperbole is naive but not foolish (*Northanger Abbey*, I. xv). Her delusion is the belief that others are above caring about money. Catherine is readily convinced that General Tilney does not care about money, except 'as it allowed him to promote the happiness of his children' (II. x). She knows nothing, but we know better from the next short sentence: 'The brother and sister looked at each other.' Having heard his 'disinterested sentiments on the subject of money . . . more than once' (II. xi), she thinks that he is 'misunderstood by his children'. But anyone who professes not to care must be a hypocrite. 'I hate money,' announces Isabella Thorpe (II. i). It will not be long before she tells Catherine, as if in implied justification of her carrying on with Frederick Tilney, 'after all that romancers may say, there is no doing without money' (II. iii). Another mercenary young woman, Lucy Steele, tells Elinor Dashwood, 'I have always been used to a very small income, and could struggle with any poverty for him' (II. ii). This is cant. Lucy is ruthless about money – a fact nicely illustrated by her final theft from her sister of all her cash (III. xiii). We should not forget that Marianne Dashwood shares this supposed scorn of wealth with these two calculating girls. When Marianne is burbling about the 'remarkably pretty' upstairs sitting room at Allenham (just right, she is thinking, for a lucky wife), she regrets its 'forlorn' furniture. All it needs is to be 'newly fitted up—a couple of hundred pounds, Willoughby says, would make it one of the pleasantest summer-rooms in England' (I. xiii). The casual extravagance of this – all the worse as it is the imagining of wealth that will only come when Willoughby's aunt dies – should stop us short. The two lovers have been thinking of spending twice Miss and Mrs Bates's annual income on furnishing one small private room. One of Austen's attentive first readers would surely have come close to despising Marianne when he or she heard her saying this, a woman possessed by her suitor's extravagant spirit. It is further proof that those who declare themselves above caring about money are those who are most governed by it.

FOURTEEN

Why Do Her Plots Rely on Blunders?

'Wretched, wretched mistake!'

Pride and Prejudice, III. iv

Near the end of *Persuasion,* slowly, happily pacing the gravel walk in Bath, Anne Elliot listens to Captain Wentworth tell her of his feelings for her and explain his recent conduct. After Louisa Musgrove's fall in Lyme, he says, he went to stay with his brother in Shropshire, hoping to loosen 'by any fair means' Louisa's supposed attachment to him (II. xi). Edward Wentworth had asked after Anne, 'asked even if you were personally altered, little suspecting that to my eye you could never alter'. The earnest hyperbole of a lover is more resonant than he knows. 'Anne smiled, and let it pass. It was too pleasing a blunder for a reproach.' It is a 'blunder' because it reminds Anne and us of what he said just a few months earlier, when he met her again after eight years apart. Her sister Mary told her that he thought 'You were so altered he should not have known you again' (I. vii). Anne smiles now because he so blithely contradicts what he has said before. She says nothing to show him that she knows this. The comparison with his 'former words' delights her, for his opinion must be 'the result, not the cause of a revival of his warm attachment'. His love convinces him of her charms, not the other way round.

Pleasing blunder: it is a kind of oxymoron. A foolish mistake, an instance of clumsiness, opens up his feelings to her and gives her more pleasure than any successful compliment. Having misunderstood him for much of the book, Anne for a moment understands him better than he understands himself. A blunder is a way into truly knowing a person. It is the first time that the word is used in the novel, but it is used for a second time in the very next paragraph, which reports Captain Wentworth recalling his time at his brother's home in Shropshire, spent 'lamenting the blindness of his own pride, and the blunders of his own calculations'. It is as if he has caught the word from Anne, even though it was a word only in her thoughts. He is thinking of his attempt, out of 'angry pride', to attach himself to Louisa Musgrove, which could have led him into a wholly unwanted engagement. When he thought he was being manipulative he was, in fact, making the clumsiest of mistakes. For a blunder is not just an error, it is an error that another person has noticed. So it serves an oddly powerful double purpose in Austen's fiction: it can embarrass or mortify, but it also reveals a person's true feelings.

In *Emma*, the word 'blunder', used fifteen times in the novel, is like a guide to the plot. In a famous episode of coded revelation (understood by the reader, glimpsed by Mr Knightley, missed by Emma), it is made the word at the heart of the game that is itself at the heart of the novel. Having made his mistake of showing the other characters that he knows about Mr Perry's planned purchase of a carriage, and therefore showing the reader that he has been in secret communication with Jane Fairfax, Frank Churchill uses the silly diversion of anagram making with children's spelling letters around the table at Hartfield to signal to his lover. Foolish Harriet seizes on the letters that he has put in front of Jane Fairfax and, with Mr Knightley's help, finds the answer. 'The word was *blunder*; and as Harriet exultingly proclaimed it, there was a blush on Jane's cheek which gave it a meaning not otherwise ostensible' (III. v). We see all this through Mr Knightley's eyes; he knows that the word means something hidden, but does not know what. 'These letters were but the vehicle for gallantry and trick.' 'Blunder' signifies Frank Churchill's covert communication with Jane Fairfax. 'Blunder' is the word for the stupid mistake made by the clever person, a mistake that might have allowed a really ingenious interpreter to understand just what has been going on.

Frank Churchill, the cleverest character in *Emma*, seems to have alighted on a word that has been on others' lips and in the heroine's thoughts. In the work of a less skilful writer, the novel's insistence on the word might seem an authorial insertion, an advertisement of her consciously contrived theme. Not in *Emma*. Here the coincidence of its use tells us of the conditions of life in this little world, where polite social exchanges have to cover unspoken desires, and where characters are made to guess, often wrongly, at each other's true feelings. Sometimes you can hear Austen pursuing a word like this through one of her novels, as Shakespeare does, testing its powers. And as in Shakespeare, the word will often turn up in the speech or thoughts of different characters, as they all come across the same knot in the language. Though *blunder* is most often used when recounting Emma's thoughts, its first appearance in the novel is in a remark made by Mrs Weston, out of Emma's hearing, in a conversation she has with Mr Knightley. She is vindicating Emma from Mr Knightley's premonition that she will do 'harm' through her friendship with Harriet Smith. 'No, no; she has qualities which may be trusted; she will never lead any one really wrong; she will make no lasting blunder; where Emma errs once, she is in the right a hundred times' (I. v). Her attempted exoneration is more like a warning. What Mrs Weston says about Emma's mistakes is itself mistaken: we know that Emma is already leading Harriet Smith very 'wrong'. Yet more than this, her use of that peculiar phrase 'no lasting blunder' sensitises us to the mix of comedy and potential disaster in the errors that follow. For what is to prevent a blunder being 'lasting'? Why might not Emma's misperception about Mr Elton's intentions lead to the ruin of Harriet's and Robert Martin's chance of happiness together? We recall Elinor Dashwood's thought about Mr Palmer's marrying foolish Charlotte Jennings: 'his kind of blunder was too common for any sensible man to be lastingly hurt by it' (I. xx). Common – and irreparable. The results of some blunders last for the rest of a person's life.

Emma, the great blunderer, fancies herself alive to the blunders of others. When Mr John Knightley suggests to her that Mr Elton might be courting her, and that she might seem to him to be 'encouraging', she confidently contradicts him: 'she walked on, amusing herself in the consideration of the blunders which often arise from a partial knowledge of circumstances, of the mistakes which people of high pretensions to judgment are for ever falling into' (I. xiii). We are fully inhabiting Emma's thoughts and therefore her delusions, and we can hear how the word *blunder* is like a little trap for her. The person who lives by cleverly intuiting the motives of others, of knowing a blunder when she encounters it, is doomed to blunder herself. She almost recognises this as she sits down 'to think and be miserable' after the embarrassing disaster of Mr Elton's proposal, and that word inserts itself into her thoughts. 'She would gladly have submitted to feel yet more mistaken—more in error—more disgraced by mis-judgment, than she actually was, could the effects of her blunders have been confined to herself' (I. xvi). The narrative subtlety of this is that we can hear her capacity for self-delusion beginning to reassert itself even in the train of apparent self-condemnation: 'gladly have submitted' is her turn of phrase or turn of thought, as she tells herself that she would be happy to be 'disgraced' if only Harriet were to escape the consequences of her errors. She acknowledges to herself that she has 'blundered most dreadfully', yet she does so in a passage where most of her delusions remain intact (I. xvi). She sleeps well and awakes the next day with her 'spirits' restored.

By naming her mistakes Emma trivialises and rises above them. As in that first use of the word by Mrs Weston, *blunder* has become a term for a foolish little error, an embarrassing tripping up. When Emma and Harriet later make their necessary visit to the vicarage to meet the new Mrs Elton, our heroine is conscious of irksome recollections, rather than truly mortified. 'A thousand vexatious thoughts would recur. Compliments, charades, and horrible blunders' (I. xiv). Those 'vexatious thoughts' do not yet comprehend any acknowledgement of her own manipulativeness. The word that she uses when she thinks about getting things wrong seems to have been overheard by others, even though Emma has never spoken it, only thought it. When Jane Fairfax fends off Mrs Elton's highly unwanted offer to send one of her own servants to collect her letters, she tries to change the subject, veering off into praise of the post office. 'So seldom that any negligence or blunder appears! So seldom that a letter, among the thousands that are constantly passing about the kingdom, is ever carried wrong' (II. xvi). In this novel of blunders, of motives misunderstood and secret attachments almost betrayed, the word comes naturally. By the time that Frank Churchill uses *blunder* in the word game at Hartfield, there is a moment's illusion that, like Captain Wentworth being passed the word by Anne Elliot, he has intuited it from Emma herself. When he later writes his long letter accounting for his conduct to Mrs Weston, passed by her to Emma and Mr Knightley, he curses the post in a sentence that uses the word 'blunder' twice. 'Imagine the shock; imagine how, till I had actually detected my own blunder, I raved at the blunders of the post' (III. xiv). You might think that he was picking up on what Jane Fairfax said earlier, except that he was not actually present to hear her words. He is expressing his feelings on finding that his letter of explanation never reached his lover, and then finding the mistake is his, not the post's. (He absent-mindedly placed his letter to Jane Fairfax in his desk.) This sophisticated plotter is almost undone by the simplest of blunders.

Eventually, as a half-confession to Mr Knightley, Emma herself actually speaks the word when discussing the behaviour of Mr Elton. 'I was fully convinced of his being in love with Harriet. It was through a series of strange blunders!' (II. ii). The secret engagement between Frank Churchill and Jane Fairfax means that everyone in this novel gets things wrong, but Emma tells Mrs Weston that at least her error has been confined to a passing comment in confidence. 'Your only blunder was confined to my ear, when you imagined a certain friend of our's in love with the lady' (III. x). She refers to Mrs Weston's thought that Mr Knightley might have a *tendresse* for Jane Fairfax. Mrs Weston seizes on Emma's special word when she replies, 'True. But as I have always had a thoroughly good opinion of Miss Fairfax, I never could, under any blunder, have spoken ill of her.' The exchange demonstrates why foolish mistakes are made not just narratively but even morally interesting by Austen. Frank Churchill and Jane Fairfax have ensured that everyone will make mistakes, but some people's mistakes, like Mrs Weston's, are inert and harmless. Blunders show people up, and Mrs Weston, keeping her matchmaking ideas almost to herself, will do no damage with hers. A careful speaker, she is confident that she was never at risk of saying something derogatory about Jane Fairfax to her son-in-law. If she blundered, it was safely.

Emma's mistakes are different and dangerous – dangerous to herself. Her realisation of this comes when Harriet tells her that she believes that Mr Knightley will propose to her. Emma is forced to see that it is she who has inadvertently encouraged her protégée towards Mr Knightley. "'Good God!" cried Emma, "this has been a most unfortunate—most deplorable mistake!—What is to be done?'" But nothing is to be done. Like Frankenstein, it seems, Emma has created the being who will take what she loves and destroy her happiness. It is all her own doing. 'How to understand it all! How to understand the deceptions she had been thus practising on herself, and living under!—The blunders, the blindness of her own head and heart!' (III. xi) Blunders indeed – no longer just embarrassing mistakes, but disastrous errors, born, as she now acknowledges, of her own skills of self-deception. For the moment it appears that her blunders have built a plot that will end most unhappily for her. But at least her blunders, *felix culpa*, have shown her what she truly feels about Mr Knightley, if only by making it likely that she will lose him. Her stupid mistakes have shown her and us the way to her heart. Luckily Harriet is wrong about Mr Knightley; she too has misunderstood, and Emma is to be saved from a life as her father's nurse and backgammon companion. It is naturally that other great causer of blunders, Frank Churchill, who finally waves the word away. He jestingly asks Emma to look at Jane Fairfax and see her remembering his error over knowing about Mr Perry getting a carriage. 'Do not you see that, at this instant, the very passage of her own letter, which sent me the report, is passing under her eye—that the whole blunder is spread before her' (III. xviii). Even in his state of grateful happiness, Frank Churchill is characteristically flippant about the painful mistakes of the past.

Not all Austen's heroines blunder. Tony Tanner identifies just what it is that has always made Fanny Price a hard heroine to like. 'She is never, ever, wrong.'[1] This is not a matter of morality; it is a matter of fact. There are other Austen heroines whose moral judgement is impeccable: Elinor Dashwood and Anne Elliot can be trusted to be 'right' in their principles and moral sentiments. Yet both of them are mistaken about certain matters of fact. Fanny is not just morally unimpeachable, she is also right in her factual judgements. It is the novel's great psychologist, Mary Crawford, who blunders. It is mostly Fanny whom she misunderstands, but not only her. Early on in her insertion of herself into the favours of the Bertram family, things go badly wrong on the visit to Sotherton, when, in the chapel, she launches into mockery of any family practice of religion. Imagine how tedious it was when attendance was mandatory for those young ladies and their servants, 'especially if the poor chaplain were not worth looking at' (I. ix). Edmund gently disputes her caricature, before she finds out from Julia that he is himself destined to become a clergyman. 'Miss Crawford's countenance, as Julia spoke, might have amused a disinterested observer. She looked almost aghast under the new idea she was receiving.' She has put her foot in it. She is so taken aback that Fanny pities her, though soon enough she is 'rallying her spirits, and recovering her complexion'.

Mary Crawford's 'lively mind', as Edmund calls it, sometimes leads her into tactless sallies. Yet when she applies herself she can find how to please anybody – except Fanny. The Mansfield Park ball is a cameo of her psychological canniness, as she supplies each principal character with the lines they want to hear. To Sir Thomas, who has arranged the ball to honour Fanny, she speaks in warm praise of his niece. To Lady Bertram she gives the opportunity of boasting that

Fanny's elegant appearance is the creation of her own lady's maid. To Mrs Norris she exclaims, with wonderful dishonesty, 'Ah! Ma'am, how much we want dear Mrs. Rushworth and Julia tonight!' (II. x). But Fanny she gets wrong. 'Miss Crawford blundered most towards Fanny herself, in her attentions to please.' She tries to give her heart 'a happy flutter' by talking to her confidentially of her brother's mysterious mission to London the next day. She has been 'misinterpreting Fanny's blushes'; Fanny is pained, not pleased. She does not relish Henry Crawford's attentions. Her secret, fiercely guarded, keeps her safe from Mary Crawford's knowing remarks. She loves Edmund. Mary Crawford never divines this, and so she will always misinterpret her. Her failure to see Fanny's secret, and the blunders to which this failure leads, immunise Fanny against her charms.

For such a psychologically astute person, soon able to play the Bertrams at will, Mary Crawford's tendency to blunder towards Fanny is extraordinary. She imagines, for instance, that she will win Fanny to her brother's favour by telling her about all the London ladies who have been desperate for his attentions. 'He has now and then been a sad flirt, and cared little for the havock he might be making in young ladies' affections' (III. v). When she sees Fanny blush at being told that she is the only young woman who 'can think of him with any thing like indifference', she imagines that she sees that she is not after all 'so insensible'. The reader knows that the blush comes from embarrassed indignation. When she later lets Fanny know by letter that her brother has been seeing Mrs Rushworth in Twickenham, it is with some purpose that she wryly signals, 'Now do not make yourself uneasy with any queer fancies . . .' (III. xiv). She must think that she is making Fanny jealous, rather than outraging her. What a miscalculation to suppose that her insinuations would actually pique

Fanny's romantic interest in her brother. Miss Crawford's blunders reveal her – to the reader as much as to the heroine – but perhaps they go some way to explain the preference for Mary Crawford over Fanny that readers have expressed down the years. We like people who make mistakes.

Catherine Morland in *Northanger Abbey* is all blundering, of a thoroughly sympathetic kind. When solicited by Captain Tilney for an introduction to Isabella Thorpe in order to ask for a dance, she assures him through Henry Tilney that Isabella would not be interested (being engaged to her brother James). 'Your brother will not mind it I know . . . because I heard him say before, that he hated dancing' (II. i). Her naivety is complete: Captain Tilney's disdain for dancing is an affectation that he will drop for any pretty girl, and Isabella will prove perfectly open to the attentions of a handsome new dancing partner. 'How very little trouble it can give you to understand the motives of other people's actions,' comments Henry, smiling. Her mistakes please him. The parody plot of this novel all derives from Catherine's egregious error in supposing that life might follow the plot of a Gothic novel. Yet most of her mistakes about other people are the consequences not just of naivety but of good nature. She misunderstands people who are mean-minded or selfish in ways that are foreign to her. Her blunders are charming and disarming.

Redundant blunders can feel like penalties for Austen's heroines, destined for happiness but given an extra twist of pain first.

Mistakes and misunderstandings are central to *Northanger Abbey*, but Austen elsewhere likes to create them where they are surplus to her plots. In *Sense and Sensibility* there is a peculiar little episode where Mrs Jennings is allowed to make an

unnecessary mistake about Elinor's relationship with Colonel
Brandon. In the most extraordinary shift of viewpoint in the
novel, we see him suggesting to Elinor that he might offer
Edward Ferrars 'the living of Delaford' through the eyes of
Mrs Jennings, who can hear only fragments of what is being
said (III. iii). She has 'hopes' that the Colonel will propose
to Elinor, and believes that she is witnessing this happening
(while rather disapproving of his 'unlover-like' manner of
addressing her). For much of a chapter she and Elinor manage
to talk at perfect cross-purposes, Mrs Jennings assuming that
she has just become engaged to Colonel Brandon, before the
misunderstanding is cleared up. It is a little narrative cul-de-
sac – wholly unnecessary to the plot – but perhaps comically
irresistible in a novel so concerned with the pains of waiting for the right proposal. In *Pride and Prejudice* Elizabeth
is summoned into her father's library to be told something
astonishing. A letter from Mr Collins has suggested that she
will soon be marrying Mr Darcy. 'Now, Lizzy, I think I *have*
surprised you' (III. xv). Mr Bennet jokes with Elizabeth about
the very thought of Mr Darcy being in love with her. 'Never
had his wit been directed in a manner so little agreeable to
her.' He has completely misunderstood her. 'It was necessary
to laugh, when she would rather have cried.' She is not yet
sure of Mr Darcy's affection, and so finds Mr Bennet's jests
peculiarly painful. She is being 'mortified', punished for the
prejudice against Mr Darcy that has given her father good
reason for his blunder. It is a special taste of the intimacy
between the father and his favourite daughter. This relationship is about to be displaced by Elizabeth's intimacy with her
husband-to-be and the scene is a kind of rehearsal for this.

Redundant blunders can feel like penalties for Austen's heroines, destined for happiness but given an extra twist of pain
first. One example comes near the end of *Sense and Sensibility*

and is a mistake that is produced by Lucy Steele's contrivance. The Dashwoods' manservant, Thomas, has just returned
from Exeter with news. 'I suppose you know, ma'am, that Mr.
Ferrars is married' (III. xi). Elinor turns pale and Marianne
falls back in her chair 'in hysterics'. While Marianne is helped
into another room, Elinor questions Thomas, who has met
Lucy and her new husband in a chaise. He punishes her more
by recounting how well and 'vastly contented' Lucy looked.
Now Elinor knows what it is to relinquish all hope. 'Day after
day' passes (III. xii). And then Edward suddenly appears, 'white
with agitation', and clears up the torturing misunderstanding
by explaining that Lucy has in fact married his brother Robert.
Elinor almost runs from the room and bursts into 'tears of joy'.
The misunderstanding has been Lucy's parting gesture. 'That
Lucy had certainly meant to deceive, to go off with a flourish
of malice against him in her message by Thomas, was perfectly
clear to Elinor' (III. xiii). She told Thomas to give Elinor and
Marianne 'her compliments and Mr. Ferrars's', apparently
confident that the message would be misinterpreted. It may
seem a little far-fetched to the modern reader, but Lucy knows
well how a servant will report things. A mistake about a name,
as we know from Austen's own letters, is the commonest kind
of blunder.

> On inquiring of Mrs. Clerk, I find that Mrs. Heathcote made a
> great blunder in her news of the Crooks and Morleys; it is young
> Mr. Crook who is to marry the second Miss Morley—& it is the
> Miss Morleys instead of the second Miss Crooke, who were the
> beauties at the Music meeting.—This seems a more likely tale, a
> better devised Impostor. (*Letters*, 27)

Elinor's Lucy-induced misconception, which dispirits her for
days, is a peculiar narrative trick, surplus to the requirements

of the plot. Elinor has to be taught how powerful were her only partially acknowledged hopes of marriage to Edward – by having them dashed. It is reminiscent of the mistake in *Persuasion*, when Anne meets Captain Wentworth's sister, Mrs Croft, who asks her if she knows that her brother is now married. 'She could now answer as she ought; and was happy to feel, when Mrs. Croft's next words explained it to be Mr. Wentworth of whom she spoke, that she had said nothing which might not do for either brother' (I. vi). Anne is made to wait only a moment before her false impression is corrected. Austen likes to create these secret bubbles of feeling, which we experience with the heroine for some brief span before the mistake is corrected and relief floods in. Except that here she does something even cleverer. Anne has been defending her feelings so effectively that she is able to 'answer as she ought', even at the moment when the death sentence to her love for Captain Wentworth is pronounced. In imitation of her suppression of her feelings, the sentence goes on, after the tiniest of pauses at a semicolon, to register her mistake, and the relieving fact that it is Captain Wentworth's brother of whom she speaks, with the barest flicker: 'happy to feel'. She has managed to deny the stab she must experience when she briefly thinks he is married.

Misconceptions drive *Persuasion*. In one telling use of the title word near the novel's end, 'persuasion' becomes a synonym for misunderstanding. Meeting Captain Wentworth at the White Hart, Anne recalls how, at the previous day's encounter, 'the same unfortunate persuasion, which had hastened him away from the concert room, still governed' (II. x). This 'persuasion' is his idea that she is becoming attached to Mr Elliot. The misconception stirs him into acknowledging the force of his own love and Anne begins to see it. For much of the novel she has interpreted the man she loves wrongly. Yet the only true mistake is that made by Mrs Smith, nexus of all Bath gossip, who assumes wrongly that Anne has fallen for the attentive Mr Elliot. When Anne postpones their next meeting because she wants to go to the concert, Mrs Smith speaks to her 'with an expression half serious, half arch', predicting that she will not be getting many more visits from her friend (II. vii). Why does Austen allow this mistake? To let us see that, despite Mrs Smith's knowledge of her suitor, the marriage would have gone ahead if he had been minded and she had been receptive. After the concert Anne visits her friend and finds her reading her face. 'I perfectly see how the hours passed . . . Your countenance perfectly informs me that you were in company last night with the person, whom you think the most agreeable in the world' (II. ix). Anne is amazed at her penetration, imagining that she is talking about Captain Wentworth. What is the point of this error? Partly to cement the internalisation of Anne's drama of feeling: truly, no one knows of her love, of what is going on between her and Captain Wentworth. Though it takes place entirely in the view of others, though they are never alone together until he has finally declared himself to her, it is completely hidden. But it is also to push Anne and her friend to the reali-sation of what could have happened. The blunder – licensed by Mrs Smith's correct inference that love is in the air – has chilling implications. Mrs Smith is self-interested enough to have hoped that her friend might influence her new husband, Mr Elliot, to regain her inheritance. Anne cannot understand why she spoke so favourably of him. 'My dear . . . there was nothing else to be done' (I. ix).

The most powerful example of such brief misunderstand-ing, happily corrected, occurs in *Emma*, when Mr Knightley struggles to declare himself to the heroine. 'I must tell what you will not ask' (III. xiii). Emma thinks that he is about to tell her of his love for Harriet and stops him: 'don't speak it, don't speak it'. He complies, in 'deep mortification', and for just a moment Austen lets you see how a misunderstanding might end hopes of a happy ending. Only some better instinct – 'Emma could not bear to give him pain' – makes her change her mind, allowing the revelation that 'Harriet's hopes had been entirely groundless, a mistake, a delusion, as complete a delusion as any of her own'. Mr Knightley is allowed to declare himself, but not before we have known that hesitation, that possibility of failure. Austen loves blunders because they show the difference between what we can understand of her characters, and what they can understand of each other. This final near-blunder allows Emma, for once, to understand everything, while Mr Knightley never grasps and will never grasp that Emma imagined him as Harriet's future husband. 'Seldom, very seldom, does complete truth belong to any human disclosure.' It might be the motto of Austen's fiction.

FIFTEEN

What Do Characters Read?

'He never read The Romance of the Forest, nor The
Children of the Abbey. He had never heard of such books
before I mentioned them, but he is determined to get them
now as soon as ever he can.'

Emma, I. iv

In Ang Lee's 1995 film version of *Sense and Sensibility*,
scripted by Emma Thompson, Kate Winslet, in the character
of poetry-loving Marianne Dashwood, reads Shakespeare's
Sonnet 116 ('Let me not to the marriage of true minds . . .')
aloud with Willoughby, played by Greg Wise. Shakespeare's
paean to lovers' constancy (in fact addressed to a young man)
is a popular choice for contemporary wedding services and
must have seemed a natural choice for the screen Marianne.
Lee and Thompson clearly thought it even more significant
given Willoughby's later inconstancy. To push the point home,
they had Winslet recite it again later in the film, her love now
disappointed, as she looks at Combe Magna (the marital home
that never was) through the rain.

The film-makers were on to something. Austen's novel is
much concerned with the influence of reading, and Marianne

puts a premium on literary discernment. Willoughby is qualified to be her partner by his ability to talk in the right way
about the right books. In her first conversation with him, she
excitedly discovers their shared tastes: 'her favourite authors
were brought forward and dwelt upon with so rapturous a
delight, that any young man of five and twenty must have
been insensible indeed, not to become an immediate convert
to the excellence of such works, however disregarded before'
(I. iii). Willoughby happily agrees with her every literary
opinion. He has quite enough 'sensibility' to respond in the
right way to books, or to know that this beautiful girl rates
such responsiveness very highly. Perhaps he senses what
Austen's first readers were expected to infer: that Marianne's
'sensibility' – apparently all instinct and spontaneity – was
itself learned from her reading. Books instruct her strong-
est feelings. As far as Marianne is concerned, Willoughby has
himself walked out of a book. 'His person and air were equal
to what her fancy had ever drawn for the hero of a favourite
story' (I. ix).

It is difficult to think of a novelist who makes reading a
more animating part of her characters' lives than Jane
Austen. Her completed fiction begins, in *Northanger Abbey*,
with a heroine whose errors are entirely the product of books:
the Gothic novels that she devours and then confuses with
reality. The novel on which she was working when she died,
Sanditon, has at its centre a character, Sir Edward Denham,
who 'had read more sentimental Novels than agreed with him'
(Ch. 8) and has begun to fancy himself the seductive rake
from a Samuel Richardson novel. Reading takes possession
of Austen's characters; how and what they read reveals them.
Yet the film's use of one of Shakespeare's sonnets is poetic
licence. The Sonnets were little regarded in Austen's day, and
unlikely reading matter for either Marianne or her dashing

lover, alert as they both are to literary fashion. In the novel, what does Willoughby read with the Dashwoods? Something surprising. When he is unaccountably called away to London, promising no return and sending Marianne into a histrionic 'violent oppression of spirits', his departure brings to an end the book that they have been enjoying *en famille*:

> one evening, Mrs. Dashwood, accidentally taking up a volume of Shakespeare, exclaimed,
>
> 'We have never finished Hamlet, Marianne; our dear Willoughby went away before we could get through it. We will put it by, that when he comes again . . . But it may be months, perhaps, before *that* happens.' (I. xvi)

It is jolting to think of Willoughby and the Dashwoods sharing the parts of a play whose protagonist dwells so often on the sexual urges of his mother and stepfather, and where 'the rank sweat of an enseaméd bed' is so vividly imagined. (It is just possible that they were reading a safer version: a *Family Shakespeare*, expurgated by Thomas Bowdler's sister Harriet, had been published in 1807.) The choice of play testifies to the literary seriousness of the Dashwoods, and to the willingness of Marianne's suitor to take on the most demanding literary parts, for we are surely invited to imagine that Willoughby will have been rendering Hamlet himself.

Willoughby reads his way into the Dashwoods' hearts – 'he read with all the sensibility and spirit which Edward unfortunately wanted' (I. x). Reading is important to the Dashwoods, and Elinor has to assure her sister that Edward's 'enjoyment of books is exceedingly great' (I. iv). The hyperbole is a measure of her anxiety. Reading matters. Reading sets the Dashwood girls apart from the empty-headed ladies and gentlemen on whose company they are forced.

Though nothing could be more polite than Lady Middleton's behaviour to Elinor and Marianne, she did not really like them at all. Because they neither flattered herself nor her children, she could not believe them good-natured; and because they were fond of reading, she fancied them satirical: perhaps without exactly knowing what it was to be satirical; but *that* did not signify. It was censure in common use, and easily given. (II. xiv)

Why 'satirical'? Because she is made to feel uneasy: Elinor and Marianne are too clever by half and take themselves off elsewhere, to a world of books. Those who spend much time reading are evidently not satisfied with Lady Middleton's world. Austen cannot resist the clever speculation, 'perhaps without exactly knowing what it was to be satirical'. Lady Middleton senses that she might be laughed at, and yet cannot quite imagine why.

The Dashwoods are readers in a non-reading world. As Elinor weeps over her discovery of Edward's secret engagement to Lucy Steele, she knows that he will not be happy 'with a wife like her—illiterate, artful, and selfish' (II. i). It is an extraordinary combination of adjectives, never used before or since. Lucy *can* read and write (though the grammar of her letters is highly faulty). 'Illiterate' means that she has not read books. The word reflects Elinor's judgement. 'Lucy was naturally clever . . . but her powers had received no aid from education, she was ignorant and illiterate' (I. xxii). To Austen's heroine the deficiency seems severe. Lucy's ignorance of books will be as much a torment to poor Edward, her future husband, as her cunning and self-interestedness. Such a devastating character sketch presumes that reading is good for you, especially if you are a woman. Austen herself had less than two years' formal schooling and relied on her father's instruction and access to his library of some

500 books, a large collection for a country clergyman (*Letters*, 31). You can sense something personal to the author when she distinguishes in *Mansfield Park* between the rich Bertram girls, who have a governess and suppose Fanny 'stupid at learning', and the heroine herself, with her native 'fondness for reading which, properly directed, must be an education in itself' (I. ii).

Those who do not read are the worse for it. When we hear in the opening sentence of *Persuasion* that Sir Walter Elliot 'never took up any book but the Baronetage', we catch not just his aristocratic self-regard but also his stupidity. Sir Walter being so preoccupied with the signs of his status, Kellynch Hall must have its stock of books, probably a library. And this is all he reads! Some at least know well enough to pretend to 'literacy'. 'I declare after all there is no enjoyment like reading!' exclaims Miss Bingley in *Pride and Prejudice*, failing in her attempts to draw Mr Darcy away from his book (I. xi). Three chapters and a day earlier, this paragon of disingenuousness was aiming a barb at Elizabeth for not playing cards because she was 'a great reader, and has no pleasure in anything else'. Now, seeing what Mr Darcy is doing, Miss Bingley has a book in her hand, but chosen, idiotically, only 'because it was the second volume of his'. She knows that books do furnish an impressive home, and disloyally dissociates herself from her own father who, though rich from 'trade', failed to stock enough shelves with these genteel objects. '"I am astonished," said Miss Bingley, "that my father should have left so small a collection of books"' (I. viii). She knows enough, too, to compliment Mr Darcy on his books. 'What a delightful library you have at Pemberley, Mr. Darcy!' Proudly and stiffly he observes that building it has been 'the work of many generations'. Her response is intended flattery. 'And then you have added so much to it yourself, you are always buying books.' With the emphasis on expenditure, this is just tactless enough to let us sense her evaluation of books by cost and yardage.

Lack of reading in a man is a sure sign of worthlessness. In *Mansfield Park*, Sir Thomas Bertram sees 'some part of the truth' about Mr Rushworth, his daughter's proposed spouse: he is 'an inferior young man, as ignorant in business as in books' (II. iii). In *Northanger Abbey*, Catherine may be foolish to believe too thoroughly in Mrs Radcliffe's novel, but the boorish John Thorpe is worse, revealing his 'illiteracy' by not knowing that Radcliffe is the author of *The Mysteries of Udolpho*, and calling Fanny Burney unreadable because she 'married an emigrant' (I.vii). The best men read, though their reading does not seem quite so health-giving when they tell women of its benefits. Mr Darcy is deliciously absurd, to us and Elizabeth, in his pompous pro forma of a woman's necessary accomplishments. He rounds off his list – 'a thorough knowledge of music, singing, drawing, dancing, and the modern languages' – with, 'To all this she must yet add something more substantial, in the improvement of the mind by extensive reading' (I. viii). Elizabeth has done this reading, but naturally now wants to deny it. More resigned is Mr Knightley, with his ironical approval of the reading lists that Emma has drawn up for herself over the years. 'I have seen a great many lists of her drawing-up at various times of books that she meant to read regularly through—and very good lists they were—very well chosen, and very neatly arranged—sometimes alphabetically, and sometimes by some other rule' (I. v). When Emma takes up Harriet Smith, conducting her through the right books is part of her plan.

> Her views of improving her little friend's mind, by a great deal of useful reading and conversation, had never yet led to more than a few first chapters, and the intention of going on to-morrow. It was much easier to chat than to study; much pleasanter to let

her imagination range and work at Harriet's fortune, than to be
labouring to enlarge her comprehension. (I. ix)

Emma understands what 'improvement' entails, but hardly
embarks on it. The wit of these sentences is their sympathy
with her avoidance of labour. Trying to make Harriet more
'literate' is probably a fool's errand, when 'prettiness' is much
more likely to assure her a contented future.

Being well-read is not beyond suspicion. There is one
quotation in all Austen's fiction from *Paradise Lost*, and who
supplies it? Henry Crawford, naturally – his literacy another
aspect of his dangerous charm. In private conversation at the
Parsonage with his sister Mary and half-sister Mrs Grant, he
fends off the latter's wish that he marry one of the Bertram
girls with a fragment of Milton: 'I consider the blessing of a
wife as most justly described in those discreet lines of the poet,
"Heaven's *last* best gift"' (I. iv). His emphasis nicely misinterprets Adam's enraptured description of Eve ('My fairest, my
espous'd, my latest found') in Book V of *Paradise Lost*. The
turning on its head of the poem's intended sentiment is his
witty literary blasphemy. Wonderfully, the only other Austen
character who quotes Milton is the appalling Mrs Elton in
Emma. Recalling her courtship by Mr Elton, she tells the
utterly uninterested Mr Weston, 'he was apt to be in despair,
and exclaim that he was sure at this rate it would be *May*
before Hymen's saffron robe would be put on for us' (II. xviii).
Her adaptation of lines from Milton's 'l'Allegro' ('There let
Hymen oft appear/In Saffron robe, with Taper clear') invok-
ing the Greek God of marriage is a gloriously pretentious
euphemism, all the more satisfying because she should not be
broadcasting details of her courtship at all.

Those who truly love reading attract the misjudgements
or suspicions of others. In *Persuasion* Anne overhears, from

behind a hedge, Louisa Musgrove telling Captain Wentworth of her rejection, some six years earlier, of Charles Musgrove's proposal of marriage. Louisa says that her parents 'think Charles might not be learned and bookish enough to please Lady Russell, and that therefore, she persuaded Anne to refuse him' (I. x). This is all wrong: Anne rejected Charles's proposal because she was still in love with Wentworth. The brilliance of the passage is that we overhear the dialogue with Anne, sensing the pressure of her feelings. Louisa's misconception reflects the easy belief that book-lovers are a species apart. Anne herself confirms this. When she hears the news of Louisa's engagement to Captain Benwick, the narrative follows the surprised sequence of her thoughts. 'Captain Benwick and Louisa Musgrove! The high-spirited, joyous-talking Louisa Musgrove, and the dejected, thinking, feeling, reading, Captain Benwick, seemed each of them everything that would not suit the other. Their minds most dissimilar! Where could have been the attraction?' (II. vi) This use of 'reading' as an adjective has passed out of our vocabularies. The OED cites an example from the *Monthly Magazine* of 1797, which tells you how unusual a 'reading man' was by talking of 'my residence at the university, and a constant intercourse with both reading and non-reading men'. Captain Wentworth reverts to the same adjective when expressing to Anne his own astonishment at the engagement of Captain Benwick and Louisa Musgrove.

'I confess that I do think there is a disparity, too great a disparity, and in a point no less essential than mind.—I regard Louisa Musgrove as a very amiable, sweet-tempered girl, and not deficient in understanding, but Benwick is something more. He is a clever man, a reading man—and I confess, that I do consider his attaching himself to her with some surprise.' (II. viii)

Benwick is an odd sort of person. 'I am sure Lady Russell would like him,' says Charles Musgrove, 'He is just Lady Russell's sort. Give him a book, and he will read all day long' (II. ii). It is clearly a form of eccentricity.

Anne is appointed as his companion at Lyme because of her own relish of reading, revealed earlier during an autumnal walk.

> Her pleasure in the walk must arise from the exercise and the day, from the view of the last smiles of the year upon the tawny leaves and withered hedges, and from repeating to herself some few of the thousand poetical descriptions extant of autumn, that season of peculiar and inexhaustible influence on the mind of taste and tenderness, that season which had drawn from every poet, worthy of being read, some attempt at description, or some lines of feeling (I. x).

Anne carries in her head a selection of poetical 'beauties', as anthologies of the 'best' extracts were called in Austen's day. However, she is rueful about the self-indulgent pleasures of autumnal verse: 'after another half mile of gradual ascent through large enclosures, where the ploughs at work, and fresh-made path spoke the farmer, counteracting the sweets of poetical despondence and meaning to have spring again, they gained the summit . . .' Life pushes poetic melancholy aside. When she walks with Benwick, it is contemporary poetry that he wants to discuss – and declaim:

> having talked of poetry, the richness of the present age, and gone through a brief comparison of opinion as to the first-rate poets, trying to ascertain whether *Marmion* or *The Lady of the Lake* were to be preferred, and how ranked the *Giaour* and *The Bride of Abydos*; and moreover, how the *Giaour* was to be pronounced, he showed himself so intimately acquainted with all the tenderest

songs of the one poet, and all the impassioned descriptions of
hopeless agony of the other; he repeated, with such tremulous
feeling, the various lines which imaged a broken heart, or a mind
destroyed by wretchedness, and looked so entirely as if he meant
to be understood, that she ventured to hope that he did not always
read only poetry . . . (I. xi)

It is 1814, the mid-point of what we now call the Romantic
period, but he does not have Wordsworth or Coleridge or
Blake in mind. He names Walter Scott and Lord Byron, the
two best-selling poets of the day.

For the discerning reader there would be an edge of comedy
in the English naval man's taste for Byron's 'impassioned' tales.
The Bride of Abydos is a 'Turkish Tale' about the illicit passion
of the Pasha's daughter Zuleika for her cousin Selim. In *The
Giaour*, Leila, a haremite of the Turk, Hassan, has a clandes-
tine love affair with 'the Giaour' (the word means 'infidel'). Her
master sews her into a sack and casts her into the sea. The
Giaour kills Hassan and many years later, having become a
monk, he makes his dying confession to a fellow monk, denying
religious consolation and clinging only to a vision of his lover.

> I would not, if I might, be blest;
> I want no paradise, but rest.
> 'Twas then, I tell thee, father! Then
> I saw her; yes, she lived again;
> And shining in her white symar,
> As through yon pale gray cloud the star
> Which now I gaze on, as on her,
> Who look'd and looks far lovelier;
> Tomorrow's night shall be more dark;
> And I, before its rays appear
> That lifeless thing the living fear.[1]

When Benwick and Anne discuss this poem, it is the latest thing. Later, Anne reflects on Benwick's engagement to Louisa:

> She saw no reason against their being happy. Louisa had fine naval fervour to begin with, and they would soon grow more alike. He would gain cheerfulness, and she would learn to be an enthusiast for Scott and Lord Byron; nay, that was probably learnt already; of course they had fallen in love over poetry. The idea of Louisa Musgrove turned into a person of literary taste, and sentimental reflection was amusing, but she had no doubt of its being so. (II. vi)

She is entertained by the cliché that has become reality: Benwick and Louisa have 'fallen in love over poetry'. Benwick has been reading poetry out loud at Louisa's bedside, she his captive audience.

Novel-readers were also novel-listeners.

For both Austen and her characters, reading commonly means reading aloud. Benwick-like, in June 1808 Austen's brother James read Scott's *Marmion* aloud to her, their brother Edward and his wife Mary. 'Ought I to be very much pleased with Marmion?—as yet I am not.—James reads it aloud in the Even^g' (*Letters*, 53). Reading was a shared familial experience. When Austen wrote to her sister Cassandra, who was staying with their brother Edward and his wife Elizabeth in Kent, she imagined the scene. 'How do you spend your Evenings?—I guess that Eliz:th works, that you read to her, & that Edward goes to sleep' (*Letters*, 14). Hearing a book was as common as silently reading it. 'I come to you to be talked to, not to read or hear reading,' Austen tells Martha Lloyd, her brother James's sister-in-law. 'I can do *that* at home' (*Letters*, 26). Books are performed or listened to. 'We have got the 2d vol. of Espriella's Letters [by Robert Southey],' Austen tells her sister, '& I read it aloud by candle-light' (*Letters*, 56). In *Sense and Sensibility* Marianne finds Edward Ferrars lacking in 'sensibility' – the prized capacity for finer feelings – giving as evidence his poor performance in reading out loud: 'it would have broke *my* heart had I loved him, to hear him read with so little sensibility' (I. iii). Her sister, she absurdly supposes, 'has not my feelings, and therefore she may overlook it, and be happy with him.' Edward has been reading the poetry of William Cowper, a test of emotiveness as far as Marianne is concerned. Cowper was also a favourite of Austen, who has Fanny quote him twice with intense feeling in *Mansfield Park* (I. vi and III. xiv). The Austen family apparently shared Marianne's predilection. 'My father reads Cowper to us in the evening, to which I listen when I can' (*Letters*, 14).

As a would-be clergyman, an ability to read aloud would be expected of Edward Ferrars. (Austen's father, Rev. George Austen, was proficient.) On Mr Collins's first evening with the Bennets, he is naturally, as a clergyman, invited to read aloud to the family. As a vicar, Mr Elton is given the duty of reading aloud to Emma and Harriet as the former draws the latter. Another clergyman, Henry Tilney, puts his professional expertise to good (if incongruous) use by reading *The Mysteries of Udolpho* aloud to his sister Eleanor, before deciding that he would rather read it more rapidly to himself. 'I remember that you undertook to read it aloud to me, and that when I was called away for only five minutes to answer a note, instead of waiting for me, you took the volume into the Hermitage Walk, and I was obliged to stay till you had finished it' (*Northanger Abbey*, I. xiv). Vicar-to-be Edmund

Bertram earnestly discusses the importance of reading aloud with Henry Crawford.

> The subject of reading aloud was farther discussed. The two young men were the only talkers, but they, standing by the fire, talked over the too common neglect of the qualification, the total inattention to it, in the ordinary school-system for boys, the consequently natural, yet in some instances almost unnatural, degree of ignorance and uncouthness of men, of sensible and well-informed men, when suddenly called to the necessity of reading aloud, which had fallen within their notice, giving instances of blunders, and failures with their secondary causes, the want of management of the voice, of proper modulation and emphasis, of foresight and judgment, all proceeding from the first cause: want of early attention and habit; and Fanny was listening again with great entertainment. (III. iii)

Edmund goes on to speak of this skill as if it were one of the most important qualifications of a clergyman, and regrets that 'the art of reading' has often been insufficiently studied by those joining this profession. Crawford, whom we presume to be untroubled by actual religious beliefs, engages earnestly in discussion of 'the properest manner in which particular passages in the service should be delivered'. It is all to impress the listening Fanny, naturally, but the discourse could not be sustained if her admirer did not have a considered judgement of how liturgical sentences should be read out.

Mary Crawford, we might remember, blandly tells Edmund that a vicar had best not try writing his own sermon for Sunday, but should instead read out an elegant published sermon (I. ix). Characteristically, she imagines a genteel clergyman as a polished performer of other men's words. Her brother is the most resourceful reader of all, admired by Fanny in his

performance of the very Shakespeare play that she herself
has been reading to Lady Bertram: 'She often reads to me
out of those books; and she was in the middle of a very fine
speech of that man's— what's his name, Fanny?—when we
heard your footsteps' (III. iii). Fanny has been at yet another
of her duties – reading aloud – though Lady Bertram's vague-
ness about text and character indicate that the book has been
genteel muzak to her. Henry takes up the volume and begins
to read out highlights from *Henry VIII*; Fanny 'was forced to
listen; his reading was capital, and her pleasure in good reading extreme'. Henry leaps from character to character and
has her rapt – until 'the book was closed, and the charm was
broken' (III. iii). Fanny may be able to resist Henry Crawford's
courtship, but his reading powers disarm her.

However droll the image of Benwick reading himself
and Louisa Musgrove into love, reading aloud is what a
male lover should be able to do. When we hear that Robert
Martin, in *Emma*, is able to do this, we know he is not the
clown that Emma wants him to be. Harriet Smith recalls
how he would read to her from a book on which Austen was
herself schooled: 'sometimes of an evening, before we went
to cards, he would read something aloud out of the Elegant
Extracts—very entertaining' (I. iv). (The chosen anthology, edited by Vicesimus Knox, was one of those mockingly
taken as standards of respectable reading in Chapter v of
Northanger Abbey.) Nothing speaks more strongly of Robert
Martin's affection for Harriet than his willingness to join her
in the formulaic Gothic that is her preferred reading matter. 'I
know he had read the Vicar of Wakefield. He never read the
Romance of the Forest, nor the Children of the Abbey. He had
never heard of such books before I mentioned them, but he is
determined to get them now as soon as ever he can' (*Emma*, I.
iv). Goldsmith's *The Vicar of Wakefield*, an eighteenth-century

updating of the Book of Job that is also a brilliant parody of sentimental fiction, was just the novel to read if you did not read many novels. Anne Radcliffe's *The Romance of the Forest* and Regina Maria Roche's *The Children of the Abbey* are both sensational tales, thick with mystery and coincidence. Robert Martin's choices have the sobriety of a man trying to improve himself, which makes Emma's unevidenced description of him to Harriet as 'illiterate and coarse' peculiarly unjust.

Robert Martin reads agricultural reports to himself, but reads novels aloud to the women of his household. Fiction is something you share: 'if a rainy morning deprived them of other enjoyments, they were still resolute in meeting in defiance of wet and dirt, and shut themselves up, to read novels together. Yes, novels . . .' (*Northanger Abbey* I. v). This has become one of the most famous outbursts in all Austen's fiction, apparently prompted by contemporary disparagement of novels, and leading into the author's vindication of the genre. The girls' togetherness is not just metaphorical. They are reading passages aloud to each other. In the next chapter Isabella promises Catherine, 'When you have finished Udolpho, we will read the Italian together.' This reading together was Austen's own habit. 'Fanny & I are to go on with Modern Europe together, but hitherto have advanced only 25 Pages' (*Letters*, 89). In her letters to Cassandra, she talks of particular novels as shared experiences between the two women, probably because they had been read aloud. In 1807 she tells Cassandra how Charlotte Lennox's novel *The Female Quixote* 'makes our evening amusement, to me a very high one, as I find the work quite equal to what I remembered it' (*Letters*, 49). It is being read out loud at her Southampton home. Her brother Frank's wife 'to whom it is new, enjoys it as one could wish'. Her brother James's wife, however, 'has little pleasure from that or any other book'.

Mr Collins affects to be shocked when a book is produced to be read aloud whose cover 'announced it to be from a circulating library' – and therefore almost certainly a novel (*Pride and Prejudice*, I. xiv). He is absurd, and his behaviour perhaps evidence that the disapproval of fiction was no longer a serious matter. Fanny Price joins the circulating library in Portsmouth, and Mary Musgrove and Lady Russell, in *Persuasion*, visit circulating libraries. Austen herself frequented these institutions, recalling in a letter to her niece Anna that the one in Dawlish 'was particularly pitiful & wretched 12 years ago, & not likely to have anybody's publication' (*Letters*, 104). Noting the opening of a local subscription library (possibly in Basingstoke) in 1798, Austen herself mocked those affected to disdain novels.

> I have received a very civil note from Mrs Martin requesting my name as a Subscriber to her Library which opens the 14th of January, & my name, or rather Yours is accordingly given ... As an inducement to subscribe Mrs Martin tells us that her Collection is not to consist entirely of Novels, but of every kind of Literature &c &c—She might have spared this pretension to *our* family, who are great Novel-readers & not ashamed of being so;—but it was necessary I suppose to the self-consequence of half her Subscribers (*Letters*, 14).

Novel-readers were also novel-listeners. Private, silent reading could accommodate a more robust choice of fiction. The great eighteenth-century novels of Fielding were deplored for their sexual amorality, and those of Sterne for being bawdy: neither was suitable for family consumption. Yet Austen's allusions to *Tom Jones* and *Tristram Shandy* indicate her close knowledge of both.[2] Her own novels were not for private consumption: they were read out loud to family and friends before they were ever published. This began with *Elinor and Marianne*, the early version in letters of what would become *Sense and Sensibility*.[3] Her niece Anna recalled in later life how as a child she heard her aunt reading *First Impressions* (the early version of *Pride and Prejudice*) aloud to the family circle.[4] The reading aloud continued. When *Pride and Prejudice* was first published, the author and her mother read out a large part of it to a neighbour, Miss Benn, who had come for dinner, without ever telling her who the author was: 'in the evening we set fairly at it & read half the first volume to her ... I believe it passed with her unsuspected— she was amused, poor soul! *that* she could not help you know, with two such people to lead the way; but she really does seem to admire Elizabeth' (*Letters*, 79). Reading the book in shifts, it seems, the Austen ladies got through perhaps thirteen chapters, probably taking at least two hours to do so. Austen's account implies considerable animation, on the part of Miss Benn as well as the readers. It is a vignette of how for Austen (as for her characters) reading could be essentially social.

Pace Mr Darcy, books for Austen are not just the solemn matter of improvement. They are the means by which people live out their desires or their follies. Marianne Dashwood is not entirely wrong to believe that reading takes you to a person's heart. In *Mansfield Park*, the first reason given for Fanny loving Edmund is that 'he recommended the books which charmed her leisure hours' (I. ii). Nothing, we sense, can be more intimate. In Whit Stillman's clever 1990 film *Metropolitan*, loosely based on Austen's novel, the hero wins the Austen-adoring heroine only when he himself learns to appreciate *Mansfield Park*. Which is as it should be.

SIXTEEN

Are Ill People Really to Blame for Their Illnesses?

'I do not think I ever was so ill in my life as I have been all this morning: very unfit to be left alone, I am sure. Suppose I were to be seized of a sudden in some dreadful way, and not able to ring the bell!'

Persuasion, I. v

You might think people really were to blame for their own illnesses, if you were as easily tricked by Frank Churchill as Emma is. The day after their first meeting, Emma asks him about visiting Miss Bates's house, where, he says, he found himself kept much longer than he had intended by 'the talking aunt'. What about his acquaintance from Weymouth, Miss Fairfax (whose name he has not mentioned)? How was she looking?

'Ill, very ill—that is, if a young lady can ever be allowed to look ill. But the expression is hardly admissible, Mrs. Weston, is it? Ladies can never look ill. And, seriously, Miss Fairfax is naturally so pale, as almost always to give the appearance of ill health.—A most deplorable want of complexion.' (II. vi)

He speaks as if illness were Jane Fairfax's natural condition. Her reserve, even insipidity, he implies, makes her look
unhealthy. Emma might begin 'a warm defence of Miss
Fairfax's complexion' but his judgement is surely half-
pleasing to her. She is herself, after all, the character who
claims 'I am always well, you know' in response to an anxious
enquiry from Mrs Weston (III. xii). When Frank Churchill
goes on to declare that 'nothing could make amends for the
want of the fine glow of health', he seems to be preferring
one woman rather explicitly to the other. 'Ill' is his word for
Jane Fairfax's very character.

It is all a blind. He loves Jane Fairfax. So hastily and passion-
ately has he rushed her into a secret engagement that we must
also infer strong sexual attraction. That pale complexion must
allure him. Yet he is clever enough to know how she appears
to others and to know that Emma will be ready to believe
that her rival for elegance actually looks 'ill' – her own robust
health being, in her own mind, the sign of her superiority. In
claiming that she is always well, Emma is saying something
peculiar for her age. A diligent reader of Jane Austen's letters
would be hard put to find one which did not mention illnesses
among family and friends. More than muslin or money, illness
is her consistent concern and surpasses even the weather as a
natural topic of epistolary conversation. Occasionally Austen
describes her own indispositions, but mostly she reports the
ailments of family members and close friends. In an age when
diagnoses were unconvincing and treatments rarely produc-
tive, a slight illness might always seem like a harbinger of
something worse. Take this, from a letter of June 1808:
'There has been a cold & sore throat prevailing very much in
this House lately, the Children have almost all been ill with it,
& we were afraid Lizzy was going to be very ill one day; she
had specks & a great deal of fever.—It went off however, &

they are all pretty well now' (*Letters*, 53). The relief of this is something that we can hardly feel any more. It gives us some idea of how our usually comfortable distinction between trivial and serious ailments was much less secure.

There was good reason to worry over each new indisposition, but therefore also more to be gained from hypochondria. There are suggestions in Austen's correspondence of reined-in exasperation at others' supposed afflictions: a jaundiced reader might think that her mother and her brother Henry, both often ill and both notably long-lived, were possible valetudinarians. 'Dearest Henry! What a turn he has for being ill!' she exclaimed in a letter to her sister in 1813, as she reported yet another of his ailments (*Letters*, 96). In November 1815 she wrote from London to Cassandra describing Henry's slow recovery from another bout of illness, 'but still they will not let him be well' (*Letters*, 128). She seems divided between exasperation ('He is so well, that I cannot think why he is not perfectly well') and concern ('The fever is not yet quite removed'). Occasionally she lets loose about some notable hypochondriac, as in a letter of September 1813, where she describes Edward Bridges' wife as 'a poor Honey—the sort of woman who gives me the idea of being determined never to be well—& who likes her spasms & nervousness & the consequence they give her, better than anything else' (*Letters*, 90). For the most part, however, Austen fusses over symptoms without mockery. 'Henry is not quite well.—His stomach is rather deranged. You must keep him in Rhubarb & give him plenty of Port & Water' (*Letters*, 88). Sometimes it seems that Mr Woodhouse's pseudo-medical twitterings were all too easy for her to generate.

A cold or an attack of bile might be nothing – or it might be something. It is a shock for the modern reader when he or she begins to realise from the dates of letters that Austen's

comments on her own health, as inconsequential as the bulle-
tins that she has been issuing on friends and family for twenty
years, tell us of the onset of a fatal illness. The shock is the
greater as most of her reports talk of her improving health.
'We are all in good health & I have certainly gained strength
through the Winter & am not far from being well; & I think
I understand my own case now so much better than I did, as
to be able by care to keep off any serious return of illness'
(*Letters*, 149). Less than six months later she was dead.

Illness shapes the plots of several of her novels. Illness takes
Catherine Morland to Bath, whence Mr Allen has been sent
for his gout. Mrs Allen is naturally delighted. 'A neighbour of
ours, Dr. Skinner, was here for his health last winter, and came
away quite stout' (I. viii). 'That circumstance must give great
encouragement,' replies Mr Tilney, with his special brand of
unnoticed irony. It is usefully unclear what the reader is to
think of going to Bath for your health. Mrs Allen is foolish,
but her husband is not. That exemplary couple Admiral and
Mrs Croft also come to Bath to minister to illness. According
to Mary Musgrove, the Crofts are in the town because 'they
think the admiral gouty' (*Persuasion*, II. vi). The report comes
originally from Charles Musgrove, so might be thought to be
reliable. Yet there is always the suspicion that the therapeutic
powers of the Bath waters are illusory. The waters are, after
all, sampled by Mr Woodhouse and recommended by Mrs
Elton. Jane Austen's brother Edward was one of those who
came to Bath for his ill health, drinking the waters and bathing and attaching himself to a Bath physician, Dr Fellowes
(*Letters*, 20 & 22). The novelist knew well the fashionable vale-
tudinarian culture of Bath, though we do not know how
absurd she found it . . .

The difficulty of distinguishing between the merest hypochondria and the first signs of a fatal ailment produces a comic

coup with the death of Mrs Churchill in *Emma*. For much of the novel illness, so-called, has appeared to control Frank Churchill's movements. He is about to enjoy the ball that he has begun to organise in Highbury when a letter arrives. 'Mrs. Churchill was unwell—far too unwell to do without him' (II. xii). He must leave immediately for Yorkshire. Later he writes to Mrs Weston from Mrs Churchill's home to say that she is 'recovering', but that 'he dared not yet, even in his own imagination, fix a time for coming to Randalls again' (II. xiii). Frank Churchill is eventually liberated to return by Mrs Churchill's ill health. She and her husband decide to travel to London, as Mr Weston reports: 'she has not been well the whole winter, and thinks Enscombe too cold for her—so they are all to move southward without loss of time' (II. xviii). Mr Weston has 'not much faith in Mrs. Churchill's illness', he tells Mrs Elton, before half-recollecting that hypochondria is made possible by the reality of death around the corner. "'I hope," said he presently, "I have not been severe upon poor Mrs. Churchill. If she is ill I should be sorry to do her injustice."' His self-correction is like a reminder of the paradox at work in all the novels: most people are merely imagining themselves ill; however, anybody might die at any time. The former is possible because of the latter. On Frank Churchill's next visit to Highbury we get intimations that Mrs Churchill's condition is no longer a mere *malade imaginaire*. 'That she was really ill was certain; he had declared himself convinced of it' (III. i). Now she has decided that she cannot stand the noise of London and is moving to Richmond. 'Mrs. Churchill had been recommended to the medical skill of an eminent person there, and had otherwise a fancy for the place.' We are still in the balance between illness and 'fancy', but one or the other is manoeuvring her adopted son closer and closer to Highbury.

Fancy bested by reality might seem to be the pattern of

Sense and Sensibility. After Willoughby's abrupt departure, Marianne performs the business of suffering, complete with insomnia, headaches and inability to speak (I. xvi). After she is rejected by him in London, however, her affliction becomes real. Austen ensures that her almost fatal illness has its origins in her own self-indulgent folly ('imprudence' is Austen's unhesitating word): Marianne pleases herself with a twilight walk in the grounds of the Palmers' country house, where the grass is 'the longest and wettest', and then sits around in wet shoes and stockings (III. vi). Disappointment in love may have weakened her, but she sets her own sickness in train. Once she is ill Elinor forces 'proper medicines' on her (III. vii), but what might these be? The apothecary is sent for, 'pronouncing her disorder to have a putrid tendency' and 'allowing the word "infection" to pass his lips'. On his second visit he admits 'His medicines had failed', but he is full of confidence in some further treatment or other. This confidence is his business. Mrs Jennings, meanwhile, assumes that the illness will be fatal. Sir John Middleton tells Willoughby in the lobby of the Drury Lane Theatre that Marianne is 'dying' (III. viii). Mrs Dashwood arrives in 'terror', convinced that Marianne is 'no more' (III. ix). Much later Marianne's own self-diagnosis seems to confirm this. 'My illness, I well knew, had been entirely brought on by myself, by such negligence of my own health, as I felt even at the time to be wrong. Had I died,—it would have been self-destruction' (III. x).

In recent decades, critics and readers have been willing to find Marianne a victim rather than a culprit. Perhaps the most influential has been Tony Tanner, whose introduction to the Penguin Classics edition of *Sense and Sensibility* scintillatingly invokes Freud and Foucault to argue that socialisation makes Marianne ill. She suffers from 'neurosis brought on by repression'. Illness is the price she pays for bending her nature to society: 'sickness is precisely the cost of her entry into the sedate stabilities of civilised life envisaged at the end'.[1] The problem with this argument is that it is Marianne's proud sensibility, rather than her eventual socialisation, that makes her susceptible. Marianne's sickness begins with being 'hysterical'. Even after her recovery, her susceptibility remains, producing her 'hysterics' when a servant announces that 'Mr. Ferrars is married' (III. xi). 'Hysterics' might not have the pejorative force that it now has, but the other Austen characters with whom it is associated are models of self-indulgence. In *Persuasion* Mary Musgrove has to be kept from 'hysterics' when her son breaks his collarbone (I. vii). Finding excuses to go out in the evening, she brandishes her 'hysterical' symptoms as an excuse for not looking after her son: 'I am not at all equal to it. You saw how hysterical I was yesterday.' When Louisa Musgrove has her accident, Mary suffers from 'hysterical agitations' (I. xii) and continues to be 'hysterical' the next day (II. i).

Austen's characters live with the expectation of illness.

Marianne's fellow hysterics are a dubious crew. 'My mother was in hysterics,' Jane Bennet tells Elizabeth on the confirmation of Lydia's elopement (II. v). Mrs Bennet subsequently embarks on an enumeration of her symptoms: 'such tremblings, such flutterings, all over me, such spasms in my side, and pains in my head, and such beatings at heart, that I can get no rest by night or by day' (III. v). In *Sense and Sensibility* Marianne seems to share her susceptibility with the appalling Fanny Dashwood, who falls into what Mrs Jennings calls 'violent hysterics' when she hears of Edward's engagement to Lucy Steele (III. i). Mrs Jennings returns from one of her daily visits to her daughter Charlotte, who has recently given birth to her first child, and brings the report, which she has had from the doctor, Mr Donavan, attending her daughter. He has been called to see Mrs John Dashwood, and readily gossips with Mrs Jennings about his other patient's condition. Mr Donavan, opportunist attendant of family disappointment, has, says Mrs Jennings, returned to the Dashwood residence in Harley Street so that 'he may be within call' when Mrs Ferrars is told the news – 'for your sister was sure *she* would be in hysterics too'. A wonderful little comic subplot: what does the doctor say to his medical friends? 'What! Is Fanny ill?' asks Elinor (III. i). One hardly knows the answer.

Austen's characters live with the expectation of illness. In *Persuasion*, when Anne is in a stir of emotions after reading the letter to her from Captain Wentworth, everybody assumes that she must be ill. Comically, Mrs Musgrove first wishes that her servant Sarah – evidently the illness specialist – were available, and then, really thinking of her own daughter, tries to assure herself that this is not another case of a fall (II. xi). Yet there really is such a thing as illness, which we suddenly remember when we hear Lady Denham in *Sanditon* opine, 'It would be only encouraging our Servants and the Poor to fancy themselves ill, if there was a Doctor at hand' (Ch. 6). Failure to understand the seriousness of an illness is a special quality of the foolish or ill-judging. So, as her son Tom's fever goes, Lady Bertram thinks her son out of danger. Edmund and his father, however, note some new 'hectic symptoms' and, advised by the physician, fear for Tom's lungs. Tom Bertram has been brought near death (and into penitence) by an illness that is entirely self-inflicted. He has gone from London to Newmarket (for the races and gambling), 'where a neglected fall, and a good deal of drinking, had brought on a fever' (*Mansfield Park*, III. xiii). His friends desert him and his 'disorder' becomes worse and worse. It is the proper lesson for a young man who is always talking of some 'particular friend' or other.

Yet the expectation of illness is the reflex of the hypochondriac. In *Emma* Mr Woodhouse sees illness everywhere. 'But poor Mrs. Bates had a bad cold about a month ago' (I. xii). He and his daughter Isabella embark on a contest of judgements from their favoured quacks: Mr Wingfield thinks that there has never been such an autumn for colds; Mr Perry does not call it a 'sickly season'. Isabella's hypochondria comes in useful when Emma wishes to speed Harriet out of Highbury. She has 'a tooth amiss', and so must be sent to London to a dentist. (Jane Austen herself endured a series of unpleasant visits to a fashionable London dentist in 1813: see *Letters*, 87 & 88) 'Mrs. John Knightley was delighted to be of any use; any thing of ill health was a recommendation to her' (III. xvi). Hypochondria makes a person a sure topic of conversation, so that when Emma and Harriet visit Miss Bates she must, on a cold day, make 'anxious enquiries after Mr. Woodhouse's health' (II. i) – rather than envying him his untroubled affluence. He calls himself 'a sad invalid' (II. xiv), but in fact there is no evidence that he is in anything but robust health.

Mr Woodhouse and his eldest daughter are joined by Mary Musgrove, who invites her sister Anne to stay because she already foresees 'that she should not have a day's health all the autumn' (I. v). 'I am so ill I can hardly speak' is the wonderfully self-contradicting complaint of this garrulous hypochondriac (I. v). In her first conversation with Anne she reveals that she has been out to dinner the day before, despite her supposedly delicate condition. Between the two sisters there is something like an acknowledgement of the real cause of Mary's indisposition. 'You know I always cure you when I come,' says Anne. In her wonderfully self-revealing, blithely contradictory letter to Anne in Bath, Mary cannot decide if she is ill ('I am far from well') or just about to be ill ('I dare say I shall catch it'), though all is summed up by the true egomania of self-pity in the final sentence: 'my sore-throats, you know, are always worse than anybody's' (II. vi).

Hypochondriacs have their different ways in Austen. In her final, uncompleted novel *Sanditon* she created a family of hypochondriacs, the Parker siblings. The chief sufferer appears to be Diana Parker, who writes letters that detail the horrors of her 'Spasmodic Bile' (Ch. 5) and lament her incapacity, but who is active to the point of mania. She is the very opposite of what she pretends to be. Meanwhile her portly brother Arthur has joined in the same family business of being ill, but only as a cover for his own indolence and greed. He pretends to be self-denying for the sake of his constitution while industriously brewing himself thick hot chocolate and explaining to Charlotte why he needs plenty of butter on his toast in order to safeguard 'the Coats of the Stomach'. He is but a glutton in not very complete hiding, responsible for one of the great lines in the oeuvre. 'The more Wine I drink (in Moderation) the better I am' (Ch. 10). Diana, meanwhile, is too expert on her ailments to trust any practitioner. 'We have entirely done with the whole Medical Tribe' (Ch. 5). Theirs is what Charlotte calls 'the habit of self-doctoring'.

Medical practitioners do not come in for the anti-medical satire of Sterne or Smollett. The nameless 'surgeon' who is summoned to attend Louisa Musgrove in *Persuasion* is presumed to be competent and authoritative, though he can only predict, not intervene (I. xii). A surgeon is a specialist that only a town would afford. In the opening chapter of *Sanditon*, Mr Heywood is thoroughly amused by the notion that there might be a surgeon living in his village. The novel is kicked into life by Mr Parker's search for 'some medical

Man' to establish at Sanditon, whose presence 'would very materially promote the rise and prosperity of the Place' (Ch. 2). A surgeon is a cut above an apothecary, though not genteel in the eyes of some: in *The Watsons* the wealthy Miss Edwards loves Emma Watson's brother Sam, but Emma's sister Elizabeth assures her that marriage is impossible. 'Her father and mother would never consent to it. Sam is only a Surgeon you know'.[2]

The 'intelligent, gentlemanlike' Mr Perry, the apothecary in *Emma*, is first seen tactfully failing to contradict Mr Woodhouse's absurd opinion that wedding cake is harmful. He agrees that it 'might certainly disagree with many—perhaps with most people, unless taken moderately' (II. ii). Thus the joke about 'all the little Perrys being seen with a slice of Mrs. Weston's wedding-cake in their hands'. Their father is a man who makes his handsome living from bending to the prejudices of his clients. No wonder he is called 'intelligent' (a rare adjective in Austen's lexicon) – the only other men called 'intelligent' by Austen are Mr Allen and Henry Tilney, though Mr Knightley uses the word of Robert Martin. At just the time that *Emma* was published the status of the apothecary was a question of public debate.[3] Physicians and surgeons, with their respective Royal Colleges, did all they could to establish their professional superiority to the apothecaries who were often the first resort of genteel patients, especially outside large towns. Mr Woodhouse says that 'there is not so clever a man any where' (I. xii), and we are inclined to agree. He is certainly profiting handsomely from all these hypochondriacs: 'he is always wanted all round the county'. Naturally, when Emma steps for a moment out of Ford's the draper's shop the first person she sees is 'Mr. Perry walking hastily by' (II. ix). He is always around and always busy.

The plot of *Emma* turns on Mr Perry's increasing affluence,

Frank Churchill blurting out his knowledge of Mr Perry's 'plan of setting up his carriage' (III. v). His charges are clearly large. Miss Bates talks of her niece being so ill that 'we will call in Mr. Perry. The expense shall not be thought of' (II. i). Being poor, Miss Bates is the only character who actually mentions Mr Perry's bills. She thinks that he is 'so liberal' that he might offer not to charge them, but they will insist: 'He has a wife and family to maintain, and is not to be giving away his time.' There seems little danger of this. Miss Bates's little meditation on the propriety of charging and paying fees speaks for the size of those fees. It seems likely that Mr Perry inspires confidence by being expensive. Frank Churchill even tries a joke about the lucrative business of tending to the ailing inhabitants of Highbury, suggesting that if a ball were to be held at the Crown instead of at Randalls there would be less danger of anyone catching a cold. 'Mr. Perry might have reason to regret the alteration, but nobody else could' (II. xi). Mr Woodhouse replies 'rather warmly', deeply offended at the suggestion that his apothecary relishes minor ailments: 'Mr. Perry is extremely concerned when any of us are ill.' Near the end of the novel Mrs Weston speaks of her recent worries about her baby daughter's health, and how she nearly called for Mr Perry. The listening Mr Woodhouse commends her for thinking of Mr Perry and regrets only that she did not call this minister to anxiety. 'She could not be too soon alarmed, nor send for Perry too often' (III. xviii). Mr Perry, charging for each call-out, would be grateful if this became accepted wisdom. What does he imagine that Perry can actually do? For he goes on to say that, though the baby girl does now seem well, 'it would probably have been better if Perry had seen it'. His logic is as incontrovertible as it is nonsensical.

On the crucial evening of Mr Knightley's proposal, Emma is liberated for her walk in the garden by the fact that Mr Perry has 'a disengaged hour to give her father' (III. xiii). Perhaps he has been summoned (the bad weather of the previous day has afflicted Mr Woodhouse); perhaps he simply calls when time is available to him, knowing that he will always find a welcome (and, presumably, a payment for his consultation). Mr Knightley has looked into the dining room, where patient and apothecary are sequestered, and found 'he was not wanted there'. The length of his visit – 'I should like to take another turn. Mr. Perry is not gone' – also provides the pretext for the further circuit of the Hartfield grounds that gives him the opportunity for his declaration. The next day Emma receives a note from Mrs Weston in which she says that she 'felt for your father very much in the storm of Tuesday afternoon', but has been reassured by Mr Perry 'that it had not made him ill'. Mr Perry's visit has been a kind of precautionary measure.

Perhaps it is only in *Persuasion* that we get a picture of illness that is neither imaginary nor self-inflicted. This is the novel in which the flesh is frailest – there is the Musgrove child with his broken collarbone, Captain Harville with his wound, Louisa Musgrove and her head injury – and death is closest. Though Anne's old school friend Mrs Smith has come to Bath, the very oasis of hypochondriacs, there is no doubt that she has been ill. As one critic notes, she is 'the first invalid in Jane Austen's novels whose distresses are indubitably real'.[+] She had been 'afflicted with a severe rheumatic fever, which finally settling in her legs, had made her for the present a cripple' (II. v). The reality check is made sharper when Mrs Smith's account of her friendship with Mrs Rooke, her nurse, prompts Anne to some pious reflections about the virtues to which illness prompts sufferers and those who care for them. 'A sick chamber may furnish the worth of volumes.' Mrs Smith speaks 'more doubtingly', putting Anne right:

sickness reveals the 'weakness' of 'human nature . . . and not its strength'. Mrs Smith even explains how this allows Mrs Rooke to sell her patients the handicraft items that she has made – just at the point where 'they have recently escaped from severe pain, or are recovering the blessing of health'.

There are certainly Austen characters who are made ill by others. When Fanny Price in *Mansfield Park* gets a headache it is because she has been forced into labour by Lady Bertram and Mrs Norris (I. vii). When Jane Fairfax in *Emma* is ailing, it is because of Frank Churchill. 'Jane caught a bad cold, poor thing! So long ago as the 7th of November,' says Miss Bates (we are now well past Christmas) (II. i). 'I am afraid we must expect to see her grown thin, and looking very poorly.' Her niece is indeed suffering. Jane Fairfax is ill as a response to her life's vicissitudes. No wonder the Campbells are sorry for her: 'She had never been quite well since the time of their daughter's marriage' (II. ii). She has the 'slight appearance of ill-health' that makes her seem a little too thin. 'Jane caught no cold last night,' announces Miss Bates to Emma, as if this were in itself a lucky achievement. Jane Fairfax's illnesses are further evidence of the true state of her affections – and her relationship with Frank Churchill. No sooner does he leave Highbury, summoned by Mrs Churchill, than we hear that she has been 'Particularly unwell . . . suffering from headache' (II. xii). Miss Bates says that, had there been a ball at the Crown, her niece would have been too ill to attend, but we should know that this is not true, for if Frank Churchill had stayed in Highbury there would have been no illness. When Emma visits the Bates home after the Box Hill outing, she overhears Miss Bates saying 'I shall *say* you are laid down upon the bed, and I am sure you are ill enough' (III. viii).

With Frank Churchill absent, Jane Fairfax becomes so afflicted that Mr Perry is sent for. 'Her health seemed for the moment completely deranged . . . Mr. Perry was uneasy about her' (III. ix). He has nothing to offer, beyond the sensible suggestion that 'Her spirits seemed overcome'. When Frank Churchill returns from Richmond after his stepmother's death, he has to face the depth of Jane Fairfax's affliction, 'the shock of finding her so very unwell' (III. x). Emma's diagnosis is brusque and pointed: 'Jane, whose troubles and whose ill health having, of course, the same origin must be equally under cure' (III. xi). Mrs Elton seems to come to a similar conclusion. '"Do not you think her cure does Perry the highest credit?"—(here was a side-glance of great meaning at Jane' (III. xvi). 'Is not she looking well?' Frank Churchill asks Emma in the penultimate chapter. It is the last adjective any one would think of using of Jane Fairfax earlier in the novel. Yet now, with marriage assured, health is restored to her. It is a blessed illusion for those, like some modern readers, who think that ill health is usually in the imagination. Austen liked to amuse her family with accounts of what would happen to her leading characters after the endings of the novels in which they had featured. Jane Fairfax, she told them, would enjoy but nine or ten years of marital felicity before she died.[5] It seems that her husband-to-be was in fact detecting a mortal frailty when he found that deceptive way of talking about her looks.

SEVENTEEN

What Makes Characters Blush?

'No, read it yourself,' cried Catherine, whose second
thoughts were clearer. 'I do not know what I was thinking
of' (blushing again that she had blushed before) . . .

Northanger Abbey, II. x

In Austen's novels, a person can be made to blush by someone
else's failure to do so. In *Sense and Sensibility*, Elinor Dashwood
is engaged in confidential conversation with Lucy Steele
about the latter's secret engagement to Edward Ferrars and
is endeavouring to conceal her own feelings. The suspicious
Lucy is testing those feelings: she so values Elinor's judgement, she says, that if Miss Dashwood were to advise her to
give up her engagement, she would do so 'immediately' (II. ii).
'Elinor blushed for the insincerity of Edward's future wife.'
Elinor can keep from betraying her own love for Edward,
but not from exhibiting a kind of vicarious shame at Lucy's
shameless attempts to trick her into self-betrayal. *Blushing for*
someone else is usually just a figure of speech, meaning little
more than disapproving of them. 'I blush for you, Tom,' says
Sir Thomas Bertram in *Mansfield Park*, admonishing his elder
son for gambling debts that will deprive his brother of his

'living' (I. iii). He uses the phrase twice, but it cannot literally be true, given the massive dignity of his address. Elinor
Dashwood, however, does physically experience this almost
embarrassed response to her companion's dishonesty. It is
a sign that, in this novel of secrets, she cannot keep unex-
pressed her consciousness of what is really going on. The
blush is more evidence of Elinor's struggle to remain self-
possessed – a struggle so invisible to her own sister.

Austen requires her reader to be an interpreter of blushes.
For a novelist so reticent about describing her characters'
features and facial expressions, blushing is extraordinarily
important. If there is one form of expression that is missing from all those dramatisations of Austen's novels it is the
blush. Weeping is easy for any accomplished performer, but
the Austen blush – that most truly involuntary signal of feeling – is almost impossible. Young women had been dependably
blushing in novels for decades before Austen began writing:
it was a proper sign of modesty and sensibility. In Austen's
novels, however, the blush becomes a challenge to the intui-
tion of other characters, and often the reader too. When,
like Elinor, one character blushes for another, it is usually a
sign of displeasing insight. In *Northanger Abbey*, Catherine
suggests to Henry Tilney that his brother Frederick should
cease his 'attentions' to Isabella, who is supposedly engaged
to Catherine's brother James (II. iv). Henry Tilney counters
that the problem is Isabella's 'admission' of these attentions
and it is a palpable hit: 'Catherine blushed for her friend.'
Isabella is not exactly unblushing herself, but her blushes
are beyond Catherine's understanding. She encourages
Catherine to imagine teasing her that she and James Morland
were 'born for each other': 'my cheeks would have been as
red as your roses' (I. x). But the provocation and the maid-
enly response are both imaginary. When Isabella does blush

it is from a more deceitful intent. Catherine looks forward to their being 'sisters' (on Isabella's planned marriage to James) and Isabella replies '(with a blush)' that 'there are more ways than one of our being sisters' (II. iii). She is thinking of her nascent romance with Frederick Tilney. That blush is there to tell us of her fickleness, but also of Catherine's lack of comprehension.

Catherine's eventual blush for her friend is a rush of understanding. Elizabeth Bennet's blushes for her mother in *Pride and Prejudice* are, we imagine, not the first. Elizabeth literally blushes for her mother when she rudely and stupidly disputes Darcy's observations about the 'unvarying society' of country life (I. ix). Mrs Bennet is so embarrassing because she is immune to embarrassment. Later, at the Netherfield ball, her loud indiscretions bring the blood to Elizabeth's cheeks again. 'Elizabeth blushed and blushed again with shame and vexation' (I. xix). Blushing bespeaks a social awareness that others lack. When Wickham and Lydia arrive unblushingly at Longbourn after their wedding, Elizabeth and Jane do their blushing for them. '*She* blushed, and Jane blushed; but the cheeks of the two who caused their confusion, suffered no variation of colour' (III. ix). We and Elizabeth know that her friend Charlotte remains the clear-eyed person that ever she was from the 'faint blush' that occasionally appears as she listens to her husband, Mr Collins (II. v). He says things of which she is 'ashamed' precisely because he is not. Elizabeth has to watch her face because the newly married Mrs Collins must keep her true thoughts about her husband to herself.

In his brilliantly single-minded analysis of blushing in the writings of John Keats, Christopher Ricks hazards the thought that the blush is of peculiar interest to writers of the Romantic Age. Citing Charles Darwin's idea that blushing is a consequence of human 'self-attention', he argues that, for the Romantics, 'self-attention had become the supreme subject and animus for the artist'.[1] Blushing now deserved 'serious, wide, and deep scrutiny'. Austen, writing at just the same time as Keats, expects her reader to exercise this scrutiny, for the reasons for blushing can be complex indeed. In *Persuasion*, Lady Russell pretends not to have seen Captain Wentworth in the street in Bath and Anne notices her pretence. 'Anne sighed and blushed and smiled, in pity and disdain, either at her friend or herself' (II. vii). Anne's self-attention is dramatised by the way the sentence stumbles through these different responses and explanations. Such is her confusion of feelings by this stage of the novel that the reason for the blush is almost buried. She blushes in vicarious shame at Lady Russell's evasive dishonesty, but perhaps also, she thinks, at her own eager perceptiveness, sharpened by her hopes for Captain Wentworth's affections. Anne has begun to learn the importance of blushing. Earlier in the novel, she had thought herself beyond a blush. When Mrs Croft refers to the fact that Anne is 'acquainted with' her brother, she is 'electrified' – the only time that Austen ever uses this word. (The OED records the earliest use of 'electrified' to mean 'very excited' or 'thrilled' in 1801: an unusual word is needed for the strong surprise of Anne's response.) Yet concealment of this response is apparently possible. 'Anne hoped that she had outlived the age of blushing; but the age of emotion she certainly had not' (I.vi). Blushing is for a young woman.

Yet she has not truly outlived blushing: this is just another of her virtuous self-delusions. In the aftermath of Louisa Musgrove's fall, Captain Wentworth breaks through his reserve and appeals for her help 'with a glow, and yet a gentleness, which seemed almost restoring the past' (I. xii). 'She coloured deeply.' She is all too ready to blush. When she is first introduced to Mr Elliot, conscious as he must be of the

looks that passed between them at Lyme, we find her 'blushing and smiling' (II. ii). Lady Russell hints at his 'possible
attachment' and 'the desirableness of the alliance': Anne 'only
smiled, blushed, and gently shook her head' (II. v). Blushing
is the sign of her reanimation. In fact, she becomes a great
blusher. When Captain Wentworth converses with her before
the concert in Bath, we find him halting in his talk of Louisa
Musgrove's engagement with 'some taste of that emotion
which was reddening Anne's cheeks' (II. viii). Now that she
has hope again, the thought of Captain Wentworth's past flirtation excites her self-consciousness. When they get on to the
topic of Lyme she declares her 'very agreeable' impressions
of the place – 'with a faint blush at some recollections'. It
was at Lyme that Captain Wentworth began to turn to her
again. The reader is left to infer the 'emotion' and the 'recollections' that bring the blood to Anne's cheeks. The next day
she visits Mrs Smith, who suggests that Anne has been in
the company of 'the person who interests you at this present
time, more than all the rest of the world put together' (II. ix).
'A blush overspread Anne's cheeks.' Mrs Smith is thinking of
Mr Elliot, so Anne starts to put her right, before she stops,
'regretting with a deep blush that she had implied so much'.
At which Mrs Smith instantly grasps the truth. Blushing
cannot lie.

One of the few critics who has written on blushing in
Austen's fiction describes a blush as 'a truth yielded against
one's well-behaved will'.[2] Yet the truth that a blush yields
is not always what an observer presumes. Jane Austen
uses blushing to alert us not just to the secret feelings that
possess her characters, but also to the habits of misinterpre-
tation that secrecy engenders. When Mrs Jennings, watching Colonel Brandon talking quietly to Elinor Dashwood in
the window of her London drawing room, sees that 'Elinor

changed colour' at something he says, she imagines that she is witnessing a proposal (*Sense and Sensibility*, III. iii). In fact, he is offering to provide a living for Edward Ferrars so that he will be able to marry Lucy Steele, and Elinor's colouring registers her feelings on being asked to convey the news to him. She is to be the one to tell the man she loves that he will have enough money to marry another woman. Mrs Jennings is observant enough to notice the stir of emotions in Elinor's face, but wholly mistakes them. Similarly in *Emma* the heroine recognises signs that she blithely misreads. At the party at the Coles, Emma is watching Jane Fairfax when the subject of the piano is mentioned and she sees Jane Fairfax's 'blush of consciousness', followed by the 'blush of guilt' when she mentions Colonel Campbell (II. viii). The next day Emma visits the Bateses, where Jane plays the piano while Frank Churchill makes veiled jokes about Weymouth. Emma notes Jane's 'deep blush of consciousness', along with 'a smile of secret delight' (II. x). 'This amiable, upright, perfect Jane Fairfax was apparently cherishing very reprehensible feelings.' For Emma, these blushes are evidence that Jane Fairfax has an illicit admirer in Mr Dixon; the reader will be able to interpret them better.

Mansfield Park has the most blushful of Austen's heroines, not just because Fanny is a modest and sensitive soul, but also because she is governed by feelings at which no one must guess.[3] People think they understand Fanny Price, but no one does. At the opening of Chapter iii of *Mansfield Park*, we find that some five years have passed since the end of the previous chapter, Fanny is 'about fifteen' and Mr Norris has died. Edmund is recommending to the reluctant Fanny her new residence, as he imagines, with Mrs Norris, telling her that she has 'good sense, and a sweet temper, and I am sure you have a grateful heart'. '"You are too kind," said Fanny, colouring at such praise.' This is our first sign of a new kind of attachment, a sign that is the more important for being unnoticed, or at least uninterpreted, by Edmund. She blushes in acknowledgement that she is no longer a child. When the returning Sir Thomas compliments her on her appearance he raises 'a fine blush' (II. i). It is Henry Crawford, that connoisseur of female desires, who notices her 'soft skin . . . so frequently tinged with a blush' (II. vi). Her blushes alert him to her sexual attractiveness.

Fanny also blushes because she is good. She 'colours' in righteousness in response to some of the Crawfords' thoughtless jests: when she contradicts Mary Crawford's opinion of men's perfunctory letters (I. vi), or listens to her views on the inferiority of parsons (I. ix), or when Henry Crawford talks disparagingly of Mr Rushworth (II. v). The Crawfords should be able to interpret these responses, but often only the reader can know what brings the colour to her cheeks. When Edmund talks to Fanny about his feelings for Mary Crawford, she asks him not to confide in her. 'The time may come—' she says, thinking of the possibility of their marriage, and breaking off (II. ix). 'The colour rushed into her cheeks as she spoke.' Edmund presses her hand to his lips, utterly failing to understand her response. He thinks she is being delicate: she does not want to hear any of his private reservations about a woman who might end up as his wife. In fact her rush of blood tells us of her pained consciousness that her own love for him is doomed — and that he is entirely oblivious of it. Later, when Edmund says that she will surely learn to love Henry Crawford, Fanny exclaims 'Oh! never, never, never; he will never succeed with me' (III. iv). She speaks with a warmth that surprises the unsuspecting Edmund, and when she sees this 'she blushed at the recollection of herself'.

Sometimes indignation and secret pain combine. When Sir Thomas addresses her on the subject of Crawford's proposal, he notices her 'colour rising' and has to suppress a smile, for he imagines that this is her acknowledgement of pleasure (III. i). Bemused by her rejection of the proposal, he begins to wonder if her affections are engaged elsewhere. He does not finish the thought, and she does not reply: 'her face was like scarlet'. Sir Thomas chooses to take this deepest of blushes as a sign of her innocence, though he has just come as close as any character ever does to divining the truth. It is a truth that clever Mary Crawford, interpreting every blush wrongly, keeps missing. When she tricks Fanny into choosing to borrow a necklace that was her brother's gift, she then teases her about suspecting 'a confederacy between us' (II. viii). Fanny protests against the thought 'with the deepest blushes', allowing Miss Crawford to infer that she does truly relish her brother's attentions. She is wrong, but why then are Fanny's blushes so deep? Because she does think that Henry Crawford is up to something, but also because she is having to acknowledge her own sexual allure. At the ball, Mary blunders by busily 'misinterpreting Fanny's blushes' when she talks of her brother, supposing that she is 'giving her heart a little flutter' rather than merely embarrassing her (II. x). In the wake of Fanny's rejection of Henry Crawford's proposal, Mary Crawford wonders playfully at her apparent 'indifference' and asks whether 'you are so insensible as you profess yourself' (III. v). 'There was indeed so deep a blush over Fanny's face at that moment, as might warrant strong suspicion in a pre-disposed mind.' Fanny blushes because she is a virtuous girl who finds all this talk of love mortifying – but also because love does govern her every thought. She is not in the least 'insensible', though Mary Crawford is simply deluded to take her embarrassment as betokening some unconfessed liking for her brother.

After all the decades of young ladies blushing virtuously in novels, Austen has realised that the blush might interestingly mix ingenuousness with something close to guilt. Marianne Dashwood in *Sense and Sensibility* blushes when teased about Willoughby by Mrs Jennings and Sir John Middleton (I. xviii). Edward is present and she cannot disguise her self-consciousness in front of him. Yet her vaunted lack of disguise is also a kind of pride. She blushes again when Edward expresses surprise that she contemplates keeping horses for hunting. She is thinking of being married to Willoughby and is hardly hiding the fact (I. xvii). She 'colours' when Mrs Jennings jokes about her trip to Allenham with Willoughby to look at his aunt's house. Elinor subsequently admonishes Marianne for 'going all over it' in its owner's absence (I. xiii). Marianne refuses to concede that she has acted wrongly, until Elinor mentions the possibility that the house and grounds might one day be hers. 'She blushed at this hint; but it was even visibly gratifying . . .' The blush comes not from shame but from an acknowledgement of her desires. Indeed, having agreed that her visit to the house was 'rather ill-judged' she proceeds to prattle about all its delightful rooms. A good reader of blushes is being shown the fallacy of Marianne's code of openness.

The blush, in other words, is a challenge to the reader's insight.

The most innocent blusher in Austen's fiction is Catherine Morland. She hardly knows how to blush aright. When she sees Mr Tilney approaching at the dance in the Octagon Room, she acts naturally rather than affectedly, and so has 'cheeks only a little redder than usual' (I. viii). Naturally she blushes when she finds herself watched while dancing by 'a gentleman', who then whispers something to Henry Tilney (I. x). But this is something wholly different from the self-consciousness of an Isabella Thorpe. Catherine blushes because she thinks the man's notice must have been attracted by 'something wrong in her appearance'. She blushes when Henry Tilney compliments her for her 'good-nature' though she has not understood what he has said about her charitable interpretation of Frederick Tilney's motives (II. i). Her blushing is wonderfully uncertain. She blushes when General Tilney suggests that she share his son's curricle, because she remembers Mr Allen saying that it might not be right for a girl to be alone in such a vehicle with a young man (II. v). But then she decides that General Tilney cannot be recommending something wrong. There is also her 'blush of mortification' when the Tilneys' servant tells her that Miss Tilney is out, 'with a look which did not quite confirm his words' (I. xii). She is entirely innocent of the affront that has led Miss Tilney to avoid her. However, innocence finally becomes chastened self-deception. First there is the 'blush of surprize' when, fired by Gothic fantasy, she opens the mysterious chest in her room, only to find a bedspread (II. vi). Then there is a more painful consciousness when, investigating Mrs Tilney's room, she excites Henry's perplexity by her foolish questions: she 'blushed deeply' (II. ix). Blushing is her intelligent awareness of her folly.

The other modest girl who blushes a good deal is Harriet Smith. She is one of the reasons that *Emma* has more blushes any other Austen novel. Her first blush is when she recalls Mrs Martin talking of how good a husband her son would make (I. iv), but thereafter her blushes are responses to Emma's manipulative suggestions about her charms. She blushes on having Mr Elton's compliments repeated to her by Emma (I. iv); she blushes when she sits before Mr Elton to have her portrait done (I. vi). When Emma asks her if Mr Martin is really the 'most agreeable' man with whom she has ever been in company, our heroine seems almost to require her to blush: 'You blush, Harriet.—Does any body else occur to you at this moment under such a definition?' (I. vii) This is the only time in Austen's novels when one character tells another that he or she is blushing. The observation would usually be unacceptable because it can only deepen the other person's blushes. Emma sees evidence of dawning 'love'; we can see evidence of Emma's coercion. 'The blush . . . in Austen's writing can be both a transparent indicator of a character's feelings, and an agent of misdirection', writes Katie Halsey in the best analysis of blushing in her novels.[4] The blush, in other words, is a challenge to the reader's insight. Emma's confidence about Harriet's blushes is blushingly confirmed by Harriet, who supposes that Emma alone might have guessed at the relationship between Jane Fairfax and Frank Churchill – 'You (blushing as she spoke) who can see into every body's heart' (III. xi). It is a complex dramatic irony, for a discerning reader knows that Harriet blushes at the thought that Emma knows of her feelings for Mr Knightley. Emma knows nothing of the kind, suggesting that she might have cared for Frank Churchill. Harriet cries out in surprise, 'colouring'. This is a pained response and very different from the Harriet Smith blush. Soon, to Emma's consternation, this is apparent. Emma has to listen to Harriet's account of Mr Knightley talking to her 'in a more particular way than he had ever done before, in a very particular way indeed!—(Harriet could not recall it without a blush)'. She blushes with just the pleased consciousness that Emma has taught her.

It takes a good deal to make Emma blush, though she thinks of herself as a connoisseur of blushing. When she considers her sister Isabella's marriage she reflects that 'She had given them neither men, nor manners, nor places, that could raise a blush' (III. vi). It is one of Emma's little phrases, used when she tells Harriet that her supposedly forthcoming marriage to Mr Elton is 'an alliance which can never raise a blush in either of us' (I. ix). Emma would like blushing to be a matter of social pride – you blush at some stooping from your proper status. As she hears Harriet recalling her cutting a 'plaister' for Mr Elton, and admits to her own supposedly cunning untruths, she says, 'I deserve to be under a continual blush all the rest of my life' (III. iv). She must be made to blush for deeper feelings than this and indeed finds herself having to blush a good deal in the last chapters of the novel. She blushes when admonished by Mr Knightley for her cruelty to Miss Bates (III. vii). When she finds out from Mrs Weston about the Churchill–Fairfax engagement, she is made sensitive to her own past folly in a way that Mrs Weston does not perceive: 'Emma could not speak the name of Dixon without a little blush' (III. x). When she thinks of her coldness towards Jane Fairfax, 'she blushed for the envious feelings which had certainly been, in some measure, the cause' (III. xii). This is having listened to Mrs Weston's account of the engagement and the blushing is an entirely private, we might say internal, experience. She experiences 'a blush of sensibility on Harriet's account' when Mr Knightley asks her for her agreement in his recommendation of 'truth and sincerity in all our dealings with each other' (III. xv). She has accepted the need for sincerity, yet cannot give 'any sincere explanation' of that blush. Mr Knightley cannot be told that she blushes to think of Harriet's feelings for him. Emma blushes when she is rendered helpless. After they have become engaged Mr Knightley begins to talk to her of Harriet Smith. 'Her cheeks flushed at the name, and she felt afraid of something, though she knew not what' (III. xviii). What *is* she afraid of? Presumably of Mr Knightley having somehow divined her earlier belief that he might love Harriet Smith. He takes her blush to come from her knowledge of Harriet's engagement to Robert Martin. That flushing is her consciousness of her own past delusion, and of her misconception about Mr Knightley's feelings that has led to her own happiness. Now she is a blusher and he is the misinterpreter.

What about men? We register the reanimated attraction, as well as the awkwardness, when Elizabeth and Darcy encounter each other unexpectedly at Pemberley. 'Their eyes instantly met, and the cheeks of each were overspread with the deepest blush' (III. i). This mutual blush is powerful and unusual in Austen's novels. Elsewhere men do not blush, they 'colour'. In *Sense and Sensibility* Mrs Dashwood hopes that Willoughby will soon be back from London. 'He coloured as he replied . . .' (I. xv). This is guilt that what he is about to say – he has no plans to return – is entirely at odds with his behaviour towards Marianne. When Mrs Dashwood tells him that he is welcome to stay with them, 'His colour increased'. Edward Ferrars (who has just been on a secret visit to Lucy Steele) responds similarly when Marianne accuses him of being 'reserved'. '"I do not understand you," replied he, colouring. "Reserved!—how, in what manner? What am I to tell you? What can you suppose?"' (I. xvii). In this secret-filled novel, 'colouring' is the acknowledgement of secrecy. Thus Edward's reaction when Marianne asks him about the ring with a plait of hair that he is wearing. 'He coloured very deeply, and giving a momentary glance at Elinor, replied, "Yes; it is my sister's hair. The setting always casts a different shade on it, you know"' (I. xviii). It is a lie, but Elinor misinterprets his blush, assuming that the hair is her own.

Men turn red (or white) but are not usually said to blush. When Wickham and Darcy first spot each other, in the company of the Bennet girls, 'Both changed colour, one looked white, the other red' (I. xv). Which is which? We infer, I think, that Darcy turns white (righteous indignation) and Wickham turns red (embarrassment, guilt). When Elizabeth rejects his proposal, Mr Darcy turns 'pale with anger' (II. xi). When she goes on to speak of his injustice to Wickham, she and we see his 'heightened colour'. This is anger, but even love does not make men exactly blush. When Captain Wentworth in *Persuasion* encounters Anne in a shop in Bath, he is 'struck and confused'; 'he looked quite red' (II. vii). Mr Knightley turns 'red with surprise and displeasure' when Emma complacently tells him that Harriet Smith has refused Robert Martin (I. viii). He suffers a rather different rush of blood when she suggests that his admiration for Jane Fairfax may some day take him 'by surprise' (II. xv). 'Mr. Knightley was hard at work upon the lower buttons of his thick leather gaiters, and either the exertion of getting them together, or some other cause, brought the colour into his face, as he answered.' Only a narrative so much told from one character's point of view can manage to be uncertain in this way. His colouring, of course, is because his admiration for Emma is taking him by surprise.

That shared blush in *Pride and Prejudice* is the surest possible sign of mutual love: her blush has spread to him. But Elizabeth goes on blushing after the encounter. 'She blushed again and again over the perverseness of the meeting' (III. i). Blushing is the means by which Austen registers Elizabeth's unadmitted feelings. Elizabeth wishes that she and the Gardiners had left ten minutes sooner – not so that she would have avoided meeting him, but so that she would have avoided the pressure of these feelings. Here the blush is our measure of the inwardness of the character. Elizabeth blushes at thoughts to which only the reader has access. Earlier she colours when Colonel Fitzwilliam says something about not having enough money to marry, but she is blushing at her own speculation, wondering for a second if he is courting her (II. x). In a laboured exchange about what might be called an 'easy distance' between two places, she blushes at Mr Darcy's apparent reference to the distance between Longbourn and Netherfield, as if he has caught her thinking about Jane's relationship with Bingley (II. ix). In fact Mr Darcy is on the brink of his marriage proposal and must be thinking, with 'a sort of a smile', of how far his home is from the Bennets'. Elizabeth does not understand him, while he cannot possibly interpret her blush correctly. He must presume it to be a sign of her pleased consciousness of his attentions, for he draws his chair 'a little towards her'. That blush is what she feels, not what he sees. The reader inhabits Elizabeth's mind through her blushes. When she enters the house after the walk on which Mr Darcy has proposed to her a second time, Jane asks her where she has been and Elizabeth says that 'they had wandered about, till she was beyond her own knowledge' (III. xvii). 'She coloured as she spoke', but apparently without awakening suspicion. That colouring is felt rather than observed, the self-consciousness of a character with whom we share a secret. It appears to be description from the outside, but in fact it is entirely a description from the inside. No one notices but Elizabeth herself.

This is the most complex kind of embarrassment, when one of Austen's heroines blushes at what she suddenly knows about her own feelings or her own behaviour. When Mrs Weston breaks the news of Jane Fairfax's engagement to Frank Churchill, Emma asks whether it was secret even from the Campbells and the Dixons. She blushes at her worse-than-folly in supposing that Jane Fairfax was conducting some kind of love affair with Mr Dixon, though Mrs Weston has known nothing of this bizarre hypothesis. This is blushing as self-consciousness, something experienced rather than observed. At the end of the third chapter of *Persuasion*, we find that Anne must walk outside to cool her 'flushed cheeks' because Captain Wentworth's name has been mentioned – but no one else has known or noticed. A little blush in *Northanger Abbey* epitomises Austen's use of blushing to let us glimpse an inner world. Catherine is worrying about Mr Tilney being too aware of Mrs Allen's folly as he talks with her, and just at this moment he asks her what she is thinking about. 'Catherine coloured . . .' (I. iii). The knowing young man has caught her – and us – in the midst of her unflattering thoughts. Blushing is the most intense experience of self-consciousness, but only the reader – the attentive reader – can know this.

EIGHTEEN

What Are the Right and Wrong Ways to Propose Marriage?

Having resolved to do it without loss of time, as his leave of absence extended only to the following Saturday, and having no feelings of diffidence to make it distressing to himself even at the moment, he set about it in a very orderly manner, with all the observances, which he supposed a regular part of the business.

Pride and Prejudice, I. xix

A reader of Jane Austen's fiction might think that the worst way to propose marriage is by letter. The plot of *Emma* relies entirely on Robert Martin's decision to ask Harriet Smith to marry him in writing. This gives the weak-minded Harriet the opportunity to go to Emma for advice about how to answer. Although Robert Martin has arrived at Mrs Goddard's, where Harriet lives, in person, the fact that he has the letter in a package with him suggests that he always intended to propose in this way. Why? Lack of genteel confidence? A sense of delicacy, perhaps: even the prejudiced Emma detects 'delicacy of feeling' in the letter itself (I. vii). He would surely know that Harriet in person would be persuadable. It is as if he wishes, by proposing in a letter, to give her some power to make her own decision. It is an honourable but a sad misjudgement. Emma herself, as she examines Harriet's reactions and schemes to get her to reject the proposal, silently acknowledges that, had Robert Martin 'come in her way' in person, he would surely have been accepted. Mr Knightley, we later find, had expected him to 'speak' to Harriet (I. viii). He has decided to write instead, and so Emma is given her chance to meddle and the whole narrative machinery is set in motion.

By the standards of the day, Robert Martin was not wrong to write. In the eighteenth century it had become conventional to propose in this way, and letter-writing manuals even provided templates for doing so.[1] In a culture that placed a premium on the penning of a well-turned letter, a young man with Robert Martin's self-improving bent would have been very likely to have read one or other of the many guides to letter-writing – usually called 'secretaries' or 'letter-writers' – that were widely available.[2] Perhaps he had digested David Fordyce's *The New and Complete British Letter-Writer* of 1800, which included model letters from 'a young Tradesman, proposing Marriage to a Lady in the Neighbourhood' and another from 'a Gentleman to a young Lady without Fortune', offering her his hand.[3] All the evidence is that epistolary proposals of marriage were entirely proper. Sir Edward Knatchbull proposed successfully to Jane Austen's favourite niece Fanny Knight by letter in 1820.[4] But Robert Martin was wrong to use this method if he hoped to achieve the desired answer. Edmund Bertram in *Mansfield Park* sees the problem clearly enough when he wonders, in a letter to Fanny, how he might propose to Mary Crawford. 'I believe I shall write to her. I have nearly determined on explaining myself by letter' (III. xiii). A letter will enable him to conquer his uncertainties and express himself as he should. Yet he hums and haws and frets. 'A letter exposes to all the evil of consultation.' A letter can be shown around. There is always her friend Mrs Fraser – surely his enemy. 'I must think this matter over a little.' He sees the risks of a letter, though he does not see that he is blunderingly causing Fanny pain by drawing her in to his ruminations.

Edmund's scheme for proposing by letter suggests that something is wrong. Can he not imagine simply speaking to Mary Crawford of his affections? A proposal in person needs an occasion, but a man has the power to find this. For a woman it is not so straightforward. Probably Charlotte Lucas need not have worried about having to give Mr Collins the right chance to declare himself, but, knowing that he is on the point of returning from Hertfordshire to Kent, she is determined to take no risks. She makes it easy for him. 'Miss Lucas perceived him from an upper window as he walked towards the house, and instantly set out to meet him accidentally in the lane' (I. xii). She has been at that window keeping watch. Her contrivance of that accident will be a fair epitome of their relationship, with Mr Collins imagining that he is shaping events when in fact he is being manipulated by her. Yet even for a man, arranging to be on your own with the object of your attentions is not always easy. Seeking to propose to Emma, Mr Elton avails himself of a 'precious opportunity', a phrase that must echo the pattern of his own eager thinking (I. xv). After a bibulous Christmas Eve dinner at the Westons', he manages to get in the coach with her. It is his heaven-sent chance. The comedy of the episode is in our sudden recognition of what it must be like from his point of view, always having the idiotic Harriet in Emma's company and in his way. Harriet has been removed by a heavy cold, for which he must be thanking his stars, and now he has the woman he really wants on her own.

Timing is all. 'Every thing that I have said or done, for many weeks past, has been with the sole view of marking my adoration of yourself,' declares Mr Elton. How many weeks? At least the twelve weeks or so since the beginning of the novel. But he arrived in Highbury 'a whole year' earlier, and has presumably been manoeuvring towards this declaration in the coach for much of that time (I. i). Austen's novels tease us to wonder how long you should know each other before a man can propose with hope of acceptance. Charlotte Lucas's notorious advice in *Pride and Prejudice* is to be as speedy as possible. In order to fix Mr Bingley's intentions, she tells Elizabeth, Jane Bennet 'should . . . make the most of every half-hour in which she can command his attention. When she is secure of him, there will be more leisure for falling in love as much as she chooses' (I.vi). A lengthy courtship has no advantages: 'it is better to know as little as possible of the defects of the person with whom you are to pass your life'. The shortest courtship imaginable is indeed Mr Collins's of Charlotte, lasting as it does from dinner-time to night-time of a single day, all of it spent in the voluble company of others. For Austen's heroines, it is Henry Tilney's courtship of Catherine Morland that is shortest, and this in a novel which is full of haste – from the progress of Catherine and Isabella's friendship, through John Thorpe's boasts about the speed of his travel, to Colonel Tilney's constant impatience and hurry (*Northanger Abbey* has more precise times of day than any other Austen novel). The shortest of Austen's novels, its love story is also the most rapid. The time between Catherine Morland's arrival in Bath and her departure from Northanger Abbey is only eleven weeks. It is a brief acquaintance on which to base a married life together. Very brief, in fact, as during those eleven weeks Henry Tilney has spent some time away at his parish, leaving Catherine at Northanger Abbey with his sister. The novelist, having elicited such a speedy proposal from Henry Tilney, at least provides some reassurance by telling us that he and Catherine in fact marry 'within a twelvemonth' of their first meeting – not much less than the year allowed Elizabeth Bennet and Mr Darcy between their first encounter and their nuptials.

When Captain Wentworth first proposed to Anne Elliot, they had known each other 'a few months', and a good deal less than the half a year during which he stays with his brother (I. iv). Eight years later, it is something over four months from their meeting again to Captain Wentworth's proposal. It is quite clear that that earlier knowledge of each other was, and is, good grounds for their future happiness. Reaching a proposal is more problematic in the two cases where Austen's heroines have known their husbands-to-be for a very long time. Emma has been familiar with Mr Knightley all her life; Fanny Price has lived in the same house as her cousin Edmund for eight years, though for long periods he has been away at school or university. In one way, this simply reflects the reality of Jane Austen's rural society. Marriages were frequently contracted between individuals who had known each other as neighbours for years and it was common for cousins to marry each other. (Jane Austen's brother Henry married their widowed cousin Eliza.) But the pairings achieved for the heroines of *Mansfield Park* and *Emma* test our belief. Edmund has been blind to Fanny's passion for him for years, so how can he be turned from her sympathetic cousin to her suitor? Mr Knightley has been a friend and monitor to Emma, so how can he change into a lover? At least Austen finds a narratively deft and psychologically compelling solution to the second question. Mr Knightley's amorous feelings for Emma have been held in suspension until Frank Churchill's arrival appears imminent. The very prospect of his appearance generates the birth of a jealousy that will make Mr Knightley a different kind of attendant upon Emma.

In Austen, a man's declaration of love is (or should be) the same as a proposal of marriage.

You might say that the narrative interest of Austen's novels stems entirely from a convention of marriage proposals: that a man must propose; a woman must wait to be proposed to. Comparing marriage to dancing in *Northanger Abbey*, Henry Tilney condenses the essential truth: 'man had the advantage of choice, woman only the power of refusal' (I. x). No woman can propose marriage. No woman can be the first to declare her feelings. This is a social rule internalised by fiction as a narrative convention. Upon its inflexibility rests the whole of the double-narrative of Austen's first published novel, *Sense and Sensibility*. Elinor wonders whether or not Edward Ferrars is courting her, but can only wait for him to say something. Meanwhile we watch the developing relationship between Marianne and Willoughby through Elinor's eyes, not knowing whether or not Willoughby has proposed. Elinor is mystified by 'the extraordinary silence of her sister and Willoughby on the subject, which they must know to be peculiarly interesting to them all' (I. xiv). That is, their presumed engagement. They do not acknowledge 'what their constant behaviour to each other declared to have taken place': i.e. a proposal (from him) – and an acceptance (from her). He calls her by her Christian name; she gives him a lock of her hair. What do these gestures mean? Mrs Dashwood refuses to ask Marianne whether the proposal has been made (I. xvi). 'Don't we all know that it must be a match,' exclaims Mrs Jennings, just moments before we read Willoughby's letter of rejection

(I. vii). Yet an actual proposal in this world, though it might take just a few words, is a kind of magic. Without it all intimacies are apparently meaningless.

When Elinor reads the letter from Willoughby that proclaims him 'to be deep in hardened villainy', she imagines that it is, in effect, nullifying an offer of marriage (II. vii). It 'acknowledged no breach of faith' – but of course there is, strictly speaking, no breach of faith. 'Engagement! . . . there has been no engagement,' cries Marianne. Elinor is amazed that her sister could have written to Willoughby even though he had not declared himself to her (II. vii). She already knows that the correspondence between Lucy and Edward 'could subsist only under a positive engagement, could be authorised by nothing else' (I. xxii). Marianne has offered Willoughby 'unsolicited proofs of tenderness' – a dangerous folly for any woman. This is why the woman must always wait for the man to declare himself. As Marianne herself soon says, 'he is not so unworthy as you believe him. He has broken no faith with me.' Mrs Jennings talks of how he 'comes and makes love to a pretty girl, and promises marriage' (II. viii), but again, this is not what he has done. Elinor explicitly tells Mrs Jennings this: 'I must do *this* justice to Mr. Willoughby—he has broken no positive engagement with my sister' (II. viii). He never proposed. In Austen, a man's declaration of love is (or should be) the same as a proposal of marriage. Emma finds Mr Elton 'actually making violent love to her' and, naturally, 'very much resolved on being seriously accepted as soon as possible' (I. xv). Anne Elliot has received Captain Wentworth's 'declarations and proposals' (I. iv), and we understand that he tells her that he loves her and asks her to marry him – these being inextricable and simultaneous. In *Pride and Prejudice*, Darcy first proposes to Elizabeth by declaring, 'You must allow me to tell you how ardently I admire and love you' (II. xi). In *Sense and Sensibility* Marianne admits to Elinor that Willoughby has 'never absolutely' told her that he loved her; he could not have done so without proposing marriage.

We do not hear the actual proposals in *Sense and Sensibility*. Edward arrives at Barton, having been 'released without any reproach to himself' from his engagement to Lucy, on a mission. 'It was only to ask Elinor to marry him;—and considering that he was not altogether inexperienced in such a question, it might be strange that he should feel so uncomfortable in the present case as he really did, so much in need of encouragement and fresh air' (III. xiii). Charlotte Lucas seems to be right about men needing to be 'helped on'. Austen declines to tell us just how the proposal gets made or received, only, rather awkwardly, that three hours later, when they sit down to table at four o'clock, 'he had secured his lady' and 'engaged her mother's consent'. We know that Colonel Brandon has declared his love for Marianne in an 'involuntary effusion' to her mother, while she lies gravely ill (III. ix). There is no chance of his saying any of this to Marianne herself. Even stranger is the imagined 'proposal' that Marianne receives from him a couple of years later, when the 'confederacy against her' of everyone's opinions hardly seems to require Colonel Brandon to say anything at all (III. xiv).

Colonel Brandon's explanation of his feelings to Mrs Dashwood is not entirely evasive. Applying to a lady's parents is conventional. Mr Collins 'made his declaration in form' in *Pride and Prejudice* by applying to Elizabeth's mother for 'a private audience with her' (I. xix). As soon as Mr Bingley has proposed to Jane Bennet he whispers something to her and leaves the room (III. xiii). Later we find that it has been for a 'conference with her father'. The day after successfully proposing to Elizabeth, Mr Darcy comes back to Longbourn to see her father. The difficulty that Emma and Mr Knightley have in dealing with Mr Woodhouse is all the more marked because the husband-to-be is supposed to apply to the father. In *Persuasion*, Captain Benwick evidently proposes to Louisa Musgrove and is accepted, but then writes to Mr Musgrove before travelling to Uppercross for his answer. Characters are preoccupied by the notion that there are matters of form in the business of making and accepting (or rejecting) a marriage proposal. 'In such cases as these, it is, I believe, the established mode to express a sense of obligation for the sentiments avowed, however unequally they may be returned,' says Elizabeth Bennet to Mr Darcy, with haughty irony (II. xi). Her pretence of attachment to convention is utterly disdainful. We know that Charles Musgrove cannot have loved Anne Elliot by the parody of formality that Austen adopts when she tells us that he proposed to her: 'She had been solicited . . . to change her name, by the young man' (I. iv). He might have said something quite unaffected, but his actual words are turned into a formula. This is nothing like the imagined flow of 'declarations and proposals' that Anne once heard from Captain Wentworth. So it is no surprise when the second half of the sentence tells us that his proposal of marriage to her sister Mary followed 'not long afterwards'. Later in the novel we overhear Louisa telling Captain Wentworth that he married Mary 'about a year' after being refused by Anne (I. x). The proposal itself must have come a good deal sooner after that rejection.

What is a proposal? It is easy to assume that it is just a matter of popping the question. But some men in Austen's novels feel that the very framing of a question is a difficult business. John Thorpe in *Northanger Abbey* is a buffoon with few conversational resources, but the problems he has proposing to Catherine Morland are comic because they are real (I. xv). He comes very close, in his words and phrases, to the purposes in his head, yet never quite manages an actual proposal, and leaves Catherine with no idea of his intent. 'A famous good thing this marrying scheme, upon my soul!' Only a few chapters later Isabella is telling her that John Thorpe is 'over head and ears in love with you' and that Catherine has given him 'the most positive encouragement' (II. iii). 'He says . . . that he as good as made you an offer, and that you received his advances in the kindest way.' Catherine is naturally flabbergasted.

Reluctance must be overcome, proper hesitation allowed its expression. The assumption is that the woman who might say yes in the end will not necessarily say yes straight away. 'You are silent . . . at present I ask no more,' cries Mr Knightley, sensing that he docs have hope of Emma accepting him. But then presumptuousness is the worst possible element of a proposal. The most enjoyable example of this is Mr Collins's proposal to Elizabeth, where his speechifying is the consequence of his assurance. Then there is Mr Elton, who is given little pause by Emma's initial resistance. He stops for a moment or two to wonder why she keeps talking of Miss Smith, but soon his flow of amatory exclamations is on him again. In *Mansfield Park*, Henry Crawford's presumptuousness is more subtle. He softens Fanny up for his proposal by telling her of the commission that has been procured for her brother William. As she is about to leave the room in excitement to tell her uncle, he pounces. 'The opportunity was too fair, and his feelings too impatient. He was after her immediately' (II. xiii). We do not hear his words, for we are inhabiting Fanny's mind, and she at first hardly realises what it is that he is saying. He is 'in the middle of his farther explanation, before she had suspected for what she was detained'. We get snatches of his likely phrasing: 'sensations which his heart had never known before' filter through her disbelieving consciousness. 'It was all beyond belief!' Yet the presumptuousness of these men is no greater than that of Mr Darcy in his first proposal to Elizabeth. He opens with a declaration that it is made despite himself: 'In vain have I struggled' (II. xi). His ardour overwhelms his reservations. He proposes because, despite all pride and all social considerations, he must have Elizabeth. It is the closest thing in all Austen's fiction to a declaration of sexual desire, and therefore not sufficient grounds for marriage. No more than Mr Collins does Mr Darcy conceive of being refused, which is why he must think again.

Mr Collins is wonderfully absurd for taking Elizabeth's first, politely phrased refusal as but the first step on a path to acceptance. There is no saying no to him. He foolishly supposes that he knows what is 'usual with young ladies'. Yet his expectation that a well-brought-up young woman would not necessarily say yes immediately is probably based on real social convention. Anything other than a rejection is encouragement. So tricky is the whole business that while some, like John Thorpe, who do want to propose do not manage to do so, others who never propose find that they have in fact offered marriage. The key example is in *Persuasion*. Captain Wentworth never proposes or comes near to proposing to Louisa Musgrove, but finds that he is being thought of as if he had. 'I found . . . that I was considered by Harville an engaged man!' (II. xi) He is not outraged; he is mortified, for on reflection, he cannot quarrel with their assumption. 'I was hers in honour if she wished it.' He has acted in such a way that she might expect a proposal – walking on his own with her, paying his attentions to her, jumping her down – and he has done this before witnesses. As he is an honourable man, all this is as good as proposing. If a man of honour does make an offer he is hooked. Thus John Dashwood's grotesque (and ill-advised) advice to Elinor about Colonel Brandon: 'his friends may all advise him against it. But some of those little attentions and encouragements which ladies can so easily give, will fix him, in spite of himself. And there can be no reason why you should not try for him' (II. xi).

It is a matter of morality as much as law. Thinking Willoughby engaged to Marianne, Elinor had expected his letter to her sister to express 'his desire of a release' from their engagement, along with 'professions of regret', this being the 'decorum of a gentleman'. So a man might ask to be released, even if the example of Lucy Steele would tell us that his fiancée's agreement might not be forthcoming. A man who broke off an engagement without permission could be sued for breach of promise by a woman, though if the case did not involve seduction, awards for damages in this periods were not usually financially crippling, and cases were often settled out of court for modest sums.[5] A good man, however, will regard himself as bound to his first proposal. So Edward Ferrars explains to Elinor that he had to stick to the arrangement with Lucy Steele, however hateful it had become to him (III. xiii). A woman, however, can change her mind. Jane Austen herself changed her mind overnight, from yes to no, when she received a proposal from Harris Bigg-Wither in 1802.[6] Lucy Steele changes her mind and 'releases' Edward Ferrars. Sir Thomas Bertram gives his daughter Maria the chance to change her mind about marrying Mr Rushworth. Anne Elliot was once persuaded to change her mind from accepting Captain Wentworth's proposal to declining it.

It is not surprising that women might like to entertain their 'power of refusal', if it is the only power available. Emma, the arch-'imaginist', entertains herself with imagining all the ways in which Frank Churchill might come to a 'declaration' and be rejected by her (II. xiii). Mrs Smith in *Persuasion*

suggests something rather dismaying about marriage proposals: that women contemplate them with disdain but respond
to them with gratitude. She talks as if a woman can usually
foresee a proposal and likes to imagine turning it down. 'Till
it does come, you know, we women never mean to have any
body. It is a thing of course among us, that every man is
refused – till he offers' (II. ix). She does not know that her
friend has already turned down two men. Yet Mr Collins's
theory about the mere conventionality of refusals finds some
backing in the refusals even of some of Austen's heroines.
Fanny rejects Mr Crawford's proposal, but the next day Sir
Thomas says that he has 'received as much encouragement
to proceed as a well-judging woman could permit herself to
give' (III. i). He is being insensitive, but not stupid. Near the
end of the novel the novelist intervenes unnecessarily to tell
us that, had Edmund married Mary Crawford, and Henry
Crawford remained dedicated to marrying Fanny, she would
eventually have complied. Only her secret love for Edmund
keeps her safe; if this had become hopeless, she would have
given in to the inevitable. Equally, Anne Elliot in *Persuasion*
is guarded from her cousin's advances only by her secret love
for Captain Wentworth. In her revelatory conversation with
Mrs Smith, she contemplates agreeing to marry Mr Elliot.
'Anne could just acknowledge within herself such a possibility
of having been induced to marry him, as made her shudder at
the idea of the misery which must have followed' (II. ix). The
dread possibility is that she might have been 'persuaded' by
Lady Russell, who, as she herself is forced to see in the final
chapter, has been 'pretty completely wrong' about everything.

Men should not necessarily take no for an answer. Anne
Elliot tells Captain Wentworth that if he had returned two
years later and tried her again he would have succeeded. He
curses himself for not having done so. Mr Darcy returns to

Elizabeth to ask her once more, having properly learned the lessons of what was wrong with his first proposal. Robert Martin in *Emma* also asks again. 'You cannot mean that he has even proposed to her again—yet. You only mean that he intends it' (III. xviii). Emma cannot believe that it has all already happened. It took just one visit with John Knightley's family to Astley's Amphitheatre, followed the next day by family dinner. Robert Martin 'found an opportunity of speaking to Harriet' – and made his proposal. Other men react to being turned down by making another speedy offer to a different woman: Mr Collins, most ludicrously, within three days, but also Mr Elton, within four weeks, and Charles Musgrove, 'not long' after being turned down by Anne Elliot. The last of these three is not so absurd, Charles Musgrove being more desperate than calculating (and being discerning enough to want to marry the neglected Anne in the first place).

The proposal is a crucial element of Austen's fiction because it imagines, in a world of concealed feelings, a moment of release. As love cannot be expressed directly without a proposal, this must always come as a kind of surprise. When Mr Darcy first declares himself to her, Elizabeth Bennet is probably the most surprised recipient of a proposal in all the novels. It is a satisfying irony, as she is the only one of Austen's heroines not to believe that the man she loves is destined for another woman. Proposing marriage is difficult because it is the first moment of explicitness in a relationship. Or rather, it should be difficult to propose. (Sometimes so much so that the novelist herself cannot put it into words.) For the right proposal is the one that can imagine the answer 'no'. Mr Knightley brings himself to the point of a declaration, but gives Emma the opportunity to halt him before he makes anything explicit (III. xiii). The 'tone of deep mortification' in which he responds to her request that he not tell her why he envies Frank Churchill comes from his (mistaken) assumption that she will not allow their nearly familial relationship to become something else. Once the proposal has been made, nothing can be the same again – or so he seems to acknowledge. He thinks that he is detecting in Emma the very unease that some readers have expressed about the possibility that his protective affection for the much younger woman should become an amorous attachment. When Darcy proposes to Elizabeth for the second time, it is with the possibility of rejection uppermost: 'one word from you will silence me on this subject for ever' (III. xvi). His declaration echoes Captain Wentworth's conclusion to his renewed proposal in *Persuasion*, 'A word, a look will be enough . . .' (II. xi). He offers himself with all the chance of being refused, and therefore we know he will be accepted. And he shows that a letter, sealing two people apart from the endless company they have to keep, can, after all, be the best kind of proposal.

NINETEEN

When Does Jane Austen Speak Directly to the Reader?

I leave it to my reader's sagacity . . .

Northanger Abbey, II. xv

In Jane Austen's unfinished novel *Sanditon* the reader gets a jolt from its heroine's pleasure in being admired by a handsome young gentleman. Charlotte Heywood, from whose point of view the story is being told, becomes aware of the attentions of Sir Edward Denham on their first meeting. 'He . . . talked much—& very much to Charlotte, by whom he chanced to be placed . . . she thought him agreable, & did not quarrel with the suspicion of his finding her equally so' (Ch. 7). The jolt is not from the heroine's susceptibility to admiration, it is from the interjection that follows, which removes us entirely from her thoughts. 'I make no apologies for my Heroine's vanity.— If there are young Ladies in the World at her time of Life, more dull of Fancy & more careless of pleasing, I know them not, & never wish to know them.' There are other nineteenth-century novelists like Thackeray or Trollope who regularly intervene in the first person to comment on their own characters and plots, but in Austen it is unusual and surprising.

What is she up to? Is she worried that we will think Charlotte flirtatious? Does she really need to fend off criticism of her heroine?

Jane Austen is not supposed to do this sort of thing. 'She is impersonal; she is inscrutable,' wrote Virginia Woolf.[1] Or, as a more recent admirer has put it, 'Here was a truly out-of-body voice, so stirringly free of what it abhorred as "particularity" or "singularity" that it seemed to come from no enunciator at all.'[2] We cannot of course know if the authorial comment in *Sanditon* would have been preserved in the completed novel, but it is not unprecedented. There is a rather similar example in *Mansfield Park*. Fanny Price is in Portsmouth, where, to her distress, she has been visited by Henry Crawford. Despite having refused his proposal of marriage, she finds that he is still thrusting his attentions on her. She is walking with him and her sister Susan down the High Street in the town when they meet her father. This is 'pain upon pain, confusion upon confusion', for though Fanny has wanted Mr Crawford's declared affection for her 'to be cured', she cannot bear that it happen this way – by means of his seeing and having to converse with the no doubt drunken Mr Price. Such are Fanny's unspoken thoughts. But then Austen cannot resist adding an explanation of their contradictoriness: '. . . and I believe, there is scarcely a young lady in the united kingdoms, who would not rather put up with the misfortune of being sought by a clever, agreeable man, than have him driven away by the vulgarity of her nearest relations' (III. x). The intervention suddenly shifts Fanny's ordeal away from us and even lets us suspect a little self-regard in her attitude towards Mr Crawford. Surprisingly, Austen appears to be laughing at her supposedly irreproachable heroine. It is especially pointed because it is a small example of the lesson that Fanny is made to learn – that most of those situations she fancies undesirable could be a good deal worse.

'I' says the narrator, and we have every reason to hear
the author speaking ('my Heroine' she says in that passage
from *Sanditon*). In *Sense and Sensibility*, she speaks as 'I' just
once, oddly, near the end of the second volume. 'I come now
to the relation of a misfortune, which about this time befell
Mrs. John Dashwood' (II. xiv). She is narrating something
relatively trivial: the mistake made by an acquaintance who
assumes wrongly that the Dashwood sisters are her guests
in London and therefore includes them in the invitation to a
musical party. 'Misfortune' is sardonic, being the word that
Mrs John Dashwood might privately use about having her
sisters-in-law accompany her. Austen's disdain for this woman
has reached its ultimate expression in this wry intervention.

In all Austen's novels but *Northanger Abbey*, the authorial use
of the first-person pronoun is extraordinarily rare and pointed.
In three novels we find it in the concluding chapter. At the
opening of the final chapter of *Pride and Prejudice*, we hear of
Mrs Bennet's happiness in having married off her two eldest
daughters. The second sentence then regrets not being able
to reform this wonderfully silly woman as part of the novel's
happy ending. 'I wish I could say, for the sake of her family, that
the accomplishment of her earnest desire in the establishment
of so many of her children, produced so happy an effect as to
make her a sensible, amiable, well-informed woman for the rest
of her life' (III. xix). It is a dazzling little reality effect, as the
author finally appears in her own book to tell us that one of her
characters is simply incorrigible. Even Austen cannot chasten
her. The author relinquishes her power and Mrs Bennet, with
her own particular life force, will go on being as she is.

Austen liked this way of signing off, and employed it again
in her next novel, *Mansfield Park*. Its final chapter again uses
the authorial pronoun in the second sentence: 'Let other
pens dwell on guilt and misery. I quit such odious subjects

as soon as I can, impatient to restore everybody, not greatly in fault themselves, to tolerable comfort, and to have done with all the rest' (III. xvii). At the end of the previous chapter Edmund and Fanny have been talking of Miss Crawford and Edmund's lingering 'disappointment' in her. He will never, he is sure, be able to forget her. The author, however, has no intention of letting him sink into despondency, and must soon stir him into love for Fanny. Fanny herself does not know that Edmund is destined to be her husband, but at least she is back at Mansfield Park, with the Crawfords and Mrs Norris banished and the remaining Bertrams grateful for her presence. 'My Fanny, indeed, at this very time, I have the satisfaction of knowing, must have been happy in spite of everything.' 'I have the satisfaction of knowing . . .': it is a winningly audacious way of tackling the narrative's failure, as yet, to supply final satisfaction: the proper culmination of its love story. It is a tease – she may be satisfied, but the reader is not – as if the author were briefly considering not contriving the consummated pairing of Fanny and Edmund.

'My Fanny'. Fanny is the only heroine to whom Austen refers with this familiarity. Catherine Morland, it is true, is five times called 'my heroine' by the narrator, but only the deceitfully intimate Isabella Thorpe (twice) and her own mother call her 'my Catherine'. 'My Fanny' is extraordinary, reminding us of the special form of intimate address used by Mr Knightley after he and Emma have plighted their troth, 'my Emma'. It denotes both affection and privilege. At the very moment at which we hear the author speak in her own person we hear her expression of fondness for this particular heroine. It is an endearment that Edmund himself has used, just once. Arriving in Portsmouth in high emotion after the elopements of both his sisters he clasps Fanny and exclaims, 'My Fanny—my only sister—my only comfort now' (III. xv).

The outburst of love immediately becomes, at the speed of that first dash, merely fraternal. Austen's tease about her 'satisfaction' in knowing Fanny's happiness registers her reader's perplexity as to how this fraternal love for Fanny can become something else. How long will it take?

> I purposely abstain from dates on this occasion, that every one may be at liberty to fix their own, aware that the cure of unconquerable passions, and the transfer of unchanging attachments, must vary much as to time in different people.—I only entreat everybody to believe that exactly at the time when it was quite natural that it should be so, and not a week earlier, Edmund did cease to care about Miss Crawford, and became as anxious to marry Fanny, as Fanny herself could desire. (II. xvii)

'I only entreat everybody to believe . . .': as in *Pride and Prejudice*, the author steps in to let her characters get away from her, turning her real challenge (how can she make us believe this?) into a witty trick.

It is no accident, then, that there is so much of the author in the last chapter of *Mansfield Park*, nudging us into accepting what the novel is not going to show. In *Persuasion*, the author again speaks in the first person in the final chapter, though here it is for the only time in the whole novel. She accosts us to assure us that when two young people are determined to marry, 'they are pretty sure by perseverance to carry their point' (II. xii). 'This may be bad morality to conclude with, but I believe it to be truth.' Again, the author speaks directly in order to signal a withdrawal from the lives she has invented, and this time, as many a contemporary reader would have noticed, with a reversal of the logic of many a successful novel. From Richardson's *Clarissa* onwards, love in English fiction existed to be hampered by foolish parents or misinformed guardians.

In a characteristic moment of liberation from the formulae of courtship novels, our author refuses to believe that people cannot get married if they want to. As she does so, she implies that other novelists are more concerned with 'morality' than probability. All three of these interventions have a flavour of repudiation, with the author finally stepping on to the stage in order to refuse to follow some established narrative pattern.

Jane Austen never speaks in the first person in *Emma*; she cannot insert herself alongside her despotic protagonist. In *Northanger Abbey*, however, Austen is *there* all the time. One of the reasons why this novel feels so different from her others is that we are so constantly reminded of the author's presence, arranging and commenting and speaking as herself. Naturally *Northanger Abbey* has the last-chapter sign-off in the first person of her other novels.

> The anxiety, which in this state of their attachment must be the portion of Henry and Catherine, and of all who loved either, as to its final event, can hardly extend, I fear, to the bosom of my readers, who will see in the tell-tale compression of the pages before them, that we are all hastening together to perfect felicity. (II. xvi)

It is a fearless reference to the fact that the reader knows from the physical reality of the very few remaining pages that a happy matrimonial ending is not far away. Suddenly there is the author, who has arranged the novel as an object that we have in our hands. Yet this is but the clinching use of a rhetorical device that has been used in the preceding chapters. Austen speaks in the first person for the first time in *Northanger Abbey* at the end of the third chapter, where she consigns her heroine to bed and wonders whether she might have dreamed of Henry Tilney, whom she has just met.

I hope it was no more than in a slight slumber, or a morning doze
at most; for if it be true, as a celebrated writer has maintained,
that no young lady can be justified in falling in love before the
gentleman's love is declared,* it must be very improper that a
young lady should dream of a gentleman before the gentleman is
first known to have dreamt of her. (I. iii)

A footnote (*) refers the reader to an essay by Samuel
Richardson for *The Rambler*, in which he declares 'That a
young lady should be in love, and the love of the young gentleman undeclared, is an heterodoxy which prudence, and even
policy, must not allow.'[3] Austen intrudes to mock the teaching
of this famous novelist that amorous fancies can be subject to
some code of propriety.

This 'I' is the same author we hear, though less often, in the
later novels, an author who wants to free her reader from any
absurd expectations learned from other novels and other
novelists. The number of times Austen speaks with the first-
person pronoun in *Northanger Abbey* (fourteen) is a consequence of the author's dedication to debunking the formulae
of other novels, but also vindicating the powers of fiction.
So the next first-person intervention is to set off on her
famous (but how ironical?) defence of the genre. 'Yes, novels;
for I will not adopt that ungenerous and impolitic custom so
common with novel-writers, of degrading by their contemptuous censure the very performances, to the number of which
they are themselves adding . . . I cannot approve of it' (I. v)
Austen's mockery of the conventions of fiction also pushes
her to speak after the small disaster of Catherine going off
with John Thorpe instead of the Tilneys. 'And now I may
dismiss my heroine to the sleepless couch, which is the true
heroine's portion; to a pillow strewed with thorns and wet
with tears. And lucky may she think herself, if she get another

good night's rest in the course of the next three months' (I. xi). Or here, when Catherine is brutally dismissed from his house by General Tilney, to travel back to Salisbury on her own:

> the author must share in the glory she so liberally bestows. But my affair is widely different; I bring back my heroine to her home in solitude and disgrace; and no sweet elation of spirits can lead me into minuteness. A heroine in a hack post-chaise is such a blow upon sentiment, as no attempt at grandeur or pathos can withstand. (II. xiv)

She names herself as 'the author', something that she never does again in any novel. Most mischievous of all is the delighted explanation of Henry's love for Catherine when she is telling us of their final engagement. 'I must confess that his affection originated in nothing better than gratitude, or, in other words, that a persuasion of her partiality for him had been the only cause of giving her a serious thought' (II. xv). 'I must confess . . .': as if the author were disappointed at the ignoble workings of his affections. 'It is a new circumstance in romance, I acknowledge, and dreadfully derogatory of an heroine's dignity.' In fact, she is repudiating the psychology of love usually served up in novels.

So in *Northanger Abbey*, 'the reader' is present too, addressed three times directly (but not in any other of Austen's completed novels). 'Monday, Tuesday, Wednesday, Thursday, Friday, and Saturday have now passed in review before the reader; the events of each day, its hopes and fears, mortifications and pleasures, have been separately stated, and the pangs of Sunday only now remain to be described, and close the week' (I. xiii). In this novel as never again, the author is joined with the reader in an amused monitoring of her ingenuous heroine. The author's presence is needed because

Catherine is so unworldly, and it assures us that she will not really come to harm. She must even be protected from her own self-condemnation. Listening to the Tilneys' educated talk of the picturesque on a walk above Bath, Catherine is 'heartily ashamed' of her ignorance of what makes for a good view (I. xiv). 'A misplaced shame,' the author immediately tells us. 'Where people wish to attach, they should always be ignorant ... A woman especially, if she have the misfortune of knowing any thing, should conceal it as well as she can.' This ends in a jaundiced worldliness that any biographer would imagine speaks from the author's own experience. Austen's reflections on her unworldly heroine give a singular tone to the narratorial irony of *Northanger Abbey*. When Catherine is first hooked by Isabella Thorpe, she forgets her interest in Henry Tilney in the excitement of her new 'amity', and the narrator comments: 'Friendship is certainly the finest balm for the pangs of disappointed love' (I. iv). This judgement comes from outside the narrative and can easily be thought of as the wry voice of the author. Catherine has not yet discovered what anyone could properly call 'love', and the 'friendship' of Isabella is entirely a cloak for self-interest, so this slice of sententiousness is the author's *faux* wisdom. Similarly, when she comments on her heroine's interest in clothes – 'She cannot be justified in it. Dress is at all time a frivolous distinction' (I. x) – it is with the confidence that her reader will hear the author's scorn for such moralism.

Sometimes Jane Austen cannot resist . . .

Austen could not always remain aloof from her creations. She knew very well the impulse to make a mocking comment on people's behaviour, and gave this impulse to her most fallible heroine, Emma Woodhouse. Thus the line preceding Emma's worst act, the mortification of Miss Bates at Box Hill: 'Emma could not resist' (III. vii). Sometimes Jane Austen cannot resist either. Take the introduction in *Emma* of Frank Churchill's plans to arrange a ball in Highbury.

> It may be possible to do without dancing entirely. Instances have been known of young people passing many, many months successively, without being at any ball of any description, and no material injury accrue either to body or mind;—but when a beginning is made—when the felicities of rapid motion have once been, though slightly, felt—it must be a very heavy set that does not ask for more. (II. xi)

This is larded with irony, but parades itself as commentary from personal experience. Even in later novels, she sometimes cannot resist, usually when awakening the reader to the difference between fact and wishfulness. In *Mansfield Park*, when the Bertrams and the Crawfords go riding in the hot weather, 'there were shady lanes wherever they wanted to go'. There is not a pause before Austen adds, 'A young party is always provided with a shady lane' (I. vii). She could not resist the remark. All that supposed shade was the excuse for the young people to do what they wanted to do anyway. When Austen describes Mrs Goddard's school in *Emma*, she really cannot resist having a stab at modern girls' schools 'which professed, in long sentences of refined nonsense, to combine liberal acquirements with elegant morality upon new principles and new systems—and where young ladies for enormous pay might be screwed out of health and into vanity' (I. iii). Where does this come from? We are being told of something that does not occur to any of the characters in the novel. Is it sharp social commentary, or a bee in the authorial bonnet?

In her last completed novel, the devil in Austen produces comments that have taken readers aback down the years. As Captain Wentworth sits on the sofa with Mrs Musgrove in order kindly to condole with her over the death of her scapegrace son, Austen fails to imitate his 'self-command'. She cannot resist reflecting on how ridiculous a fat person's grief can seem.

> Personal size and mental sorrow have certainly no necessary proportions. A large bulky figure has as good a right to be in deep affliction, as the most graceful set of limbs in the world. But, fair or not fair, there are unbecoming conjunctions, which reason will patronize in vain—which taste cannot tolerate—which ridicule will seize. (I. viii)

Ridicule, in the person of the author herself, has certainly seized this opportunity in a manner that many have often found 'not fair'. The author who occasionally intervenes in *Persuasion* cannot help laughing at what we might think sad. She steps aside from the drama on the Cobb just after Louisa Musgrove's fall to comment on the growing crowd collected 'to enjoy the sight of a dead young lady, nay, two dead young ladies, for it proved twice as fine as the first report' (I. xii). What the characters think of as tragedy is suddenly, from the author's perspective, a comedy. In this melancholy novel, a satirical author sometimes cannot stop herself from intervening. When Lady Russell calls at Uppercross at Christmas, the house is full of loud, cheerful children and she is relieved when she departs for Bath. But the author must tell us that Lady Russell's ears are not always so sensitive. 'Every body has their taste in noises as well as in other matters; and sounds are quite innoxious, or most distressing, by their sort rather than their quantity' (II. ii). She cannot abide the infant tumult at the Musgroves', but her spirits rise at the din of Bath when she enters the town in her carriage.

The literary admirer of Jane Austen does not want to know her views from her novels, for they are most apparent when her interpolated comments seem unsettlingly unironical. When, in *Mansfield Park*, Henry Crawford is not punished by the world as harshly as the former Mrs Rushworth, Austen explicitly acknowledges and regrets this inequality. 'That punishment, the public punishment of disgrace, should in a just measure attend *his* share of the offence is, we know, not one of the barriers which society gives to virtue. In this world the penalty is less equal than could be wished' (III. xvii). That 'we' is both the author and the reader, recognising together that a woman is for ever tainted by such an 'offence', while a man may go on in the world. It is in *Sense and Sensibility*, however, that we find a vein of authorial opinion that is diluted out of her subsequent novels. Take our introduction to the Steele sisters, who win over Lady Middleton by their rapturous attentions to her children. 'Fortunately for those who pay their court through such foibles, a fond mother, though, in pursuit of praise for her children, the most rapacious of human beings, is likewise the most credulous; her demands are exorbitant; but she will swallow anything' (I. xxi). This is amusing enough, but it is the dry observation of an author. The balanced and paradoxical form of her sentences in this novel seem to entice her to sententiousness. Take this, on Mrs John Dashwood's having Elinor and Marianne as companions in some of her London social forays:

> Mrs. John Dashwood was obliged to submit not only to the exceedingly great inconvenience of sending her carriage for the Miss Dashwoods, but, what was still worse, must be subject to

all the unpleasantness of appearing to treat them with attention: and who could tell that they might not expect to go out with her a second time? The power of disappointing them, it was true, must always be hers. But that was not enough; for when people are determined on a mode of conduct which they know to be wrong, they feel injured by the expectation of any thing better from them. (II. xiv)

That last sentence is just what we might expect from a well-meaning novelist of the period. Here is Maria Edgeworth in *Patronage*, published just three years after *Sense and Sensibility*, explaining why Caroline Percy's suitor Mr Barclay has not made more of an effort to persuade her to listen to his declarations of affection for her.

Love . . . let poets and lovers say what they will to the contrary, can no more subsist without hope than flame can exist without fuel. In all the cases cited to prove the contrary, we suspect that there has been some inaccuracy in the experiment, and that by mistake, a little, a very little hope has been admitted.[4]

The obligation of a serious author is to offer us insights into the paradoxes of human behaviour. Here is Mary Brunton in her novel *Self-Control*, published a year before *Sense and Sensibility*, telling us that the rakish Colonel Hargrave is likely to fall short of even the very modest reformation (no more seducing servant girls) he plans in order to win pious Laura Montreville.

It might be supposed, that when the scale of duty which we trace is low, we should be more likely to reach the little eminence at which we aspire; but experience shews us, that they who poorly circumscribe the Christian race, stop as much short of their humble design, as does he of nobler purpose, whose glorious goal is perfection.[5]

In *Sense and Sensibility*, Austen still has some of this wisdom-giving manner of her contemporaries, but she has another reason for authorial intervention that is unique to this novel: Marianne Dashwood. Austen finds the character so provoking that she sometimes cannot resist diagnosis and judgement. This is particularly clear in the wake of Willoughby's sudden departure, when Marianne retreats into an agonised display of wounded sensibility. 'She was without any power, because she was without any desire of command over herself' (I. xv). The analysis is not in Elinor's thoughts; it is the author passing judgement on Marianne's display of distress. This is Austen informing us of what we might not otherwise correctly perceive. The impression is confirmed by the next chapter, which begins with a description of Marianne's incessant weeping and her refusal to sleep or eat or even speak. She gives her mother and sisters pain, but will not be consoled by them. The author is pushed to an exclamation. 'Her sensibility was potent enough!' (I. xvi) We can hear all the author's scorn for the display of 'sensibility' in the sarcasm with which this demands to be read.

The exclamation mark indicates that the author, exasperated or disbelieving, has just had to speak. At the end of the opening chapter of *Mansfield Park*, Mrs Price, a little mystified at the Bertrams' decision to adopt one of her girls rather than one of her boys, has written to excuse Fanny's delicacy with the hope that she might be better for a 'change of air'. Austen is stopped by the truth behind the platitude. 'Poor woman! she probably thought change of air might agree with many of her children' (I. i). It is an odd device, by which the author has a good guess at the thoughts of a character she has herself invented. It is used with delicious sarcasm in *Persuasion* when Sir Walter Elliot fishes for compliments from Elizabeth and Mrs Clay by saying that women look at him and Colonel Wallis in the street in Bath because Colonel Wallis is 'a fine military figure' (II. iii). 'Modest Sir Walter!' exclaims someone who can only be the author. The opposite is surely true: Sir Walter is fully expecting to be told that his looks, not his companion's, are the cause of fluttering female attention. The character's vanity is so overwhelming that it has provoked even the author to derision. Similarly when Lady Russell, a 'good woman' who often excites ridicule from her creator, decides that Sir Walter's move to Bath is an excellent thing, Austen is nettled into an outburst. 'How quick come the reasons for approving what we like!' (I. ii). So they do. Yet the general aphorism has a special dramatic force. The author is driven to speak by the self-serving reasoning of her own character. She is struck by Lady Russell's behaviour, as if she were observing her rather than creating her. The author speaks for the best reason that an author can have: to credit her character with a life all of her own.

TWENTY

How Experimental a Novelist Is Jane Austen?

Mr. Collins, to be sure, was neither sensible nor agreeable;
his society was irksome, and his attachment to her must be
imaginary. But still he would be her husband.

Pride and Prejudice, I. xxii

Jane Austen knew that her novels were different. You can see
it in her 'Plan of a Novel, according to hints from various
quarters', which she wrote in around 1816, not long after
publishing *Emma*. Based on the 'hints' (by which she means
requests) of particular relations and acquaintances, it is also
a list of ingredients learned from the very many novels that
she had read. There was no doubt what would be expected of a
female protagonist: 'Heroine a faultless Character herself—,
perfectly good, with much tenderness & sentiment, & not
the least Wit ... All the Good will be unexceptionable in
every respect—and there will be no foibles or weaknessses
but with the Wicked, who will be completely depraved &
infamous.'[1] Her own notes indicate that her niece Fanny
Knight, whom she elsewhere recorded 'could not bear *Emma*
herself', had wanted a faultless protagonist, and that family

friend Mary Cooke had preferred a heroine without wit. No more Elizabeth Bennets. The notion that a heroine should be faultless, which now sounds psychologically so improbable, would have been entirely familiar to a keen novel-reader of the period. It went back to the hugely influential fiction of Samuel Richardson, who, according to Henry Austen, was his sister's own favourite. When he revised his great novel *Clarissa* in response to what he thought were misreadings of the novel, Richardson upbraided critics who had suggested that his heroine was at fault in her conduct towards either her family or her would-be seducer, Lovelace. 'As far as she could be perfect, considering the people she had to deal with and those with whom she was inseparably connected, she is perfect.'[2]

'Pictures of perfection as you know make me sick & wicked,' Austen wrote in a letter to Fanny Knight just a few months before her death (*Letters*, 155). Fanny had set a suitor, James Wildman, to read her aunt's novels (without telling him the identity of their author) and he had evidently objected that her female characters were not exemplary. 'I particularly respect him for wishing to think well of all young Ladies; it shews an amiable & a delicate Mind.' So 'faultless' is a word for heavy irony. In Austen's novels it is first used of a woman in *Mansfield Park*, and incredibly it is applied to Maria Bertram. 'Maria was indeed the pride and delight of them all—perfectly faultless—an angel' (I. iv). As a fragment of narration it seems extraordinary, but in context we see that it reflects Mrs Norris's opinion, and probably her words: not just 'faultless', but 'perfectly faultless'. The phrase dooms her. In *Emma*, it is Mr Knightley's word for Emma, immediately after she has accepted his proposal. 'He had ridden home through the rain; and had walked up directly after dinner, to see how this sweetest and best of all creatures, faultless

This is central to Mr K.'s love of Emma

in spite of all her faults, bore the discovery' (III. xiii). Even at his most enamoured, Mr Knightley knows that it is a lover's paradox. For has he not qualified to be her husband by being 'one of the few people who could see faults in Emma Woodhouse, and the only one who ever told her of them' (I. i)?

Austen's interest in her heroines' faults and errors was in itself something extraordinary in fiction. Yet the novelty went beyond this. She also developed techniques for showing the contradictoriness or even obscurity of her protagonist's motivations. Here is a typical heroine of a late eighteenth-century novel by probably the most accomplished woman novelist before Austen. It is from the opening chapter of Fanny Burney's *Cecilia* (1782).

> But though thus largely indebted to fortune, to nature she had yet greater obligations: her form was elegant, her heart was liberal; her countenance announced the intelligence of her mind, her complexion varied with every emotion of her soul, and her eyes, the heralds of her speech, now beamed with understanding and now glistened with sensibility.[3]

From 'her countenance . . .' onwards it is impossible to imagine Austen writing any of this. This heroine's outward and inner self are, in a sense, the same. She looks as she is. Her every feeling is apparently legible. And because she has to possess in fullest measure the qualities of a heroine – 'understanding' and 'sensibility' – we get all that beaming and glistening. Cecilia has much to endure before she manages to marry the man she loves, but, like most heroines before Austen, she never has to endure discovering that she has been fooled by her own feelings. Austen gave her readers an entirely new sense of a person's inner life, but through new kinds of narrative rather than new insights into human nature.

Nothing is more important in fiction than the means
by which a novel renders a character's thoughts.

The managing of the attraction between Elizabeth and Mr Darcy, for instance, is a triumph of technique as much as of psychological subtlety. Elizabeth Bennet is an unprecedented creation not just because of her wit and 'archness', but because Austen is able to give us a sense of her self-ignorance. At the ball at Netherfield she is disappointed by Wickham's absence and dances first with Mr Collins and then with one of the officers.

> When those dances were over, she returned to Charlotte Lucas, and was in conversation with her, when she found herself suddenly addressed by Mr. Darcy who took her so much by surprise in his application for her hand, that, without knowing what she did, she accepted him. He walked away again immediately, and she was left to fret over her own want of presence of mind. (I. xviii)

'Without knowing what she did'. It is the most innocent of phrases, but read one way directs us to perhaps the most important fact about *Pride and Prejudice* for most readers: the strong current of attraction between two characters who are superficially at odds. Elizabeth does something despite herself and by accepting the character's own version of what has happened – fretting over 'her own want of presence of mind' – the narrator encourages the reader to imagine another explanation. She does the same thing with Mr Darcy.

He wisely resolved to be particularly careful that no sign of
admiration should *now* escape him, nothing that could elevate her
with the hope of influencing his felicity; sensible that if such an
idea had been suggested, his behaviour during the last day must
have material weight in confirming or crushing it. (I. xii)

That 'wisely' is exquisite. You could call it Austen's irony, as
she commends the self-control that will eventually turn out
to have been a self-delusion. But it is also something like Mr
Darcy's self-commendation, for the sentence clearly adopts
his own stiff and self-important turn of phrase: 'nothing that
could elevate her with the hope of influencing his felicity'.
'Till this moment, I never knew myself,' Elizabeth famously
cries when she has read Mr Darcy's letter and reflects on her
own folly at having believed everything Wickham told her (II.
xiii). Austen's most powerful innovation was to realise this lack
of self-knowledge in the very voice of the narration. In *Emma*
she concentrates this effect as never before, narrating almost
entirely from her heroine's point of view and bending reality
to match her preconceptions. We hear Emma, as we heard Mr
Darcy, commending her own judgement. As Harriet Smith's
visits to Hartfield become 'a settled thing', Emma congrat-
ulates herself: '. . . in every respect as she saw more of her,
she approved her, and was confirmed in all her kind designs'
(I. iv). That 'kind' is Emma's complacent thought about her
own motivations; the approval is not so much for Harriet as
for herself. Emma's self-delusions are not the subject of the
narration, they are its very substance. Here she is with Frank
Churchill, who has been summoned back to Yorkshire, and
who she thinks is on the verge of a marriage proposal.

He was silent. She believed he was looking at her; probably reflecting on what she had said, and trying to understand the manner.

She heard him sigh. It was natural for him to feel that he had *cause* to sigh. He could not believe her to be encouraging him. A few awkward moments passed, and he sat down again . . . (II. xii)

We pass easily from what Emma supposes, to what she hears, to what seems to be fact. The cause of his sighing is not at all what she thinks. The drama of the moment is all in her imagination: he is, we later discover, considering telling her of his engagement to Jane Fairfax. Yet the narration behaves as if ruled by her consciousness.

Much later, in the twentieth century, critics came to call this technique 'free indirect style'. It is the most important narrative technique of novelists like Gustave Flaubert, Henry James, James Joyce and Franz Kafka. A third-person narrative takes on the habits of thought or even speech of a particular character. It is a style in which, as one admirer of Austen's formal daring has put it, 'the narration's way of *saying* is constantly both mimicking, and distancing itself from, the character's way of *seeing*'.[4] Nothing is more important in fiction than the means by which a novel renders a character's thoughts. This is what novels were designed to do. 'The real world becomes fiction only by revealing the hidden side of the human beings who inhabit it.'[5] The critic who wrote this, Dorrit Cohn, acknowledged Jane Austen as 'the first extensive practitioner' of what she calls 'narrated monologue' – her name for free indirect style.[6] There is some disagreement about how easy it is to find earlier examples of the technique. David Lodge acknowledges Austen as the first great pioneer of the technique, while finding some sparse examples in Fanny Burney's later fiction.[7] Jane Spencer detects glimmerings of free indirect style in the fiction of Austen's most notable contemporary, Maria Edgeworth, and something like the germ of the technique in the same novel that

Lodge scrutinises, Fanny Burney's *Camilla* (1796).[8] Certainly
it is possible to find contemporaries of Austen who inserted
the thoughts of their characters into the narrative without
quotation marks. Here is Laura Montreville, the heroine of
Mary Brunton's *Self-Control*, after she has been propositioned
by the 'impetuous' Colonel Hargrave: 'He might now renew
his visits, and how was it possible to prevent this? Should she
now refuse to see him, her father must be made acquainted
with the cause of such a refusal, and she could not doubt that
the consequences would be such as she shuddered to think of.'[9]
Yet this is close to the omniscient reporting of her thoughts
by the narrator. There is no room to doubt either what she is
feeling, or what the reality of her situation is.

Extraordinarily, Austen not only discovered the possibilities of free indirect style, she produced in *Emma* an example of its use that has hardly been matched. So confident did
she feel about her control of the technique that she made
her plot depend upon it. When Harriet tells her that there is
another man to whom she is becoming attached, Emma thinks
she knows just what her protégé is saying. After the debacle
of the Mr Elton misunderstanding, she imagines that she is
being self-controlled when she tells Harriet that they will not
actually mention the man whom she wishes to marry: 'Let no
name ever pass our lips'. In fact Emma is condemning herself
to the most painful of errors. Her mistakenness is dutifully
followed by the narrator, who shares with her the illusion
that Harriet wishes to marry Frank Churchill. So committed is the narration to this error that there is no room for
any other perspective. When Emma meets Harriet after both
women have learned of the death of Mrs Churchill, we have
this: 'Harriet behaved extremely well on the occasion, with
great self-command. Whatever she might feel of brighter
hope, she betrayed nothing. Emma was gratified, to observe

such a proof in her of strengthened character, and refrained from any allusion that might endanger its maintenance' (III ix). To wonderfully comic effect, the narration copies Emma's confidence. Utterly wrong-headed as is this vision of events – Harriet is in fact entirely apathetic about the consequences of Mrs Churchill's death – it is also unwavering. It serves the plot of the novel because it is quite likely that a first-time reader will not even discern that this passage is revealing Emma at her most deluded. For the reader who does see this, there is the deeper pleasure of seeing how Emma is working against herself. Harriet has her eyes on Mr Knightley and Emma has encouraged her. All that queenly pleasure at her own influence ('Emma was gratified, to observe . . .') means she is heading for a fall.

One of the qualities of *Emma* is that the warping of reality by its heroine is at its least obvious when it is at its most complete. This would not work so well if there were not passages where Emma's thinking is more directly dramatised. 'The hair was curled, and the maid sent away, and Emma sat down to think and be miserable.—It was a wretched business indeed!— Such an overthrow of every thing she had been wishing for!—Such a development of every thing most unwelcome!—Such a blow for Harriet!—That was the worst of all.' The exclamation marks are the sure sign that we are following the movement of Emma's thoughts. Indeed, attending to this punctuation mark should help guide us past some of the pitfalls for critics, who might mistake Emma's judgments for the author's. Here, from near the end of the novel, is the revelation of Harriet's parentage.

She proved to be the daughter of a tradesman, rich enough to afford her the comfortable maintenance which had ever been hers, and decent enough to have always wished for concealment.—Such was the blood of gentility which Emma had formerly been so ready to vouch for!—It was likely to be as untainted, perhaps, as the blood of many a gentleman: but what a connexion had she been preparing for Mr. Knightley—or for the Churchills— or even for Mr. Elton!—The stain of illegitimacy, unbleached by nobility or wealth, would have been a stain indeed. (III. xix)

Emma may have been happily relieved of some illusions by Mr Knightley's declaration, but we can still follow her prejudices.

In *Emma*, narrative is refracted almost entirely through the consciousness of one character: Emma. In both *Pride and Prejudice* and *Mansfield Park* it allows access to the minds of many different characters, even if the heroines predominate. Here is an almost surreptitious example from *Mansfield Park*. We have been watching the Crawfords and Bertrams argue over the allocation of parts in their performance of *Lovers' Vows* and have seen Maria gain the desired role of Agatha ahead of her sister Julia. Now she will be able to enjoy all her tender scenes with Frederick, played by Henry Crawford. Julia is left to sulk.

The sister with whom she was used to be on easy terms was now become her greatest enemy: they were alienated from each other; and Julia was not superior to the hope of some distressing end to the attentions which were still carrying on there, some punish-ment to Maria for conduct so shameful towards herself as well as towards Mr. Rushworth. (I. xvii)

The sentence opens with the provision of information about Julia's unstated feelings, but soon begins to slide into some-thing more indirect. If we ask ourselves what 'some distress-ing end' might actually mean, we see that it is an evasive phrase for a scandalous outcome: Maria's disgrace in the eyes of her husband-to-be. The sentence ends with a whole-hearted adoption of what must be Julia's own thought pattern, imagining Maria's punishment 'for conduct so shameful towards herself' as well as towards Mr. Rushworth'. 'Shameful' is not the author's word, it is Julia's, as she pretends to herself that she is exercising moral judgement rather than feeling mere envy. You can see her make herself believe that she feels as she does towards her sister because of her conduct towards Mr Rushworth. You might almost have forgotten that Julia really wants Henry Crawford for herself. Austen's extraordinary narrative sophistication allows us not just to know but somehow to experience Julia's hypocrisy.

One suspects that it was a special delight to Austen to smuggle in the judgements of some of her characters. A good example is Charlotte Lucas in *Pride and Prejudice* reflecting on her success in coaxing Mr Collins into a proposal of marriage, which she has just accepted. 'Her reflections were in general satisfactory. Mr. Collins, to be sure, was neither sensible nor agreeable; his society was irksome, and his attachment to her must be imaginary. But still he would be her husband' (I. xxii). Without 'to be sure', the first half of that sentence might be the narrator's assertion; the otherwise redundant phrase lets us hear it as Charlotte's internal speech. Equally, if it said 'his attachment to her was imaginary' we would be being told something. The 'must be' makes it into the character's unspoken reflection. The narration takes on the logic of Charlotte Lucas's thoughts and lets us almost hear her calculating. 'Must' often works like this in Austen's free indirect style. When Emma first has Harriet Smith visiting Hartfield, we are told that she is so becomingly deferential and 'artlessly impressed' that 'she must have good sense' (I. iii). This is the echo of Emma's self-regard. Or again, 'The friends from whom she had just parted, though very good sort of people, must be doing her harm . . . they must be coarse and unpolished.' This has nothing to do with reality: each 'must' is Emma building her own self-gratifying story. A little later, describing Harriet's traces of 'taste', the narrative adds 'though strength of understanding must not be expected', and we have the smack of Emma's complacent superiority (I. iv). When Emma thinks about Harriet's supposed attachment to Frank Churchill, a 'must' realises Emma's strange preoccupation. 'Its tendency would be to raise and refine her mind—and it must be saving her from the danger of degradation' (III. iv).

The trick is used to very different effect in *Persuasion*. We can feel the hopelessness of this self-lacerating, self-deceiving 'must' in the passage describing Anne Elliot's reaction to her sister's report of Captain Wentworth's comment about her: '"So altered that he should not have known her again!" These were words which could not but dwell with her. Yet she soon began to rejoice that she had heard them. They were of sobering tendency; they allayed agitation; they composed, and consequently must make her happier' (I. vii). 'Must make her happier'? This is self-delusion of a special kind. We might call it self-mortification. That rejoicing is an effort of correct thinking on Anne's part, beneath which we can sense her pain even more painfully. We are caught up in the very effort to make something good of something so excruciating. In *Persuasion* Austen takes to a new extreme the narrative technique she had pioneered. Take a small part of the description of Anne Elliot's meeting with Captain Wentworth after eight years apart.

> Her eye half met Captain Wentworth's; a bow, a curtsey passed; she heard his voice—he talked to Mary; said all that was right; said something to the Miss Musgroves, enough to mark an easy footing: the room seemed full—full of persons and voices—but a few minutes ended it. Charles shewed himself at the window, all was ready, their visitor had bowed and was gone. (I. vii)

As Gillian Beer notices, we often seem to be not just in Anne Elliot's mind, but in her body. 'When she looks down, the scene is described to us only through hearing; when her eyes are lowered we see only what falls within her field of vision.'[10] Even the contraction of time, an ordinary fact of much narrative report, here becomes foregrounded. It all hurries past us, as it hurried past her.

Such impressionistic effects were new to fiction and are hardly paralleled before the twentieth century. Austen carried them over into dialogue, where she showed that direct speech could be used to represent not so much what was said as what others might have heard. Here is Mrs Elton at the party at Donwell Abbey, talking as she picks strawberries.

'The best fruit in England—every body's favourite—always wholesome. These the finest beds and finest sorts.—Delightful to gather for one's self—the only way of really enjoying them.— Morning decidedly the best time—never tired—every sort good—hautboys infinitely superior—no comparison—the others hardly eatable—hautboys very scarce—Chili preferred—white wood finest flavour of all—price of strawberries in London— abundance about Bristol—Maple Grove—cultivation—beds when to be renewed—gardeners thinking exactly different—no general rule—gardeners never to be put out of their way—delicious fruit—only too rich to be eaten much of—inferior to cherries—currants more refreshing—only objection to gathering strawberries the stooping—glaring sun—tired to death—could bear it no longer—must go and sit in the shade.' (III. vi)

(Read our author's life in)

It is an extraordinarily impressionistic rendering of talk that becomes a slightly mad monologue. 'Such, for half an hour, was the conversation.' Conversation with Mrs Elton is not much like an exchange, so there is justice in stripping out all voices except hers. The ability to enter into dialogue at all is an achievement. Marilyn Butler observes of *Emma*: 'The comic characters are monologuists, whereas Emma, like Mr. Knightley, is supreme in dialogue.'[11] The condensation of Mrs Elton's outpouring is fitting because the other guests at the party must be in the habit of not listening to much of what she says. A dedicated talker, she is condemned on this hot day to talk herself into exhaustion.

In his standard work on speech in fiction, Norman Page talks of the convention 'much favoured by Jane Austen, whereby the novelist is permitted to conflate into a single speech what must probably be supposed to have been uttered as several separate speeches'.[12] In fact, this convention seems invented by Austen. At one extreme it is used for the 'incessant flow' of Miss Bates. Other people must sometimes be speaking during her unstoppable monologues, but their interventions or responses are excised. Take a slice of her talk at the ball at the Crown.

'Thank you, my mother is remarkably well. Gone to Mr. Woodhouse's. I made her take her shawl—for the evenings are not warm—her large new shawl— Mrs. Dixon's wedding-present.— So kind of her to think of my mother! Bought at Weymouth, you know—Mr. Dixon's choice. There were three others, Jane says, which they hesitated about some time. Colonel Campbell rather preferred an olive. My dear Jane, are you sure you did not wet your feet?—It was but a drop or two, but I am so afraid:— but Mr. Frank Churchill was so extremely—and there was a mat to step upon—I shall never forget his extreme politeness.—Oh! Mr. Frank Churchill, I must tell you my mother's spectacles have never been in fault since; the rivet never came out again. My mother often talks of your good-nature. Does not she, Jane?—Do not we often talk of Mr. Frank Churchill?—' (III. ii)

Other people are saying things, but their words are simply smothered. The contraction of time is part of the effect, as if the dialogue were boiling down the effects of listening to this character.

Even better, if we were to be able to hear what Jane Fairfax or Frank Churchill were saying we might detect their awkwardness. Miss Bates goes on about Weymouth and Frank Churchill's visit to mend the spectacles, and the subtext is the relationship between these two. In fact, Miss Bates is the novel's most reliable witness, being so circumstantial that no one listens to what she is saying. She provides a record of the goings-on in Highbury from which you could, if you were attentive, derive the true story. The fact that her monologues contain all the clues to the hidden plot of *Emma* was first pointed out by Mary Lascelles in her book *Jane Austen and her Art*, but readers and critics continue to miss the fact.[13] Examine Miss Bates's speeches closely enough and you will get all that is hidden and important – but you will never look closely enough. P. D. James wrote of *Emma* as a detective story, but even she missed what would properly belong to a detective story: that the important clues are to be found in the unattended ramblings of a character beneath our notice.[14]

> 'I am a talker you know; I am rather a talker; and now and then I have let a thing escape me which I should not. I am not like Jane; I wish I were. I will answer for it *she* never betrayed the least thing in the world. Where is she?—Oh! Just behind. Perfectly remember Mrs. Perry's coming.—Extraordinary dream indeed!' (III. v)

This is just after Miss Bates has revealed Frank Churchill's blunder about Mr Perry getting a carriage. In another ramble she lets anyone who is attending know that Jane Fairfax's decision to accept Mrs Elton's implicitly hellish posting a governess with the Smallridges was connected to, and directly followed, news of a chaise having been ordered to Randalls to take Frank Churchill off to Richmond (III. viii). Just listen to Miss Bates and you will understand what has been going on! As she says herself, she betrays everything.

The impression of Miss Bates's outpouring is shared by everyone present. All hear her, though none interpret her. With Miss Bates, everything is spoken. What free indirect style is able to render for Austen is the opposite of this, what cannot be spoken. *Persuasion* is characterised by the heroine's absence from speech and events around her – an inwardness so absorbing that things happen to her in a kind of blur, even though we can be sure that the other characters are not noticing. Thus when Captain Wentworth helps Anne into the Crofts' carriage – 'Yes, —he had done it. She was in the carriage, and felt that he had placed her there' (I. x). The narration is accurate to her feelings, though hardly at all to the objective reality. 'She understood him. He could not forgive her . . .': but she does not understand him at all. Austen pioneered a narration that could mimic not just how a character might think, but also how she might avoid thinking. An early, unsettling example is this description of Elinor Dashwood's reaction to the news that she, her mother and her sisters are to leave their home in Sussex for Devon.

Elinor had always thought it would be more prudent for them to settle at some distance from Norland, than immediately amongst their present acquaintance. On that head, therefore, it was not for her to oppose her mother's intention of removing into Devonshire. The house, too, as described by Sir John, was on so simple a scale, and the rent so uncommonly moderate, as to leave her no right of objection on either point; and, therefore, though was not a plan which brought any charm to her fancy, though it was a removal from the vicinity of Norland beyond her wishes, she made no attempt to dissuade her mother from sending a letter of acquiescence. (I. iv)

The language of this is very close to Elinor's own reasoning process, but in following this it fails to mention the subtext: that Elinor loves Edward, and that moving to Devon means moving away from him. The narrative has taken on all her slightly chilly self-control.

As well as allowing the narrative to be shaped by a character's thoughts, Austen also had a technique for the suggestive avoidance of those thoughts. In *Mansfield Park* Edmund and Mary Crawford are discussing the character and occupation of clergymen, with the latter using the example of Dr Grant to show that members of the clergy are often not admirable men. Miss Crawford wishes Fanny a better fate than to be married to such a man, 'quarrelling about green goose' all week.

'I think the man who could often quarrel with Fanny,' said Edmund, affectionately, 'must be beyond the reach of any sermons.'

Fanny turned farther into the window; and Miss Crawford had only time to say, in a pleasant manner, 'I fancy Miss Price has been more used to deserve praise than to hear it,' when being earnestly invited by the Miss Bertrams to join in a glee, she tripped off to the instrument, leaving Edmund looking after her in an ecstasy of admiration of all her many virtues, from her obliging manners down to her light and graceful tread (I. xi).

Fanny turns into the window, and turns away from us too, for Austen absents herself from knowing, or anyway from telling us, what her heroine feels. The turning away dramatises the pitch of Fanny's feeling. Mary Crawford senses something, and covers the awkward moment graciously, but she does not know the half of what Fanny feels. The narrator's own reserve about Fanny's feelings enacts the character's own tenderness on the subject of her love for Edmund. She hardly dare admit to herself her impossible passion. Austen's audacious narrative technique allows Fanny's feelings to be the undercurrent of the narrative, without becoming its subject. Any novelist can tell us what a character feels; Austen developed a means of declining to tell us. In doing so she bequeathed new technical possibilities to later novelists. Catch the dramatic and narrative subtlety of what Austen is doing as Fanny turns away from us and we indeed catch her in what Virginia Woolf called 'the act of greatness'. Characteristically, this moment of audacious fictional experiment is also an instance of the most perfect reticence.

Notes

Introduction

1 *British Critic*, July 1816, in Brian Southam, ed., *Jane Austen. The Critical Heritage 1811–1870* (London: Routledge & Kegan Paul, 1968), p. 71.

2 *Gentleman's Magazine*, September 1816, ibid., p. 72.

3 Henry Austen, 'Biographical Notice of the Author', in J. E. Austen-Leigh, *A Memoir of Jane Austen and Other Family Recollections*, ed. Kathryn Sutherland (Oxford: World's Classics, 2002), p. 140.

4 Henry Austen, 'Memoir of Miss Austen', ibid., p. 150.

5 Virginia Woolf, 'Jane Austen at Sixty', *Nation and Athenaeum*, 15 December 1923, reprinted in *The Essays of Virginia Woolf*, Vol. IV, ed. Andrew McNeillie (London: The Hogarth Press, 1994), p. 155.

6 *The Journal of Sir Walter Scott*, ed. W.E.K. Anderson (Oxford: Clarendon Press, 1972), 14 March 1826, p. 114.

7 Henry James, 'The Lesson of Balzac' (1905) in Brian Southam, ed., *Jane Austen*, pp. 229–30.

8 Ibid, p. 300.

9 Vladimir Nabokov, *Lectures on Literature*, ed. Fredson Bowers (San Diego, CA: Harcourt, 1982), p. 13.

10 *The Nabokov–Wilson Letters*, ed. Simon Karlinsky (New York: Harper & Row, 1979), letter of 5 May 1950, p. 241.

11 Ibid., letter of 9 May 1950, p. 243.

12 Ibid., cited in Karlinsky introduction, p. 17.

Chapter 1: How Much Does Age Matter?

1 See E. A. Wrigley and R. S. Schofield, *The Population History of England 1541–1871. A Reconstruction* (1981; reprinted Cambridge: Cambridge University Press, 2002), p. 255.

2 R. A. Austen-Leigh, ed., *Austen Papers 1704–1856*, introduction by David Gilson (London: Routledge/Thoemmes, 1995), pp. 156–7.

3 William Austen-Leigh and Richard Arthur Austen-Leigh, *Jane Austen: A Family Record*, rev. Deirdre Le Faye (London: The British Library, 1989), p. 134, and Hazel Jones, *Jane Austen and Marriage* (London: Continuum, 2009), p. 39.

Chapter 2: Do Sisters Sleep Together?

1 *London Review of Books*, 17. 24 (14 December 1995), p. 4. For Terry Castle's original article, see *LRB*, 17. 15 (3 August 1995), pp. 3–6. For the evidence, see Edward Copeland, 'The Austens and the Elliots: A Consumer's Guide to *Persuasion*', in Juliet McMaster and Bruce Stovel (eds), *Jane Austen's Business: Her World and Her Profession* (Basingstoke: Macmillan, 1996), p. 137.

2 Quoted in Kate Chisholm, *Fanny Burney: Her Life* (London: Chatto & Windus, 1998), p. 117.

3 See Amanda Vickery, *Behind Closed Doors: At Home in Georgian England* (London: Yale University Press, 2009), for contemporary evidence of husbands and wives having separate bedrooms.

Chapter 3: What Do the Characters Call Each Other?

1 Just one of the peculiarities of terms of address in Austen's fiction observed in Isaac Schapera, *Kinship Terminology in Jane Austen's Novels* (London: The Royal Anthropological Institute, 1977), p. 2.

2 The novels in which they feature are Samuel Richardson, *Clarissa* (1747-8), Fanny Burney, *Evelina* (1778), *Cecilia* (1782) and *Camilla* (1796), and Charlotte Smith, *Emmeline* (1788).

3 Maggie Lane, *Jane Austen and Names* (Bristol: Blaise Books, 2002)., pp. 12–13.

4 See E. G. Withycombe, *The Oxford Dictionary of English Christian Names* (1950; reprinted Oxford: Oxford University Press, 1973), p. 199.

5 Lane, *Names*, p. 33.

6 Ibid., p. 35.

Chapter 4: How Do Jane Austen's Characters Look?

1 Laurence Sterne, *Tristram Shandy*, ed. Melvyn and Joan New (London: Penguin, 1997), Vol. VI, Ch. xxxviii, p. 388.

Chapter 5: Who Dies in the Course of Her Novels?

1 Henry Fielding, *Tom Jones*, ed. John Bender and Simon Stern (Oxford: World's Classics, 1996), Vol. II, Ch. viii, p. 95.

2 See Anne Buck, *Dress in Eighteenth-Century England* (London: B. T. Batsford, 1979), pp. 60–6 and 82–5.

3 Phillis Cunnington and Catherine Lucas, *Costume for Births, Marriages and Deaths* (London: A & C Black, 1972), pp. 244–5.

4 Buck, *Dress*, p. 60.

5 Cunnington and Lucas, *Costume*, p. 268.

6 Fanny Burney, *Evelina*, ed. Edward A. Bloom (Oxford: World's Classics, 1982), p. 53.

7 Alison Adburgham, *Shops and Shopping 1800–1914* (1964; reprinted London: Allen & Unwin, 1981), p. 59.

8 Linda Bree, introduction to *Persuasion* (Peterborough, Ontario: Broadview Press, 1998), p. 13.

9 Jane Austen, *Catherine and Other Writings*, ed. Margaret Anne Doody and Douglas Murray (Oxford: World's Classics 1993), p. 234.

10 See Wrigley and Schofield, *The Population History of England*, p. 249.

11 See Deirdre Le Faye's biographical index to *Jane Austen's Letters* (Oxford: Oxford University Press, 1995), p. 495.

Chapter 6: Why Is It Risky to Go to the Seaside?

1 Allan Brodie, Colin Ellis, David Stuart and Gary Winter, *Weymouth's Seaside Heritage* (Swindon: English Heritage, 2006), p. 9.

2 David Selwyn, *Jane Austen and Leisure* (London: Hambledon, 1999), p. 47.

3 See Roger Sales, *Jane Austen and Representations of Regency England* (London: Routledge, 1994), pp. 141–2.

4 John K. Walton, *The English Seaside Resort: A Social History 1750–1914* (Leicester: Leicester University Press, 1983), p. 17.

5 Ibid., pp. 126–7.

6 Austen-Leigh and Austen-Leigh, *A Family Record*, p. 134.

7 Alain Corbin, *The Lure of the Sea: The Discovery of the Seaside, 1750–1840* (1994; reprinted London: Penguin, 1995), pp. 66–7.

8 Ibid., p. 272.

9 Tony Tanner, *Jane Austen* (Cambridge, MA: Harvard University Press, 1986), p. 262.

10 Austen-Leigh and Austen-Leigh, *A Family Record*, p. 124.

Chapter 7: Why Is the Weather Important?

1 *Nature*, No. 388 (10 July 1997), p. 137.

Chapter 8: Do We Ever See the Lower Classes?

1 Austen-Leigh and Austen-Leigh, *A Family Record*, p. 155.

2 See Pamela Horn, *Flunkeys and Scullions: Life Below Stairs in Georgian England* (Stroud: Sutton Publishing, 2004), pp. 213–16.

3 *Jane Austen Society Collected Reports 1949–1965*, p. 251.

4 J. J. Hecht, *The Domestic Servant Class in Eighteenth-Century England* (London: Routledge & Kegan Paul, 1956), p. 7.

Chapter 9: Which Important Characters Never Speak in the Novels?

1 Ben Jonson, *Timber, or Discoveries Made upon men and matter*, in *Ben Jonson*, ed. Ian Donaldson (Oxford: Oxford University Press, 1985), p. 574.

2 See the essays in *The Talk in Jane Austen*, ed. Bruce Stovel and Lynn Weinlos Gregg (Edmonton, Alberta: The University of Alberta Press, 2002), especially those by Juliet McMaster and Jeffrey Herrle.

3 Marilyn Butler, *Jane Austen and the War of Ideas* (1975; reprinted Oxford: Oxford University Press, 1987), p. 273.

Chapter 10: What Games Do Characters Play?

1 *The Works of Jane Austen*, ed. R. W. Chapman, Vol. VI, *Minor Works*, p. 325.

2 Charles Dickens, *Nicholas Nickleby*, ed. Michael Slater (1978; reprinted London: Penguin, 1986), Ch. 1, p. 63.

3 See David Selwyn (ed.), *Collected Poems and Verse of the Austen Family* (Manchester: Carcanet, 1996), pp. 19, 35–9 and 51–5 for Austen examples.

Chapter 11: Is There Any Sex in Jane Austen?

1 Martin Amis, *The Pregnant Widow* (London: Jonathan Cape, 2010), p. 138.

2 Ibid., p. 155.

3 See 'Biographical Notice of the Author', in *The Works of Jane Austen*, ed. R. W. Chapman, Vol. V, p. 7.

4 Samuel Richardson, *Pamela*, ed. Thomas Keymer and Alice Wakely (Oxford: World's Classics, 2001), Letter VIII, p. 20.

5 Lawrence Stone, *Broken Lives: Separation and Divorce in England 1660–1857* (Oxford: Oxford University Press, 1993), p. 26.

6 See *Sense and Sensibility*, ed. Edward Copeland (Cambridge: Cambridge University Press, 2006), p. 78.

7 See Vickery, *Behind Closed Doors*, Ch. 2.

8 See Deirdre Le Faye's biographical index to *Jane Austen's Letters* (Oxford: Oxford University Press, 1995), p. 566.

9 Its suggestiveness is definitively analysed by Brian Southam, '"*Rears*" and "*Vices*" in *Mansfield Park*', *Essays in Criticism*, Vol. LII, No. 1 (January 2002), pp. 23–35.

Chapter 12: What Do Characters Say When the Heroine Is Not There?

1 Tony Tanner, *Jane Austen*, (Cambridge, MA: Harvard University Press, 1986), p. 157.

2 See for instance Norman Page, *Speech in the English Novel* (London: Longman, 1973), p. 106: 'Jane Austen's gentlemen are shown speaking only in the presence of ladies'.

Chapter 13: How Much Money Is Enough?

1 See Maggie Lane, *A Charming Place: Bath in the Life and Novels of Jane Austen*. (1988; reprinted Bath: Millstream Books, 2003), p. 36.

2 David Nokes, *Jane Austen: A Life* (London: Fourth Estate, 1997), pp. 274–7.

3 See Austen-Leigh and Austen-Leigh, *A Family Record*, pp. 130–2.

4 W. H. Auden, 'Letter to Lord Byron', in *The English Auden*, ed. Edward Mendelson (London: Faber & Faber, 1978), p. 171.

5 Edward Copeland, *Women Writing about Money: Women's Fiction in England, 1790–1820* (Cambridge: Cambridge University Press, 1995), p. 24.

6 Bridget Hill, *Women Alone: Spinsters in England 1660–1850* (London: Yale University Press, 2001), p. 63.

7 Copeland, *Women Writing*, p. 28.

8 Edward Copeland, 'Money', in Janet Todd (ed.), *Jane Austen in Context* (Cambridge: Cambridge University Press, 2005), p. 321.

9 See G. E. Mingay, *English Landed Society in the Eighteenth Century* (London: Routledge and Kegan Paul, 1963), pp. 30–6.

10 Jones, *Jane Austen and Marriage*, p. 87.

11 Brian Southam, *Jane Austen and the Navy* (London: Hambledon, 2000), pp. 121–30.

12 Jones, *Jane Austen and Marriage*, p. 135.

13 Austen-Leigh and Austen Leigh, *A Family Record*, pp. 96 and 112. There is some dispute about the date of the purchase: see Robin Vick, 'Mr. Austen's Carriage', in *Jane Austen Society Collected Reports, 1999–2000*, pp. 226–8.

14 Copeland, *Women Writing*, p. 31.

Chapter 14: Why Do Her Plots Rely on Blunders?

1 Tanner, *Jane Austen*, p. 143.

Chapter 15: What Do Characters Read?

1 Lord Byron, *The Giaour. A Fragment of a Turkish Tale* (1813), in *Lord Byron. The Complete Poetical Works*, ed. Jerome McGann, Vol. III (Oxford: Oxford University Press, 1981), p. 80, ll. 1269–80.

2 A letter to Cassandra from Lyme Regis (14 September 1804, *Letters*, ed. Le Faye) includes a joke from *Tristram Shandy*, while her earliest surviving letter (9 January 1796, *Letters*, ed. Le Faye) involves a comparison between Tom Lefroy and *Tom Jones*. A later letter to her sister mentions the birth of her brother Frank's second son and hopes that 'if he ever comes to be hanged' she and Cassandra will be too old to care. This odd sentiment is surely an allusion to Fielding's description of Tom Jones as 'certainly born to be hanged', *Tom Jones*, Vol. III, Ch. ii, p. 103.

3 Austen-Leigh and Austen-Leigh, *A Family Record*, p. 83.
4 James Edward Austen-Leigh, *Memoir of Jane Austen*, p. 158.

Chapter 16: Are Ill People Really to Blame for Their Illnesses?

1 Tanner, *Jane Austen*, p. 99.
2 *The Works of Jane Austen*, ed. Chapman, Vol. VI, *Minor Works*, p. 321.
3 See Sales, *Jane Austen and Representations of Regency England*, pp. 147–50.
4 John Wiltshire, *Jane Austen and the Body: The Picture of Health* (Cambridge: Cambridge University Press, 1992), p. 180.
5 Austen-Leigh and Austen-Leigh, *A Family Record*, p. 216.

Chapter 17: What Makes Characters Blush?

1 Christopher Ricks, *Keats and Embarrassment* (Oxford: Oxford University Press, 1974), p. 51.
2 Mary Ann O'Farrell, 'Austen's Blush', in *NOVEL: A Forum on Fiction*, Vol. 27, No. 2 (1994), p. 127.
3 Fanny's blushes are analysed in Wiltshire, *Jane Austen and the Body*, pp. 76–89.
4 Katie Halsey, 'The Blush of Modesty or the Blush of Shame? Reading Jane Austen's Blushes', in *Forum for Modern Language Studies* (2006), Vol. 42, No. 3, p. 237.

Chapter 18: What Are the Right and Wrong Ways to Propose Marriage?

1 See Amanda Vickery, *The Gentleman's Daughter: Women's Lives in Georgian England* (London: Yale University Press, 1998), pp. 46–7.
2 An anthology of such manuals is Eve Tavor Bannet (ed.), *British and American Letter Manuals, 1680–1810*, 4 vols (London: Pickering & Chatto, 2008).
3 David Fordyce, *The New and Complete British Letter-Writer* (London, 1800), pp. 75 and 82–3.
4 Jones, *Jane Austen and Marriage*, p. 26, and Austen-Leigh and Austen-Leigh, *A Family Record*, p. 239.
5 Lawrence Stone, *The Road to Divorce: A History of the Making and Breaking of Marriage in England, 1530–1987* (Oxford: Oxford University Press, 1995), pp. 88, 91.
6 Austen-Leigh and Austen-Leigh, *A Family Record*, pp. 121–2.

Chapter 19: When Does Jane Austen Speak Directly to the Reader?

1 Virginia Woolf, 'Jane Austen', in Woolf, *Essays*, IV, p. 148.
2 D. A. Miller, *Jane Austen, or The Secret of Style* (Princeton, NJ: Princeton University Press, 2003), p. 1.
3 *The Rambler*, no. 97, in *The Yale Edition of the Works of Samuel Johnson*, Vol. IV, ed. W. J. Bate and Albrecht B. Strauss (New Haven: Yale University Press, 1968), p. 156.
4 Maria Edgeworth, *Patronage* (London, 1814), Vol. II, p. 101.
5 Mary Brunton, *Self-Control*, 2nd edition (Edinburgh, 1811), Vol. I, p. 84.

Chapter 20: How Experimental a Novelist Is Jane Austen?

1 Chapman, Vol. VI, pp. 428–30.
2 Samuel Richardson, preface to the third edition (1751) of *Clarissa* (1932; reprinted London: Dent, 1978), 4 vols, Vol. I, p. xiv.
3 Fanny Burney, *Cecilia*, ed. Margaret Anne Doody and Peter Sabor (Oxford: World's Classics, 1988), p. 6.
4 Miller, *Jane Austen*, p. 27.
5 Dorrit Cohn, *Transparent Minds. Narrative Modes for Presenting Consciousness in Fiction* (1983; reprinted Princeton, NJ: Princeton University Press, 1978), p. 5.
6 Ibid., p. 108.
7 David Lodge, *Consciousness and the Novel* (London: Secker & Warburg, 2002), pp. 46–9.
8 Jane Spencer, 'Narrative Technique: Austen and Her Contemporaries', in *A Companion to Jane Austen*, ed. Claudia L. Johnson and Clara Tuite (Oxford: Wiley-Blackwell, 2009).
9 Brunton, *Self-Control*, p. 25.
10 Gillian Beer, introduction to Jane Austen, *Persuasion* (London: Penguin, 1998), p. xxi.
11 Marilyn Butler, *Jane Austen and the War of Ideas*, p. 272.
12 Norman Page, *Speech in the English Novel* (London: Longman, 1973), p. 29.
13 Mary Lascelles, *Jane Austen and Her Art* (Oxford: Oxford University Press, 1939), pp. 177–8.
14 P. D. James, '*Emma* considered as a detective story', in *Jane Austen Society Collected Reports 1996–2000*, pp. 189–200.

Bibliography

Adburgham, Alison. *Shops and Shopping 1800–1914*. 1964; rpt. London: Allen and Unwin, 1981

Amis, Martin. *The Pregnant Widow*. London: Jonathan Cape, 2010

Ashelford, Jane. *The Art of Dress: Clothes and Society 1500–1914*. London: The National Trust, 1996

Auden, W. H. *The English Auden*, ed. Edward Mendelson. London: Faber & Faber, 1978

Austen, Jane. *The Novels of Jane Austen*, ed. R. W. Chapman. 5 vols. Oxford: Oxford University Press, 1965–6

—. *Minor Works*, ed. R. W. Chapman, rev. B. C. Southam, *The Works of Jane Austen*, Vol. VI. Oxford: Oxford University Press, 1987

—. *Persuasion*, ed. Linda Bree. Peterborough, Ontario: Broadview Press, 1998

—. *Persuasion*, ed. Gillian Beer. London: Penguin, 1998

—. *Catherine and Other Writings*, ed. Margaret Anne Doody and Douglas Murray. Oxford: World's Classics, 1993

—. *Sense and Sensibility*, ed. Edward Copeland. Cambridge: Cambridge University Press, 2006

—. *Jane Austen's Letters*, ed. Deirdre Le Faye. Oxford: Oxford University Press, 1995

Austen-Leigh, J. E. *A Memoir of Jane Austen and Other Family Recollections*, ed. Kathryn Sutherland. Oxford: World's Classics, 2002

Austen-Leigh, Richard Arthur, ed. *Austen Papers 1704–1856*, intro. David Gilson. London, 1995

Austen-Leigh, William and Richard Arthur Austen-Leigh. *Jane Austen. A Family Record*, rev. Deirdre Le Faye. London: The British Library, 1989

Bannet, Eve Tavor (ed.). *British and American Letter Manuals, 1680–1810*. London: Pickering & Chatto, 2008

Brodie, Allan, Colin Ellis, David Stuart and Gary Winter. *Weymouth's Seaside Heritage*. Swindon: English Heritage, 2006

Brunton, Mary. *Self-Control*, 2nd ed. Edinburgh, 1811

Buck, Anne. *Dress in Eighteenth-Century England*. London: B. T. Batsford, 1979

Burney, Fanny. *Evelina*, ed. Edward A. Bloom. Oxford: World's Classics, 1982

—. *Cecilia*, ed. Margaret Anne Doody and Peter Sabor. Oxford: World's Classics, 1988

Butler, Marilyn. *Jane Austen and the War of Ideas*. 1975; rpt. Oxford: Oxford University Press, 1987

Byron, Lord. *The Giaour. A Fragment of a Turkish Tale* (1813), in *Lord Byron. The Complete Poetical Works*, ed. Jerome McGann, Vol. III. Oxford: Oxford University Press, 1981

Chisholm, Kate. *Fanny Burney. Her Life*. London: Chatto & Windus, 1998

Cohn, Dorrit. *Transparent Minds. Narrative Modes for Presenting Consciousness in Fiction*. 1983; rpt. Princeton, NJ: Princeton University Press, 1978

Copeland, Edward. *Women Writing about Money: Women's Fiction in England, 1790–1820*. Cambridge: Cambridge University Press, 1995

Corbin, Alain. The *Lure of the Sea: The Discovery of the Seaside, 1750–1840*. 1994; rpt. London: Penguin, 1995

Crozier, W. Ray. *Blushing and the Social Emotions: The Self Unmasked*. Basingstoke: Palgrave Macmillan, 2006

Cunnington, Phillis, and Catherine Lucas. *Costume for Births, Marriages and Deaths*. London: A & C Black, 1972

Dickens, Charles. *Nicholas Nickleby*, ed. Michael Slater. 1978; rpt. London: Penguin, 1986.

Edgeworth, Maria. *Patronage*. London, 1814

Fielding, Henry. *Tom Jones*, ed. John Bender and Simon Stern. Oxford: World's Classics, 1996

Fordyce, David. *The New and Complete British Letter-Writer*. London, 1800

Gilbert, Sandra M., and Susan Gubar. *The Madwoman in the Attic. The Woman Writer and the Nineteenth-Century Literary Imagination*. London: Yale University Press, 1979

Halsey, Katie, 'The Blush of Modesty or the Blush of Shame? Reading Jane Austen's Blushes'. *Forum for Modern Language Studies* (2006), 42, No. 3, 226–38

Hecht, J. J. *The Domestic Servant Class in Eighteenth-Century England*. London: Routledge & Kegan Paul, 1956

Hill, Bridget. *Women Alone: Spinsters in England 1660–1850*. London: Yale University Press, 2001

Horn, Pamela. *Flunkeys and Scullions: Life Below Stairs in Georgian England.* Stroud: Sutton Publishing, 2004

Jane Austen Society Collected Reports, 6 vols

Johnson, Claudia L., and Clara Tuite (eds). *A Companion to Jane Austen.* Oxford: Wiley-Blackwell, 2009

Johnson, Samuel. *The Yale Edition of the Works of Samuel Johnson*, Vol. IV, ed. W. J. Bate and Albrecht B. Strauss. New Haven: Yale University Press, 1968

Jones, Hazel. *Jane Austen and Marriage.* London: Continuum, 2009

Jonson, Ben. *Timber, or Discoveries Made upon men and matter*, in *Ben Jonson*, ed. Ian Donaldson. Oxford: Oxford University Press, 1985

Lane, Maggie. *A Charming Place: Bath in the Life and Novels of Jane Austen.* 1988; rpt. Bath: Millstream Books, 2003

—. *Jane Austen and Names.* Bristol: Blaise Books, 2002

Lascelles, Mary. *Jane Austen and Her Art.* Oxford: Oxford University Press, 1939

Le Faye, Deirdre. *A Chronology of Jane Austen and Her Family.* Cambridge: Cambridge University Press, 2006

Lodge, David, *Consciousness and the Novel.* London: Secker & Warburg, 2002

McMaster, Juliet, and Bruce Stovel. *Jane Austen's Business: Her World and Her Profession.* Basingstoke: Macmillan, 1996

Miller, D. A. *Jane Austen, or The Secret of Style.* Princeton, NJ: Princeton University Press, 2003

Mingay, G. E. *English Landed Society in the Eighteenth Century.* London: Routledge & Kegan Paul, 1963

Nabokov, Vladimir. *Lectures on Literature*, ed. Fredson Bowers. San Diego, CA: Harcourt, 1982

— and Edmund Wilson. *The Nabokov–Wilson Letters*, ed. Simon Karlinsky. New York: Harper & Row, 1979

Nokes, David. *Jane Austen: A Life.* London: Fourth Estate, 1997

O'Farrell, Mary Ann. 'Austen's Blush', in *NOVEL: A Forum on Fiction* (1994), Vol. 27, No. 2, 125–39

Page, Norman, *Speech in the English Novel.* London: Longman, 1973

Richardson, Samuel. *Pamela*, ed. Thomas Keymer and Alice Wakely. Oxford: World's Classics, 2001

—. *Clarissa.* 1932; rpt. London: Dent, 1978

—. *Clarissa*, ed. Angus Ross. London: Penguin, 1985

Ricks, Christopher. *Keats and Embarrassment.* Oxford: Oxford University Press, 1974

Rothstein, Natalie (ed.). *Barbara Johnson's Album of Fashions and Fabrics.* London: Thames & Hudson, 1987

Sales, Roger. *Jane Austen and Representations of Regency England.* London: Routledge, 1994

Schapera, Isaac. *Kinship Terminology in Jane Austen's Novels.* London: The Royal Anthropological Institute, 1977

Scott, Walter. *The Journal of Sir Walter Scott,* ed. W.E.K. Anderson. Oxford: Clarendon Press, 1972

Selwyn, David (ed.). *Collected Poems and Verse of the Austen Family.* Manchester: Carcanet, 1996

—. *Jane Austen and Leisure.* London: Hambledon, 1999

Southam, Brian. *Jane Austen. The Critical Heritage 1811–1870.* Routledge & Kegan Paul, 1968

—. *Jane Austen. The Critical Heritage 1870–1940.* Routledge & Kegan Paul, 1987

—. *Jane Austen and the Navy.* London: Hambledon, 2000

—. *"Rears" and "Vices" in Mansfield Park. Essays in Criticism* (January 2002), Vol. LII, No. 1

Sterne, Laurence. *Tristram Shandy,* ed. Melvyn and Joan New. London: Penguin, 1997

Stone, Lawrence. *Broken Lives: Separation and Divorce in England 1660–1857.* Oxford: Oxford University Press, 1993

—. *The Road to Divorce: A History of the Making and Breaking of Marriage in England, 1530–1987.* Oxford: Oxford University Press, 1995

Stovel, Bruce, and Lynn Weinlos Gregg. *The Talk in Jane Austen.* Edmonton, Alberta: The University of Alberta Press, 2002

Tanner, Tony. *Jane Austen.* Cambridge, MA: Harvard University Press, 1986

Todd, Janet (ed.). *Jane Austen in Context.* Cambridge: Cambridge University Press, 2005

Vickery, Amanda. *The Gentleman's Daughter: Women's Lives in Georgian England.* London: Yale University Press, 1998

—. *Behind Closed Doors: At Home in Georgian England.* London: Yale University Press, 2009

Walton, John K. *The English Seaside Resort: A Social History 1750–1914.* Leicester: Leicester University Press, 1983

Wiltshire, John. *Jane Austen and the Body: The Picture of Health.* Cambridge: Cambridge University Press, 1992

Withycombe, E. G. *The Oxford Dictionary of English Christian Names.* 1950; rpt. Oxford: Oxford University Press, 1973

Woolf, Virginia. *The Essays of Virginia Woolf,* Vol. IV (1925–8), ed. Andrew McNeillie. London: Hogarth Press, 1994

Wrigley, E. A., and R. S. Schofield. *The Population History of England 1541–1871: A Reconstruction.* 1981; rpt. Cambridge: Cambridge University Press, 2002

Acknowledgements

I would like to thank all those who have given me advice and information used in the preparation of this book: Ann Channon at the Jane Austen's House Museum, Susan Allen Ford, Juliet McMaster, Sophie Missing, Charlotte Mitchell, the late Brian Southam, Elizabeth Steele, John Sutherland, Amanda Vickery and Henry Woudhuysen.

Julian Hoppit gave me guidance about money in the early nineteenth century; I owe Malthusian reflections in chapter 5 to Karen O'Brien; Deirdre Le Faye advised me on mourning habits and on money, again. I have also relied a good deal on her wonderful *Chronology of Jane Austen*.

Students whom I have taught in classes on Jane Austen's fiction at University College London over the years may well recognise their own insights in these pages. If so, I hope they will not be displeased, these classes having been my most dependable source of inspiration.

I have tested parts of this book out at talks I have given to members of the Jane Austen Society and the Jane Austen Society of North America. I would like to thank all my friends in these societies for their suggestions and unfailingly accurate corrections. Particular thanks are due to Marilyn Joice and Jill Webster for their comments on draft chapters. I am also grateful to Andrew Banks for several sharp-eyed factual corrections. It is a great sadness to me that Vera Quin, doyenne of the Jane Austen Society, died as this book was nearing completion. Vera had a knowledge of Austen and her predecessors unrivalled by most academics; I only wish she were here to read what I have written and gently put me right where necessary.

I am grateful to all those at Bloomsbury who have nudged me over the finishing line: Nick Humphrey, Emily Sweet, Catherine Best and above all my patient yet galvanising editor, Bill Swainson. I owe a special debt to my agent, Derek Johns, who gave me confidence in what I was doing from the very beginning.

I hope that my family's interest in Jane Austen will have survived what must have seemed my obsession with her writing and am grateful for their tolerance. I could never have finished the book without my wife Harriet's support and encouragement.

This book is dedicated to the memory of Tony Tanner, whose Penguin introductions to Jane Austen's novels first showed me how exciting they were. He later became my teacher at university and then a colleague; I hope that this book preserves some memories of the many conversations about Jane Austen that we had over the years.

Index